WALT DISNEY AND THE QUEST FOR COMMUNITY

For my grandparents,
Selma and Sid Mannheim

Walt Disney
and the Quest for Community

STEVE MANNHEIM

ASHGATE

Published by
Ashgate Publishing Limited
Gower House
Croft Road
Aldershot
Hants GU11 3HR
England

Ashgate Publishing Company
Suite 420
101 Cherry Street
Burlington, VT 05401–4405 USA

Ashgate website: http://www.ashgate.com

British Library Cataloguing in Publication Data
Mannheim, Steve
   Walt Disney and the quest for community
   1.Disney, Walt, 1901-1966 2.New towns - Florida - Planning
   3.Amusement parks - Florida - Design and construction
   4.Utopias 5.EPCOT Center (Fla.)
   I.Title
   307.7'6'0975924

Library of Congress Cataloging-in-Publication Data
Mannheim, Steve, 1962-
   Walt Disney and the quest for community / Steve Mannheim.
      p. cm.
   Includes bibliographical references and index.
   ISBN 0-7546-1974-5 (alk. paper)
   1. EPCOT Center (Fla.)--Planning. 2. Amusement parks--Florida--
Planning. 3. Disney, Walt, 1901-1966. I. Title.

GV1853.3.F62 E636 2002
791'.06'875924--dc21

791·068 MAN

2002074730

ISBN 0 7546 1974 5

Typeset by Manton Typesetters, Louth, Lincolnshire, UK and printed and bound in Great Britain by MPG Books Ltd, Bodmin, Cornwall.

Contents

List of Illustrations

Preface

Entertainment industry pioneer Walter Elias 'Walt' Disney (1901–66) was listed by *Time* magazine as one of the twenty innovators who changed the world during the twentieth century. In the final months of his life, Disney was preparing to build his most ambitious project yet, the Experimental Prototype Community of Tomorrow (EPCOT), in central Florida.

Disney's EPCOT concept combined company town, visitor attraction, and experimental laboratory. Unlike utopian communities, EPCOT was not advertised as the perfect solution to the urban crisis of the 1960s but instead would be in a continuous state of technological 'becoming,' drawing upon the best minds of American industry, government, research institutes, and academia. Its model urban form was a clear reaction to suburban sprawl and the diminished significance of downtowns.

Research for this book began when, in the late 1980s, a friend in the construction industry informed me that Disney had originally conceived of a different project to be built where the 1982 Epcot Center theme park now stands. It was to be a city of tomorrow. I read Bob Thomas' biography of Disney and began to piece together the missing parts of the story. At the time, there was very little material available on the subject. Ultimately, I returned to school and with the support of the University of Southern California, this project commenced.

Disney's EPCOT concept reached across many disciplines and so does this book. Broad in scope, EPCOT cannot be understood through an eye-of-the-needle perspective. The chapters are generally organized to reflect the community development process. Many chapters examine the planning and development experience of the company to identify trends and influences on EPCOT planning. This examination also yields a history of Disney's real estate activities since his earliest days in the animation business. Certain chapters require a brief explanation. Chapter 1, Physical Planning, the longest chapter, presents a general overview of the EPCOT concept, followed by an analysis of influences from planning history and from Disney's life. Chapter 3, Architecture and Construction, analyzes concepts for EPCOT buildings as well as other projects Disney supervised. Chapter 4, Site and Technology, deals with the challenging conditions of the Florida property and includes a summary of some of the technological achievements of Disney's own company. Chapter 6, Economic Analysis and Finance, examines both public and private sources of funds and also covers the EPCOT team's important tours of the research and development laboratories of the

Space Age. Chapter 9, Operations and Management, draws heavily upon the Disneyland experience to shed light on Disney's philosophies and policies. Finally, Chapter 10, EPCOT After Disney, explains how the experimental community evolved into projects like Epcot Center and the town of Celebration, Florida.

There are several nomenclature conventions used in the book. Project X and Project Future were early names for Project Florida. Project Florida ultimately became known as Disney World. After Disney's death, it was changed to Walt Disney World. In addition, Walt Disney Productions became The Walt Disney Company in 1986. These two entities are referred to as the company or the Disney organization for the sake of convenience. Walt Disney Imagineering was known as WED Enterprises prior to 1986. WED was named for its founder, Walter Elias Disney. It should be noted that in Disney's time, Walt Disney Productions was effectively a family company, not the multinational media and entertainment conglomerate it is today. This makes Disney's EPCOT concept even more ambitious.

Walt Disney the man is referred to as Disney. The EPCOT acronyms also are interesting. The original concept for the Experimental Prototype Community of Tomorrow is known as EPCOT. WED Enterprises writer Marty Sklar also referred to the concept as 'Waltopia.' In 1982, EPCOT Center opened. Eventually, it became known as Epcot. In order not to confuse the theme park with the 1966 community concept, I use Epcot Center when referring to the theme park. On October 27, 1966, Disney filmed his segments of a promotional film about EPCOT and the Florida property. The script is entitled 'Florida Film' and that name is used here.

During my research, more than one historian suggested to me that EPCOT was probably a 'figment of a publicist's imagination.' Disney's company was built on more than marketing and imagination, although these were key ingredients. Disney had selected 1,100 acres of land and a multidisciplinary team of professionals to plan and develop EPCOT. Although the city was never built, the concept evolved. It is a story Disney himself might have chosen for one of his own 1960s fairy tales.

Acknowledgments

This book would not have been possible without the inspiration and support of many people. Much gratitude goes to the University of Southern California professors who provided intellectual challenge and growth: Edward Blakely, Dowell Myers, David Sloane, and Martin Krieger. The work of Richard Peiser of Harvard University convinced me to look at EPCOT through the lenses of the real estate development process. Gerald Gast of the University of Oregon tried to keep me focused on design. Deone Zell at California State University, Northridge, helped me in numerous ways, particularly with interviewing skills. Richard Weinstein at the University of California, Los Angeles was kind enough to read an early draft of the manuscript. The EPCOT concept drew from several professions and Robert Kinton, William Tooley, William Whitney, David Wilcox, Tom Larmore, Jon Jerde, Stephen Bourcier, Alan Aronson, Arthur Ganezer, and Stuart Ketchum all served as sounding boards in design, real estate, and related fields. Tom Boles and Jeff Speaker of DeMolay International provided information about Disney's youth. I would also like to thank several people at The Walt Disney Company who helped make this project possible: David R. Smith, Robert Tieman, Collette Espino, Rebecca Cline, Lucille Martin, David Fisher, Sandy Huskins, Barbara Hastings, John Hench, Ray Watson, and Card Walker.

Several individuals at the Reedy Creek Improvement District were also especially helpful, particularly Tom DeWolf and Tom Moses. In addition, the following 'Disney veterans' were of critical assistance: Morgan 'Bill' Evans; Bill Martin; Marjorie Davis (Mrs. Marvin Davis); Nannette Latchford; Harrison 'Buzz' Price; Don Edgren; Ward Kimball and Betty Kimball; Colonel Tom Jones; Ken Klug; Robert Foster; Joanne Potter-Heine; Phil Smith; Richard Morrow; Carl Bongiorno; Bob Gurr; and Diane Disney Miller and Ron Miller. I would also like to thank retired Welton Becket & Associates design principal Robert Tyler. Valerie Rose at Ashgate Publishing was a blessing and so was copy-editor Kay Cooperman Jue. Finally, other people who provided inspiration in important ways are Sandra Quinn, Bill Quinn, Virginia Aids, and Harvey Sternbach.

Introduction

*In 1911 there were two little studios doing business, one in Los Angeles,
one in Hollywood, in two shabby old barns.*

Boyle Workman,
The City That Grew, 1935[1]

*The idea of building a city of the future where there's nothing but marsh and
cypress might seem crazy, but look at what happened at Disneyland ...
When we went there, it was nothing but orange groves.*

Roy O. Disney, 1967[2]

*And David prepared large quantities of iron to make the nails for the doors of the
gates and for the clamps, and more bronze than could be weighed;
and timbers of cedar logs beyond number.*

1 Chron. 22:3, 4

The Experimental Prototype Community of Tomorrow (EPCOT) was entertainment industry pioneer Walter Elias 'Walt' Disney's (1901–66) final dream.
After more than forty years in the entertainment industry, Disney wore the
hard hat of a builder. He had acquired experience in the planning and
development of various projects, including private residences; advanced
motion picture studios; motion picture sets; Disneyland, the world's first
theme park; a redevelopment project in St. Louis, Missouri; four notable
1964–65 New York World's Fair pavilions; the Mineral King Valley, California, ski resort; the California Institute of the Arts (CalArts) campus; and
other projects. His development concept at the time of his death would
combine company town, visitor attraction, and a device with which to help
solve the problems of cities.

In December 1963, Walt Disney Productions released the animated feature, *The Sword in the Stone,* a story about the young King Arthur. Just a
month earlier, another rendition of Camelot had come to a tragic close in
Dallas, Texas. Meanwhile, Disney was on a trip back to Los Angeles after
inspecting swampland property in central Florida. The property would be
the site for Disney's own final crusade: the quest for community.

During his last filmed appearance on October 27, 1966, he declared that
the problems of cities were the most important issues confronting society.

The company, along with potential partners in American industry, the people of Florida, and the federal Department of Housing and Urban Development (HUD), would prepare to develop an experimental community.

Disney's EPCOT conceptual model included the following features: a radial/organic plan; a 50-acre town center megastructure enclosed by a dome; a regional mall-sized, internationally themed shopping area; a hotel and convention complex of 30 or more stories; office space; a greenbelt; high-density apartments; single-family houses; neighborhood centers; a satellite community; monorail and PeopleMover systems; and underground automobile and truck tunnels. In addition, EPCOT would be closely linked to an industrial park. Drawing upon contemporary practice, historical precedent, and the company's previous experience, this planning model was designed to address the urban evils that formed what architect Victor Gruen called 'the Anti-City,' the Disney villain in this story.[3]

Perhaps the most visible manifestation of the urban crisis of the 1960s was civil unrest. Heavy smoke rose from the Los Angeles community of Watts, southeast of Disney's residence, during the summer of 1965. Civil rights demonstrations at the 1964–65 New York World's Fair, where the company had constructed pavilions, and in other parts of the nation, were hallmarks of this turbulent period in American history. Several important pieces of federal legislation grew out of the civil rights movement at the time, including the *Civil Rights Act of 1964* and the *Voting Rights Act of 1965*. In addition, in November 1966, President Lyndon Johnson signed the *Demonstration Cities and Metropolitan Development Act of 1966* ('Model Cities'). The Act's purpose was to provide financial and technical assistance to develop '*new and imaginative proposals*' [emphasis added] and

> revitalize large slum and blighted areas; to expand housing, job, and income opportunities; to reduce dependence on welfare payments; to improve educational facilities ...; to combat disease and ill health; to reduce ... crime and delinquency; to enhance recreational and cultural opportunities; to establish better access between homes and jobs ...[4]

Congress found and declared 'that improving the quality of urban life is the most critical domestic problem facing the United States.'[5] The Republican Disney and the Democratic Congress and Administration appeared to be on an unusual, common course as the company consulting firm Economics Research Associates (ERA), prepared a presentation outline seeking financial assistance for EPCOT from the newly established HUD.

Disney discussed the philosophy behind the EPCOT concept during his final filmed appearance in 1966. The following points summarize the core philosophy: showcase the development, utilize and test new materials and ideas from American industry, find solutions to urban problems, EPCOT would be in a state of becoming, focus on the needs and happiness of residents, and generate demand for new technologies.[6] Disney's faith in technological progress based on the free enterprise system was never more evident.

In this role, Disney would help focus his peers in American industry on the urban crisis as he searched for prototype products to use in the experimental community. Walt Disney Productions had a long record of technological innovation of its own in the entertainment industry. In addition, the company had established close relationships with a wide range of American industries. Disney and his team would build upon those relationships to seek financial participation and the latest in technology from the research and development laboratories of America's Space Age.

As previously noted, EPCOT would be in a constant state of becoming, as Disney's generation had seen the pace of technological change accelerate. This technological change was reflected at Disneyland, where initially futuristic attractions, such as the Monsanto House of the Future, were being retired as relics of the past. Unlike film production, Disneyland enabled Disney to alter his creations from time to time. He once reflected that 'Disneyland is like a piece of clay, if there is something I don't like, I'm not stuck with it. I can reshape and revamp.'[7] With its 20,000 residents, EPCOT would be more organic and less pliable than the theme park. Disney would be faced with a new problem: how to achieve the goals of an ordered, experimental community while maintaining something he was passionate about – the rights of the individual.

At this time, WED Enterprises was advancing technology for use outside the studio and theme park. During the 1964–65 New York World's Fair, Disney's Imagineers made strides in research and development for mass transportation and utilized aerospace technology for the robotics known as Audio-Animatronics. In addition, participation in the fair enabled the Disney organization to establish and/or solidify relationships with other corporations. These included Ford Motor Company and Thomas Edison's company, General Electric.

While King Arthur's Carousel revolved at Disneyland, General Electric's Progressland carousel took World's Fair visitors on a technological journey through time, with Audio-Animatronics hosts, beginning in the 1880s and ending with G.E.'s modern Medallion Home of the 1960s. EPCOT would be similar in some respects to G.E.'s carousel. Although EPCOT would not rotate, it also would be in a state of technological becoming. Disney's own 'carousel of life' began at the end of the Victorian Age and closed with a final act that included visits to Space Age places like NASA to help him develop his futuristic EPCOT concept.

Henry Ford's Greenfield Village in Dearborn, Michigan also served as an inspiration to Disney. It includes a park, historic buildings, and a showcase of American industry and technology. According to animator Ward Kimball, Disney and Ford enjoyed a 'mutual admiration society.'[8] Disney visited Greenfield Village more than once. Its exhibits include Thomas Edison's Menlo Park and Florida laboratories, pieces of the Kitty Hawk flyer, and early tabulation equipment. Greenfield Village is at least symbolic of the state of becoming philosophy. Its inventions and laboratories reflect the staggering pace of technological change since the Industrial Revolution.

Disney was determined to build EPCOT and brought to bear a formidable team, vision, and years of experience accomplishing what to others seemed to be the impossible. Biographer Bob Thomas notes that 'Disneyland became a crusade for Walt, more so than sound cartoons, color, animated features and all the other innovations he had planned.'[9] EPCOT was Disney's attempt to top Disneyland. It would be the final crusade. Retired General William E. 'Joe' Potter recalled that development of the EPCOT and Disney World master plan 'occupied a large part of the last year of Walt Disney's life.'[10] In 1986, Lillian Disney recalled that her husband 'wanted this city of tomorrow. I can just see him drawing a wagon wheel. He really wanted to make it work.'[11]

However, EPCOT remained a concept at the time of Disney's death. Real estate economist Harrison Price emphasizes that it was planned 'in the last stages of a man's life, in a ... hurry, to do what he said he wanted to do, which is to leave 25 years of work for his organization.'[12] Disney protégé Card Walker also recalls that 'he [Disney] had a feeling of pressure that he had to get this going.'[13] When Disney was determined to complete a project, it was difficult to deter him. At the opening of Walt Disney World in 1971, Roy O. Disney concluded that his brother had 'great determination, singleness of purpose and drive; and through his entire life he was never pushed off his course or diverted to other things.'

Disney often 'played his hunches' and usually won. Disneyland, originally viewed as a 'kiddie park' amongst the orange groves of Southern California, became the first theme park and is visited by people from around the world. *Snow White and the Seven Dwarfs* (1937), the first full-length animated feature film, was known as 'Disney's Folly' during production. The classic film introduced a new genre to family entertainment and continues to establish profit records for the studio. Imagineer Marvin Davis, who worked closely with Disney on the EPCOT plans, probably reflected Disney's feelings about that particular hunch when he said, 'I spent weeks and weeks developing this plan that I thought was damn good.'[14]

Over the years, comparisons have been made between Disney and Leonardo da Vinci. Obviously, the two men are from different times and differ immensely from one another, but there are similarities that shed light on the EPCOT concept. In 1942, Sir David Low, a noted British political cartoonist, concluded that Disney and his team were the most significant figures in graphic art since da Vinci. In 1969, urban historian Lewis Mumford stated, 'There are many lessons to be drawn from Leonardo's example; but the most important one, perhaps, is that he demonstrated that the integration of science and the humanities with life is actually possible.'[15] EPCOT planning would bring together some of the nation's most talented artists and the latest in technology from the research and development laboratories of American industry.

The need for such an approach also was identified by architect Victor Gruen in his book, *The Heart of Our Cities* (1964). According to Imagineer John Hench, Disney had been 'studying Victor Gruen a long time.'[16] Gruen concluded that one of the serious problems in planning is that specialization in the professions can result in losing sight of the overall objective. He added that the men 'of the Renaissance did not have this problem. How would one classify Leonardo da Vinci? As an architect? A city planner? An engineer? A sculptor? An industrial designer? A graphic artist? A transportation expert? He had no title, no license, no academic degree.'[17] Sharon Disney Lund, Disney's younger daughter, recalled that her father admired Leonardo.[18] In the entertainment industry, Disney was accustomed to seeking input from a wide array of professionals and, according to landscape architect Morgan 'Bill' Evans, 'Wherever he turned, he learned from experts all that he thought he ought to know about that particular endeavor.'[19]

While King Arthur had his knights, Disney was surrounded by a team of Renaissance men, or at least professionals trained to work alongside the many vocations in the motion picture business. Imagineer Randy Bright wrote, 'The WED staff became a harmonic blend of talents that was unparalleled in the entertainment industry. It consisted of designers, architects, writers, sculptors, engineers, creators of special effects, and imaginative people from many other disciplines.'[20]

This multidisciplinary approach to the future continues to have relevance today. Urban historian Sir Peter Hall writes, 'The almost certain growth drivers in this coming era are of course informational: they will combine artistic and intellectual creativity with technological innovativeness, on the model first created in Hollywood between 1915 and 1940 ... .'[21] Disney also realized that growth drivers combined art, technology, and commerce. From the outset, Disney's Medici family was the public. With all of the company's products, including EPCOT, Disney was concerned with meeting the needs of people.

Disney also understood that EPCOT would bring newer issues, such as regulation, social planning, and community governance, to the forefront. He paved the way for the enactment of three statutes by the state of Florida to create a special district for the property the company owned there as well as two municipalities. Disney did not have time before his death to work out the social aspects of the experimental community in great detail. Most of the corresponding legal issues were unresolved. Still, Marvin Davis recalled that Disney wanted to help solve all of the problems confronting society with EPCOT.[22] The concept would combine experiments in physical planning, institutional design, technology, and other disciplines.

For example, the EPCOT planning team drew freely from urban history, including stenographer Sir Ebenezer Howard's (1850–1923) classic book, *Garden Cities of To-Morrow* (1902). This utopian vision was republished in 1965 with an introductory essay by Lewis Mumford. He compared Howard's Garden City with Leonardo da Vinci's plan to reduce congestion and squalor in Milan.[23] Howard's book initially was published in 1898 as *To-morrow! A Peaceful Path to Real Reform*. It was a reaction to the horrific conditions in industrial cities like London, where raw sewage flowed in the streets.[24] Such conditions gave rise to the need for public planning. Marvin Davis, trained in architecture at the University of Southern California, probably was familiar with Howard's Garden City tradition. Beginning in 1949, Disney spent four consecutive summers in England to shoot films like *Treasure Island* with English casts and crews. He was exposed to the British New Town movement then underway.[25] The self-contained, postwar New Towns of England, with their roots in the Garden City, are reminiscent of the EPCOT planning model.

There are many reasons why Disney's experimental community concept never came to fruition after his death. These include the loss of his vision and leadership, the potential cost of such an undertaking, and the legal and community governance complexities involved. The concept changed and its influence can be seen is several other company projects, including the Epcot Center theme park and the planned community of Celebration, Florida. Still, EPCOT's transit orientation, concern for the environment, and other aspects of the original concept take on increasing relevance today. Disney introduced the preliminary plans for the EPCOT concept in his 1966 Florida Film. He stated that although the plans might change over time, the basic philosophy for Disney World would remain much the same.[26]

A full-size copy of Michelangelo's *David* stands over Forest Lawn Memorial Park in Glendale, California, where Disney is buried. Not far away are the Walt Disney Studios. Perhaps the men of antiquity and the Renaissance were correct: there really is nothing new under the ersatz Hollywood sun. But something new was 'wagging the tail' of the Audio-Animatronics dog. Man would soon set foot on the moon just decades after the Wright brothers took to the sky in North Carolina. Somewhere west of Cape Kennedy, beneath the Florida sky, 27,443 acres waited for the Sculptor to reveal solutions to the greatest challenge of all: community – The Greatest Show, right here on Earth.

CONCEPT

Chapter 1

Physical Planning

Make no little plans. They have no magic to stir men's blood and
probably themselves will not be realized. Make big plans; aim high in
hope and work, remembering that a noble, logical diagram once recorded
will never die ... Remember that our sons and grandsons are going to do
things that would stagger us. Let your watchword be order
and your beacon be beauty.

Daniel Burnham, 1907

EPCOT's conceptual physical plan drew upon elements of yesteryear, the 1960s, and tomorrow. For example, the Garden City tradition is strongly pronounced, as are Corbusian utopian elements from the 1920s. Contemporary practice, including organic planning, new town development, and mass transit-linked postwar satellite town planning also influenced the EPCOT designers. In addition, after years of seeing Disneyland's Tomorrowland attractions become obsolete and technology advance at an ever-increasing rate, Disney incorporated the state of becoming into EPCOT. Unlike film production, in which the product is finished when placed in the 'can,' EPCOT would never be completed.

EPCOT is a model for urban development based on increased development density at the urban core/transit node. This was a direct reaction to suburban sprawl and the diminished importance of downtowns in many American cities. EPCOT's large, internationally themed retail space in the town center is more a function of its location at the heart of Disney World than it is a model for a typical community of 20,000 persons.

Imagineer John Hench has drawn upon the work of psychologists to conclude that with his design of Disneyland, 'Walt wanted to reassure people.'[1] Disney's success was evident in the faces of tens of millions of children and adults at the park. However, EPCOT's final plan would have had to reconcile Disney's reassuring Midwestern notions of community with a rapidly increasing rate of technological change in the experimental community's continuous state of becoming.

As architect and planner Victor Gruen would have said, EPCOT was Disney's own multipurpose demonstration of a 'counterattack' against the sprawl and other 'evils' of the urban crisis that was definitely not a fairy tale. This chapter presents a general overview of the EPCOT concept, followed by an examination of planning influences.

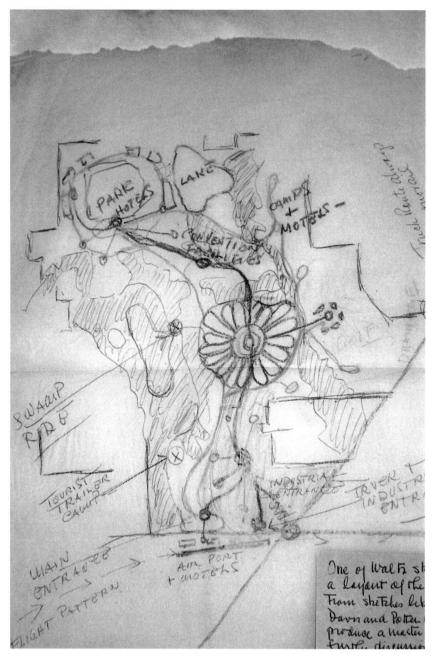

Figure 1.1   Disney's Seventh Preliminary Master Plot Plan hand sketch, 1966. This drawing embodies the EPCOT team's planning just prior to Disney's death. The organic centerpiece of the Florida property is the Experimental Prototype Community of Tomorrow. Source: Jo Ann P. Heine

Shortly before his death in December 1966, Disney personally drew a sketch of the EPCOT team's Seventh Preliminary Master Plot Plan (see Figure 1.1). As the title indicates, this was not the germinal plan.

The sketch reflects Disney's desire to leave the plan as an enduring legacy because, as an executive, he typically left drawing to his staff. The plot plan also reflects something that Disney communicated to central Florida television viewers in November 1965. He explained 'that he had learned a lesson from Disneyland and that was simply to purchase enough land to control the environment.'[2] Disney described the built environment that sprouted around his theme park on Harbor Boulevard in Anaheim, California, as a 'second rate Las Vegas.'[3]

EPCOT planner Marvin Davis was not a big fan of Las Vegas either.[4] Working under Disney, Davis prepared 69 plan iterations for Disneyland until the site plan that would ultimately have global influence was 'signed off.' At the dedication of the world's first theme park, Disney emphasized that it also would serve as a 'community center.'[5] Disneyland's Town Square, however, was a re-creation of the traditional town center that was missing in the sprawl surrounding the theme park.

This time, the planning team had 27,443 acres at its disposal, compared to Disneyland's original 160 acres. The main features of the plot plan include the Magic Kingdom, hotels, camps and motels, convention facilities, EPCOT and a satellite community, a golf course, a 'swamp ride,' an industrial park, a tourist trailer camp, a main entrance, and a 'jet airport.'[6] In addition, a monorail system runs the length of the property.

This plot plan would serve as an overall blueprint, with modification, for Walt Disney World. The conceptual airport at the southern end of the plot plan, like EPCOT, would have drawn upon an uncommon plan and the latest in technology. For example, Davis recalled that,

> The most interesting thing, I thought, was this airport which was planned after the one in Cincinnati. This circular plan cuts down the area that you need by half … Walt and I had this early plan practically sold … Of course, we would have had to get all kinds of approvals from the F.A.A.[7]

In addition, the airport concept featured new methods of expediting baggage and cargo handling, passenger loading, urban transportation linkages, and transport maintenance.[8] These features are reminiscent of what newer airports, such as the Denver International Airport, attempt to achieve. The accompanying entrance complex north of the airport would feature parking, computerized registration, and a transportation pavilion.[9] Ultimately, what became the Orlando International Airport would serve the needs of the Florida property.

Much of the planning process took place between Disney and planner Marvin Davis. The relationship, according to Davis' wife Marjorie, was 'definitely give and take.' Mrs. Davis was also Disney's niece who had lived with him when she was a child. She recalled, 'Walt was great for probing ... He would do that with me as a child. I would say something, and he'd say, "Now what do you mean by that?" I lived with him for many years. That's what he did to Marvin.'[10] Richard Irvine, a former president of WED Enterprises, shared a similar perspective.[11] In Glendale, California, at WED Enterprises headquarters, Davis created a special room with a 16-foot ceiling featuring a mosaic of aerial photographs of the Florida property. This room was off-limits to all but a few employees.[12] In 1997, Davis reflected on Disney's visits to his office, saying, 'Well, the back of my neck is pretty burnt from when he used to look over my shoulder all the time.'[13]

Another critical EPCOT team member was General Joe Potter, who served as vice president-EPCOT planning. Potter worked with Disney and WED Enterprises while he was executive vice president of the 1964–65 New York World's Fair under powerful New York planner Robert Moses. He officially joined the company in September 1965. George Rester, Davis' assistant, was also a key member of the planning team. Disney supervised and inspired the EPCOT team. Carl Bongiorno, retired president of Walt Disney Imagineering, recalls that Disney 'was over there [at WED Enterprises] three, four days a week, guiding the creative team in pursuing the concept of EPCOT.'[14] In addition, Walt Disney Productions' original Project X/Project Future Committee, initially involved in site selection, included Disney's brother Roy O. Disney, Admiral Joe Fowler, Orbin Melton (president of WED Enterprises), Lawerence Tryon (treasurer), Richard Morrow, and Robert Foster.[15]

However, not all of the plot plan elements would be completely new to the team. For example, the Disney organization was very familiar with some Florida master plan components, like the Magic Kingdom – almost a duplication of Disneyland. Other elements, like EPCOT, involved the input of consultants such as Harrison 'Buzz' Price, a close Disney advisor and founder of Economics Research Associates (ERA). It also required expert opinion, like that of Raymond 'Ray' Watson, now vice chairman of the Irvine Company and a director of The Walt Disney Company. In addition, Disney had close friends in the design professions, including Welton Becket, Charles Luckman, and William Pereira.[16]

Disney outlined the EPCOT philosophy on film on October 27, 1966. The philosophy would become one of the guiding forces within the Disney organization. It was intended not only for physical planning but crossed as many disciplines as possible. Disney asked Martin 'Marty' Sklar, who worked as a writer for WED Enterprises at the time and is now vice chairman and principal creative executive of Walt Disney Imagineering, to help him express the concept in writing. The following points summarize the EPCOT philosophy: EPCOT would be in a state of becoming; use and test new construction materials, systems, and ideas from American industry; use EPCOT as a showcase; find solutions to urban problems; generate demand for new technologies, and focus on the public need and happiness of people.

Within the physical planning discipline, the philosophies of integrating new systems, showcasing the concept to visitors through PeopleMover exposure, solving urban problems, meeting the public need, being in a continuous state of change, providing for the happiness of residents and visitors, and generating consumer demand would ultimately all have to be reflected in Disney's plans. Whether or not these philosophies would have been compatible remains an open question.

Marvin Davis elaborated on Disney's view of technological applications, noting that Disney wanted to take a prototype product 'right off the research & development boards, and put it into EPCOT ... and let people that are *living* there be the ones that are market-testing it ... .'[17] EPCOT's field testing also was intended to create market demand for new products, presumably at a faster rate than the world beyond its radial plan. This was the real Progress City (see below).

But while technology was a critical component of the concept, Disney was also concerned with the well-being of EPCOT's residents. During a press conference in Orlando in November 1965 announcing the conceptualization of a city of tomorrow, Disney stressed that he envisioned a community with human qualities:

> I would like to be part of building a model community, a City of Tomorrow, you might say, because I don't believe in going out to this extreme blue-sky stuff that some architects do. I believe that people still want to live like human beings. There's a lot of things that could be done. I'm not against the automobile, but I just feel that the automobile has moved into communities too much. I feel that you can design so that the automobile is there, but still put people back as pedestrians, you see. I'd love to work on a project like that.[18]

In addition, Disney spoke about a concept to build two cities on the property, one called 'Yesterday' and the other, 'Tomorrow.'[19]

Former planner Ray Watson emphasizes that the EPCOT planning model was dedicated to highlighting transportation systems and rebuilding the urban core.[20] The specific land use elements consisted of four major zones within an overall radial plan: central commercial, apartment ring, greenbelt and recreation, and low-density, neighborhood residential/'radiential.' Urban electric transportation was based on monorails, radiating 'WEDway' PeopleMovers, and an underground transportation hierarchy. As mentioned, the concept also provided for a satellite community.

Naturally, the EPCOT site plan was the result of a process of conceptualization and evolution. For example, Disney was quite serious initially about the word *experimental*. He considered other alternatives early in the planning process, even use of fill from the creation of an artificial lake to construct a mound city, similar to some of the concepts drawn by the British Archigram Group during the 1960s.[21] Despite the risk inherent in such a bold concept, EPCOT team members were enthusiastic about it.

Perhaps General Joe Potter put it most clearly in 1981. He believed that if Disney had lived longer, 'We would've started on the other activities on EPCOT ... and through the monorail exposure people would've seen EPCOT coming out of the ground ... .'[22]

At the focal point of EPCOT is the so-called town center. EPCOT's town center is in many respects a themed shopping mall designed for only 20,000 residents and millions of visitors. Nevertheless, in its showcase capacity, the dense urban core model, linked to electric mass transit, was intended to serve as a demonstration to visitors. The primary town center components in the plan are as follows: a landmark hotel and convention center, an internationally themed retail core, theaters, restaurants, other nightlife attractions, and resident-serving and corporate office space.[23]

In addition, the 50-acre town center area would be enclosed to protect it from central Florida weather, which is uncomfortably hot, humid, and rainy, especially in the summer. EPCOT's international shopping area anticipated many of today's themed, enclosed 'mega-malls.' From a prototype community development standpoint, the wedge-shaped parcels created by the radial plan in the town center would yield inefficient building floorplates for a typical developer. From an entertainment retailing perspective, however, visitors could wander aimlessly through 'canyons' and foreign lands on a motion picture set design scale similar to New Orleans Square at Disneyland.

This aspect of the plan also provides education through design. For instance, Disney envisioned Swiss, German, and Chinese sections in the international shopping areas using 'Disney façades.'[24] Marvin Davis estimated that each 'country' would occupy a city block (approximately 1,500 feet across) and that the area would be comparable to Disneyland's Main Street, U.S.A. in scale.[25] Like Disneyland, EPCOT's town center would be a 'show.' Songwriter Richard Sherman recalls that 'one of the things he [Disney] was going to do, was to have a resident company of players that would do original musicals there. He asked us [with brother Robert] to write them.'[26]

The hotel would be the visual center of EPCOT, featuring a seven-acre recreation deck situated above the pedestrian areas of the center city. The downtown hotel is an element of a megastructure that connects with the shopping area, office buildings, and transportation lobby. A visual magnet in the center of the radial plan, the hotel orients and reassures visitors and residents, much like Sleeping Beauty's Castle did at Disneyland or strong points have for centuries in ancient cities. The recreation deck would have included trees, waterfalls, and swimming pools. While cities like Los Angeles closed at night, 'EPCOT would be most exciting at night.'[27] Of course, like a shopping mall, this would be easier to implement in a privately-controlled environment.

Order-of-magnitude conceptual estimates of building space requirements for the town center were prepared by ERA. These included 549,200 square feet of non-retail space and 935,200 square feet of retail space in Year 10 of operation.[28] The non-retail land uses included a fire station, post office, library, theaters, banks, office space, hospital, television studio, service shops, warehouse space, and community administration. In keeping with the Garden City tradition, ERA also prepared conceptual acreage requirements for an EPCOT satellite community.[29] A residential community east of the EPCOT site appears in a Disney World Phase One plan from January 1966.[30]

Turning back to EPCOT proper, the planning team began to address the issue of neighborhoods. EPCOT planner Marvin Davis recalled that Disney had given some thought to details of neighborhood planning before he died but the scheme was not fully worked out.[31] The EPCOT plans feature neighborhood facilities adjacent to the WEDway PeopleMover stations. This compares to Ebenezer Howard's six wards for the Garden City, each with a store or depot. Most important in EPCOT's neighborhood concept is that the facilities would be placed within walking distance of residences.

The issue of residential privacy presented a challenge to EPCOT planners. Disney advisor Ray Watson recalls that he raised the issue directly to Disney in 1966, saying, 'Now, you're not going to go out and get it [the milk] in your pajamas. You're going to have to dress up and put a tie on because these people that live there are now on exhibit, just like your cast members are elsewhere.'[32] Putting himself in an EPCOT resident's place, Watson envisioned visitors peering down at his house from PeopleMovers and told Disney just that. While the EPCOT concept remained at a conceptual stage at the time of Disney's death, Watson's concern was a real one; EPCOT's goals of being both a showcase and a community dedicated to the needs of residents may not have been compatible.

The site plan includes apartment land uses situated between the town center and greenbelt. The single-family houses are located in the 'organic petals' outside the greenbelt, extending to the perimeter of EPCOT. Houses are grouped around open space in large circles. Moreover, the 'radiential' area includes traffic circles for residents' cars only, and streets run behind the houses. Each 'petal' of EPCOT's plan looks like a spacious golf course community without the links with very low development density. The interior open space includes light recreation activities for adults, play areas for children, circulating paths for pedestrians, electric carts, and bicycles. Art historian Karal Ann Marling describes the single-family areas as 'idyllic suburban subdivisions.'[33] This seemingly idyllic environment, however, would have had to confront EPCOT's technological state of becoming and visitors. Apartment and commercial land uses are separated from single-family residences in a typical Euclidian zoning pattern. Thus, households falling under different income categories would be separated. However, one of EPCOT's goals would be to adopt new types of land use policies (see Chapter 8, Regulation and Community Governance/Social Planning). Overall, EPCOT's dense urban core model can be contrasted with its 'radiential' areas, which are more akin to the Jeffersonian ideal reflected in Frank Lloyd Wright's utopian Broadacre City (1930–35). Wright actually visited the studios during

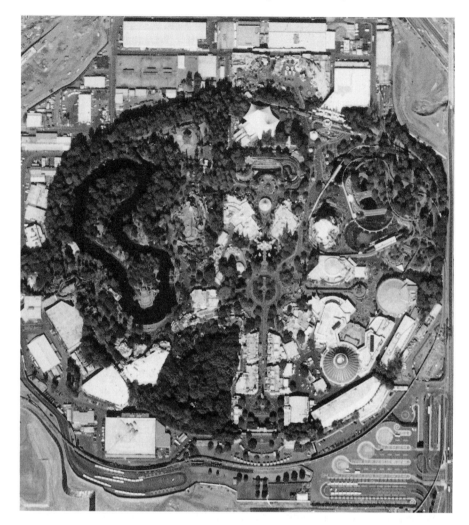

Figure 1.2   Aerial photograph of Disneyland Park, 1998. The hub and
spoke layout of Disneyland would influence Disney's thinking
about urban form. Note the large amount of open space in the
park. Source: I.K. Curtis Services

the production of *Fantasia* (1940). Disney's planning addressed transportation needs with PeopleMovers and monorails as opposed to freeways or
buses. Conceptually, the PeopleMover replaced the streetcars that Disney
saw disappear in Los Angeles.[34]
     The greenbelt was a key element in Ebenezer Howard's Garden City. In
EPCOT, the greenbelt is situated between the apartments and the single-
family houses. The greenbelt includes recreational facilities, playgrounds,

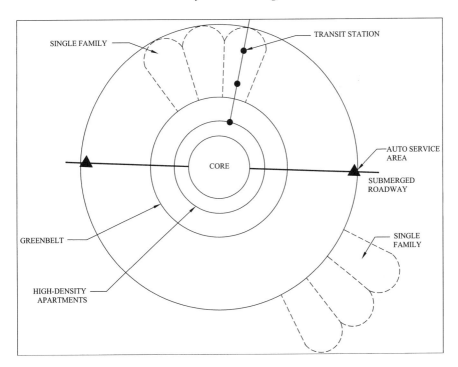

Figure 1.3 Simplified diagram of EPCOT. Based on ideas expressed by Disney, Marvin Davis, Herbert Ryman, and George Rester

churches, and schools. From the profit perspective of most real estate developers, however, land is expensive and does not produce an adequate return on investment with low coverage ratios, especially when swampland site improvements are required. The single-family and greenbelt areas together provide a seeming abundance of open space in the plan. A typical community developer would be hard pressed to provide reasonably priced housing to consumers when there is insufficient return on the investment in land due to a large amount of non-income-generating space. Still, cities require open space and WED Enterprises had a pioneering team in that department.

After development of Disneyland, Disney seemed to be sold on the radial plan. As Marvin Davis recalled, Disney 'wanted to solve everything with the radial idea.'[35] At Disneyland, Disney believed that the hub and related traffic flow gave 'people a sense of orientation – they know where they are at all times.'[36] This urban design element provides reassurance (see Figures 1.2 and 1.3).

Certainly the radial plan was not a new concept. In fact, it dates at least to the first century B.C. The problem with such plans over time is the difficulty of keeping growth within the boundaries. Urban historian Spiro Kostof concluded that the radial plan became 'a favorite device of traffic engineers and their transportation plans, and it remains so to this day.'[37]

The plot plan also included a 1,000-acre industrial park, located south of EPCOT along the monorail route. Similar to EPCOT proper, there would be a central transportation station at the industrial park. Passengers would disembark from the monorails and board WEDway PeopleMover cars that would radiate to each industrial complex. According to the plan, the industrial park would employ some of the EPCOT residents and visitors would be able to look backstage at plants, research and development laboratories, and computer centers for major corporations.[38] In 1967, the company expanded on the concept. For example, the industrial park would feature an industrial conference center for all participants. It also would house automated warehousing.[39] The research and development activities at the industrial park also might provide prototype applications for EPCOT. Disney probably was familiar with the landscaped Stanford Industrial Park (1951) with its strong ties to academic research.[40] In addition, Disney's friend, architect William Pereira, envisioned a research park for the University of California at Irvine in the late 1950s. A new technology institute was located west of Orlando which would later become the University of Central Florida.

If EPCOT had actually been built, it might look a lot like a model of a futuristic city that was created for display at Disneyland. Progress City was a massive, one-eighth scale model that was closely intertwined with the EPCOT planning process. It was placed on display on the upper one-half floor of General Electric's Carousel of Progress (now Innoventions) at Disneyland beginning in July 1967 and removed in 1973 (see Figure 1.4).[41]

Progress City could be viewed by visitors on foot or riding the PeopleMover. It was incredibly detailed: it measured 6,900 square feet (115 feet wide), contained 22,000 miniature trees and shrubs, 4,500 buildings (lit from within), 1,400 street lights, a climate-controlled center city, amusement park rides in motion, sports stadiums, an airport, an atomic power plant, underground passageways, residential cul-de-sacs, retail establishments, monorails, electric sidewalks, schools, churches, electric trains, electric carts, and PeopleMovers.[42] Disney did not live long enough to oversee the model's production. However, his wishes for the model appear to have been carried out, including his insistence that the interiors of the model's tiny buildings be finished, furnished, and lit.[43]

Florida Film writer Marty Sklar describes the relationship of the model to EPCOT:

I went through a lot of material with Marvin Davis, and with other people who were in the trenches on it ... [A]s we began developing the model of the idea, ... we called it Progress City. That model almost exactly matched all our planning for EPCOT. I think Walt got a kick out of doing that model, without having to say that he was going to build this big city, but it was all there for anybody to see.[44]

Figure 1.4   Photograph of the Progress City model built in 1967 and displayed at Disneyland. Like EPCOT, Progress City's dense urban core focused on a hotel skyscraper as PeopleMover cars transported residents and visitors to and from the central transportation lobby. Source: author's photograph

With General Electric as sponsor, it was no surprise that Progress City was all-electric. A portion of the model is still on display at the Magic Kingdom in Florida's Walt Disney World. It is estimated that more than 31 million visitors viewed Progress City at Disneyland before it was removed.[45] The model communicated EPCOT's physical plan and overall building massing. Interestingly, the model did not rely on ERA's conceptual acreage and/or building space estimates.[46]

Model production had a long and important role in the company's history. Disney himself enjoyed building models. Michael Broggie recalls, 'Walt thoroughly enjoyed building and painting brass locomotives, freight and passenger cars, and buildings that come in kits requiring hours of intricate and painstaking assembly.'[47] The lead model builder for Progress City was Fred Joerger. There is no doubt that Disney's own vision, combined with his love of model building, would have yielded a somewhat different Progress City model had he lived to see it built. Still, John Hench notes that Disney had not gotten into the 'particulars' of the model's construction because he thought that what was needed was 'a simple statement for people and that would be enough. And so the other things were still in his head and still crystallizing.'[48]

The three-dimensional Progress City developed out of Marvin Davis' plans and Herbert Ryman's paintings. Ryman spent a harried weekend with Disney and turned Davis' Disneyland site plan into a rendering that Roy O. Disney could present to financiers in New York in September 1953.[49] Animator Ward Kimball recalls that Ryman was good at doing 'big paintings' and 'bird's-eye views.'[50] According to Kimball, Disney was very visually-oriented and 'had to see everything ...'[51] As far as Ryman's work on Progress City/EPCOT was concerned, his friend Bill Evans recalls, 'Walt was telling Ryman what he wanted to see, and it was the same team [as Disneyland].'[52] Working with Davis and Ryman, Disney got the visual he needed. Ryman's conceptual renderings of Progress City communicate many of the ideas Disney would use in EPCOT, everything from white WEDway stations to shimmering satellite communities in the distance. With such devices and talent, Disney almost had a form of virtual reality in the mid-1960s.

As previously noted, several prior Disney organization projects helped to prepare the Disney team for the conceptualization of EPCOT. One was a proposed ski resort in California. Disney wanted to introduce higher development standards to the ski resort genre with the Mineral King project.[53] The site is located approximately half way between Los Angeles and San Francisco in the Sequoia National Forest. This was a work in progress at the time of his death and was never built. Even so, planning a self-contained ski village gave the Disney organization some experience in community planning.

Disney wanted Mineral King to resemble a resort he had seen and admired while making a film in Switzerland. Disney also had been Pageantry Committee Chairman for the 1960 Winter Olympic Games at Squaw Valley, California.[54] The architectural firm of Ladd & Kelsey was retained to design the Mineral King village, Marvin Davis worked on the project in-house, and a model was constructed.[55] Elements of the plan included a chapel, an ice-skating rink, convenience shops, restaurants, 14 ski lifts, a conference center, a heliport, various lodging types, and a 60,000-square-foot facility below the village. Like at Disneyland, the service facilities would be hidden to provide a more aesthetically pleasing 'stage.' Moreover, housing was planned to accommodate 2,400 permanent beds and 4,800 temporary summer units. Finally, no automobiles would be permitted in the Mineral King Valley and the 2,500-car parking area would be linked by mass transit, similar to the PeopleMover.

A second Disney project is the California Institute of the Arts (CalArts), located north of Los Angeles in Valencia, California. The school was formally established in 1961 and combined the Chouinard Art Institute and the Los Angeles Conservatory of Music. Disney's involvement with Chouinard dated to the 1930s when he sent studio artists there. He originally envisioned a Seven Arts City concept that would be similar to the Bauhaus.[56] It was Disney's goal, therefore, to utilize a multidisciplinary approach and fieldwork in the training of students. In 1960, Disney considered adding a commercial complex with theaters, galleries, shopping centers, and restaurants. However, Harrison Price determined that this concept was not financially feasible and no real design work was ever performed.[57] The architectural firm of Ladd & Kelsey was engaged to design CalArts. In addition, Disney consulted his architect friend William Pereira who had planned the University of California at Irvine campus.

Price, who is a longtime CalArts board member, believes that CalArts as it is today is the facility that Disney envisioned at the time of his death.[58] The campus plan includes a central school and administrative complex, student housing, recreation facilities, and open space. The CalArts campus opened in 1971, after considerable leadership from Roy O. Disney, and offers degree programs in art, design, music, dance, film, video, and theater.[59]

Planning experience with world's fairs and expositions also contributed to EPCOT conceptualization. In preparation for participation in the 1964–65 New York World's Fair, Disney sent many staff members to the 1958 World's Fair in Brussels and the 1962 World's Fair in Seattle.[60] At the 1964–65 New York World's Fair, the Disney organization handled a total of 150,000 visitors per day in its four pavilions.[61] Architect Victor Gruen noted that there had been a bid to locate the 1964 fair on a site in Maryland, which would later be converted to a circular Washington, D.C., satellite town of 100,000 persons.[62] Its proportions, concentric rings, and core are reminiscent of EPCOT. The proposed concept for Maryland also featured a raised platform for the fair (and later city) buildings, underneath which infrastructure would be placed. Marty Sklar has said he believes that Disney was influenced by this proposed Maryland fair concept.[63] The underground component is similar to Disney's 'utilidor.' Disney could have learned of the proposal through Robert Moses, fair president, or General Joe Potter, the fair's executive vice president. Furthermore, historian John Findlay believes that the 1962 Seattle fair's City Century 21 model, with its central climate-controlled dome, anticipated EPCOT.[64]

Harrison Price remembers flying on an airplane with Moses and Disney and they were 'talking at the same time for about an hour.'[65] Disney and Moses definitely were not always in agreement. According to Imagineer Richard Irvine, Disney believed that Moses overlooked the success of Norman Bel Geddes' Futurama exhibit at the 1939 New York World's Fair, which showed that industry could reach the public through showmanship.[66] Ward Kimball recalls that Disney attended the 1939 fair. He also emphasizes, 'Of course they also had films out on it.'[67] The Futurama model, designed by Bel Geddes, was a vision of the year 1960, obsessed with cars and superhighways to permit the nation to spread out.[68] This stands in contrast to Disney's Progress City model nearly 30 years later.

In the 1960s, the company's proposal for the Riverfront Square redevelopment project in St. Louis helped to make Disney aware of the problems of America's inner cities. Disney initially was approached by the Civic Center

Redevelopment Corporation in 1963 to produce a film about the city. Instead, he suggested that his company explore participation in the redevelopment of a two-block area along the riverfront. Similar to EPCOT, the downtown area would exclude automobile traffic. In early 1964, Marvin Davis prepared preliminary plans for a five-level atrium structure which included a town square, the Old St. Louis Gaslight Plaza, and New Orleans.[69] In addition, plans featured early concepts for a pirates attraction. Versions of both New Orleans and a pirates ride would eventually appear at Disneyland. The St. Louis plans also would include an underground level. ERA performed site and economic analyses for the planned project.

Disney's sense of nostalgia (he spent a part of his youth in Missouri), in addition to the company's contacts at Monsanto and other companies in St. Louis, almost resulted in company participation in a project with a modest projected financial return.[70] By July 1965, the company, which already was in the midst of the complex Project Florida, withdrew from Riverfront Square. Company attorney Robert Foster, looking back over the decades, believes that this was the period when Disney 'began really coming out with all these problems and things that had gone wrong with inner cities.'[71] Still, some would criticize Disney for planning his urban laboratory on virgin land and not in an inner city environment.

In the end, Disneyland provided Disney with most of his planning experience. First and foremost, Disneyland is a 'show.' Disneyland planner Marvin Davis stressed that 'no one before Walt had used movie making experience and techniques to tell a story visually in a three-dimensional park setting.'[72] The three-dimensional visual sequencing of the environment put the visitor on a stage conceived primarily by a team of art directors from the motion picture industry.

Disneyland's castle was a forerunner of EPCOT's landmark hotel. The hotel in the center of EPCOT's plan is a 'wienie.' According to John Hench, '[Disney] didn't want to walk down an alley or a passageway that didn't have something interesting that beckoned to him. He called it the "wienie" … And when we had one of those places, we put a rocket in one place, a ship in another …'[73] Richard Irvine added that a wienie also provides transition to the next 'scene.'[74] The 30-plus-story EPCOT hotel wienie beckons and also provides orientation for people on the ground. The term derives from the early carnival days. The most prominent wienie at Disneyland is Sleeping Beauty's Castle, conceptualized by Disney and Herbert Ryman and refined by architect Bill Martin.

With Disneyland, the design team learned an old lesson: total control in planning does not always yield intended results. For example, the original Disneyland site plan did not provide for sufficient paths between the themed lands; visitors were required to return to the hub to reach another land. In such cases, total design control could occasionally mean relinquishing control to the visitors. Paraphrased by Hench, Disney instructed the team to 'Just remember, if … [visitors] make a path through there, there's probably a very good reason for them to do that ... Don't put a fence there. You just pave that path.'[75]

Hench also points to Disney's well-known attention to detail in planning his projects and that he was a highly intuitive man.[76] In planning and development, it is often attention to detail that separates the 'cookie cutter' projects from developments that set new standards. In 1963, legendary community builder James Rouse made a surprising speech about Disneyland at the Harvard Graduate School of Design:

> I hold a view that may be somewhat shocking to an audience as sophisticated as this, and that is, that the greatest piece of urban design in the United States today is Disneyland. If you think about Disneyland and think of its performance in relationship to its purpose – its meaning to people more than its meaning to the process of development – you will find ... [that] it took an area of activity – the amusement park – and lifted it to a standard so high in its performance, in its respect for people, in its functioning for people, that it really became a brand new thing ... I find more to learn in the standards that have been set and the goals that have been achieved in the development of Disneyland than in any other single piece of physical development in the country.[77]

The Disneyland plan, according to Rouse, was a people-oriented design executed with high development standards. The park was far removed from the seedy amusement parks Disney had frequented with his daughters. Still, Disneyland was far removed from the problems of the 1960s urban ghetto. If Disney could elevate the old, dirty amusement park to the level of Disneyland, what might he and his team have been able to accomplish in the field of community design? This appears to be a question Disney was asking himself at the end of his life.

One of the important maxims at WED Enterprises was, according to Bill Martin, 'we never threw anything away and a lot of these ideas ended up in other plans years later.' Examples include the proposed International Street at Disneyland and a Chinatown district, neither of which was built.[78] Of course, international theming has a long tradition in fairs and exhibitions and would be featured in the EPCOT concept (see Figure 1.5).

Edison Square, another historically themed street proposed for Disneyland, evolved into General Electric's Carousel of Progress. Also, an American Liberty Street was scheduled to open at Disneyland in 1959.[79] Disney visited Williamsburg, Virginia, with his family near the end of his life and possessed several books about colonial Williamsburg. Instead, Liberty Square eventually became part of the Magic Kingdom at Florida's Walt Disney World in 1971. The WED Enterprises' maxim that an idea sometimes must wait until its time illustrates that a concept and the final show installation can end up being two very different things. The EPCOT plan was only conceptual when Disney died.

Disneyland's plan has had an impact on the design professions outside the 'berm,' as the park's elevated perimeter was called. For example, Main

Figure 1.5   A miniature international village from Disneyland's
Storybook Land (1956) attraction. Disney loved miniatures
and this would be reflected in his planning of the Progress
City model. Source: author's photograph

Street, U.S.A. has had a profound influence on the built environment. It has
helped to encourage adaptive re-use of historic town centers, influence the
design of shopping malls and entertainment venues, and discourage the
invasion of the automobile into pedestrian areas.[80] Several critics, however,
view some of these trends as ultimately contributing to the decline of 'authentic' public space in the United States. John Hench notes that Walt
Disney Imagineering still gets 'contacted by little towns in Nebraska and
other places that want to do their Main Street over and they want it to be
"authentic" like ours.'[81] Of course, Main Street, U.S.A. is Disney's idealized
thoroughfare. The Main Streets of the period were unpaved, muddy, and
featured uncontrolled signage and telegraph poles.

   On July 24, 1966, shortly before Disney's death, the three-acre, $15
million historically themed New Orleans Square partially opened to Disneyland visitors.[82] Imagineer Sam McKim, a key Main Street, U.S.A. designer,
developed early concepts for New Orleans Square. Don Edgren was the
structural engineer and Bill Martin served as architect. In addition, Ken
Anderson, John Hench, and Herbert Ryman all were sent to New Orleans in
preparation for design and construction. Building elevations were based on
photographs of the real city. Such steps reflect Disney's attention to detail in

his projects. The result was a pedestrian-oriented, architecturally detailed shopping area of the kind Disney envisioned for EPCOT's core. In fact, Ryman's 'New Orleans Candy Shop' painting appeared in the Florida Film.

In 1964, architect Charles Moore observed that the success of Disneyland was partially attributable to the 'megalopolitan' sprawl of the surrounding region. He noted that 'it is engaged in replacing many of those elements of the public realm which have vanished in the featureless private floating world of southern [sic] California, whose only edge is the ocean, and whose center is otherwise undiscoverable.'[83] The 1966 EPCOT model was conceived to help address these issues. It should be emphasized, however, that both Disneyland and EPCOT would be privately-controlled demonstration spaces as opposed to the often gritty urban landscapes of America in the 1960s.

In addition, Disneyland's idealized Town Square reflected what the designers believed to be the essential elements of the 'true American town center' of yesteryear. As Richard Francaviglia notes, 'Significantly, the buildings around the public square represent some of the key institutions in American life, the railroad station, bank, city hall, fire station, and "emporium."'[84] While Town Square was located near the park's entrance, EPCOT's 'town center' would be placed in its hub. Instead of Town Square's nostalgic train station, monorails and PeopleMovers would handle large volumes of people in a futuristic, subterranean Union Station in EPCOT. The more intimate functions of a town commons would have had to be handled at the neighborhood level in EPCOT. There, an easy trip downtown was available via the WEDway, the intermediate transit mode that was faster and cleaner than the horse-drawn trolley of Disney's yesteryear. The most difficult EPCOT planning challenge, perhaps, was that Disney's experimental community would present his team with 20,000 residents, as opposed to visitors like those at Disneyland, who could board a tram and return to the suburbs after the fireworks.

There is no question that the planning of Disneyland strongly influenced Disney. Disney's planning of his own backyard had an impact on planning the Anaheim theme park. Disney's house, located on Carolwood Drive in the Los Angeles community of Holmby Hills, featured a landscaped, bermed, model railroad system in the backyard. Disney and his staff installed 2,615 feet of track, a 90-foot-long tunnel to avoid Lillian Disney's flower garden, and a 46-foot trestle.[85] The backyard was influenced by the 1948 studio film, *So Dear to My Heart*. The film, set in 1903, was nostalgic and featured a barn and railroad station. Disney's backyard barn is now on display in Los Angeles' Griffith Park. Film authority Leonard Maltin quotes Disney in *The Disney Films*, as saying, '*So Dear* was especially close to me. Why, that's the life my brother and I grew up with as kids out in Missouri.'[86] While EPCOT would be the community of tomorrow, the word *community* undoubtedly held Midwestern meanings for Disney. Disneyland is a direct descendant of the Holmby Hills backyard. Roger Broggie, who helped

Disney develop the Carolwood Pacific Railroad, would go on to oversee development of the monorails and PeopleMovers at Disneyland.

Development of the Walt Disney Studios in Burbank also gave Disney planning experience. The success of the Walt Disney Studios plan is that it is laid out like a pedestrian-oriented college campus but is still based on the needs of animated film production. Animator Frank Thomas remembers that Disney used wooden models of the buildings in Burbank to develop the plan for the studio.[87] Similar to later plans for EPCOT's industrial complex recreation areas, the studio campus featured ping-pong tables and horse-shoe, badminton, and basketball courts.[88] Also, as he would later do in Florida, Disney once considered building apartments on the lot for employees, according to story artist Joe Grant.[89]

The original Walt Disney Studios buildings were arranged to permit the maximum amount of sunlight and green space between them.[90] Disney began to plan the studio in 1939 with an in-house design team. The buildings were designed by architect Kem Weber. The Burbank studio provides a human-scale environment, with lawns, paths, trees, and separation of the automobile. The conceptual plans for EPCOT would draw upon several of these design elements.

Naturally, there were countless influences on the planning of EPCOT in addition to the company's own experience. For example, Diane Disney Miller recalls that her father read city planning books during the summer of 1966.[91] Harrison Price prepared an overview of community planning for Disney in September 1966. Of particular relevance to EPCOT planning are outline points including the potential need for further studies relating to institutional analysis, climatic control, and analysis of building materials and methods. Price's memorandum also includes a thumbnail sketch on planning history. The Garden City, neighborhood unit, and Radburn, New Jersey plans are presented.[92]

Ebenezer Howard's *Garden Cities of To-Morrow* (1902), influenced by company towns, attempted to blend the best physical qualities of town and country.[93] Howard's recommended plan included a circular form, a garden and town center, central park, Crystal Palace glass arcade, greenbelt, industry, and railway-linked 'off-shoots' (see Figures 1.6, 1.7).

The Garden City's core features a garden surrounded by a town hall, museum, gallery, hospital, library, and theater. Howard suggested a population of 32,000. His plans incorporated his lengthy social agenda, a quasi-public Central Council, and a semi-rural appearance. Letchworth, approximately 34 miles from London, was the first Garden City. Urban historian Sir Peter Hall notes that Letchworth architects Raymond Unwin and Barry Parker 'believed that creativity came from an imaginative understanding of the past.'[94] Their reproduction of a medieval village no doubt would have appealed to Disney.

Planner Clarence Perry developed the neighborhood unit plan for New York City in 1926. The principle behind the plan was to bring facilities

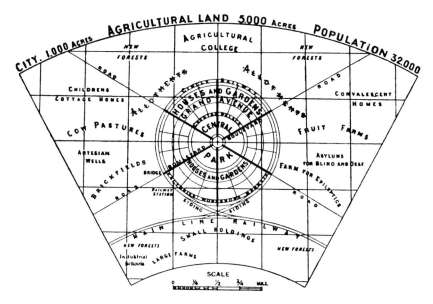

Figure 1.6 Ebenezer Howard's Garden City diagram, 1898. The EPCOT planners were strongly influenced by the Garden City tradition in planning. Source: Howard 1898

residents need on a daily basis within walking distance of their houses. The neighborhood unit population was to number approximately 5,000 persons. Perry hoped to restore political participation through community centers. As urban historian Lewis Mumford observed, Perry identified the fundamental social cell of the city and established the principle of cellular growth.[95]

Another landmark in planning history is Radburn, New Jersey, which Clarence Stein and Henry Wright designed in 1928. It followed in the Garden City tradition but would be characterized by superblocks of residential cul-de-sacs, abutting greenbelts and recreation areas, specialized roads, separation of the pedestrian, and living rooms facing toward open space.[96] Another key element of the plan was a town center. The EPCOT planners would apply each of these elements in some form.

Scottish biologist Sir Patrick Geddes reasoned that the Garden City concept was a good device to use for planning entire regions. Geddes is known for his Garden City-inspired plan for Tel Aviv in the 1920s. In the United States during the 1920s, this regional philosophy was adopted by people like Mumford, Stein, Wright, and Catherine Bauer, who influenced the Roosevelt Administration's New Deal planning policy. Ultimately, the self-contained Garden City gave way to decentralized residential sprawl made possible by the proliferation of the automobile.

Victor Gruen, the father of the enclosed shopping mall, believed that the Garden City's central Crystal Palace was a precursor of the modern mall.

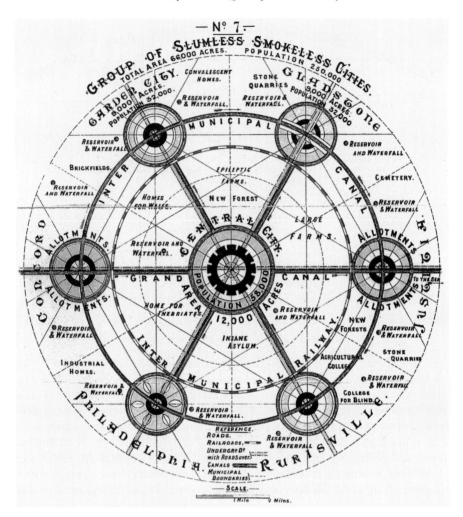

Figure 1.7   Ebenezer Howard's 'Social Cities' diagram, 1898. Instead of
monorails, Howard would incorporate an inter-municipal
railway into his plans. Source: Howard 1898

However, EPCOT's replacement of the car with mass transit systems reflects another criticism of the Garden City: that a centralized plan like
Howard's inevitably would result in traffic congestion in the automotive
age. The postwar, subway-linked satellite town of Vällingby, Sweden, a
descendant of the Garden City, would be a popular urban planning model in
the 1960s and have a strong influence on the EPCOT planning team (see
Chapter 2, Transportation: The End of 'Autopia').

In the United States, Rexford Tugwell's Resettlement Administration's
New Deal communities of Greenbelt, Maryland, Greenhills, Ohio, and

Greendale, Wisconsin, were the closest the country came to developing Howard's Garden City model. Greenbelt (1935) was heavily influenced by Radburn, New Jersey, as well as Perry's neighborhood unit. The plan consists of five superblocks forming a semicircle around open space, and all residents have direct pedestrian access to parks, retail, and community facilities.

EPCOT also would reflect a strong contemporary British influence. As John Hench recalls, 'Walt had shot pictures in England ... He thought they knew something about different things.'[97] In addition, Ray Watson compares the self-contained New Towns of Britain during the 1960s with EPCOT.[98] Finally, General Joe Potter spoke approvingly of going 'to the English law, which says that's all the bigger it gets!'[99] This is called growth control. The origins of modern public planning trace to England in the late 1800s and the shocking public health conditions at the time in cities like London. Public health and safety are the foundations of public planning in the United States. Disney's privately controlled planning approach would raise classic questions about private property rights and regulation.

Perhaps the best known British New Town is Milton Keynes, located 60 miles northwest of London, planned in 1966. Its distance from the capital was a reflection of the desire to make the New Town self-contained in the tradition of Howard's Garden City. The site is located on a main radial transportation corridor to London. Planners Llewelyn-Davies originally envisioned a population of 40,000 persons. The plans for the New Town focus on Central Milton Keynes, including a large enclosed shopping center and office space. Outside the center, 13 residential villages have their own commercial centers. The plans also include separate roads for pedestrians, open space, and bicycle paths. The Milton Keynes Development Corporation was established in 1967. ERA's HUD presentation outline for Disney made reference to community developer planning authority under the British system of development corporations (see Chapter 8, Regulation and Community Governance/Social Planning). This British precedent would become a key element in Disney's preliminary community governance and regulatory thinking for EPCOT.

In addition to Howard, architect Charles-Edouard Jeanneret Le Corbusier (1887–1965) ranked among the great utopians and profoundly influenced the built environment in the twentieth century. His most significant work in urban planning includes his large-scale urban plans of the 1920s: the Contemporary City for Three Million Inhabitants (1922) and the Plan Voisin (1925). His basic vision was that of skyscrapers set in a park-like environment based on orthogonal plans with radiating boulevards.

The Contemporary City's land use plan consists of a Great Central Station, skyscrapers, housing, public services, museums, universities, parks, sports facilities, protected habitats, and an industrial city. The open ground floors of the towers are surrounded by parks, restaurants, shops, and related uses. The Contemporary City's central multi-level station is similar to

EPCOT's transportation lobby. Its housing plan groups dwellings of various densities around open space.

The Plan Voisin was, in Le Corbusier's words, the result of 'drift and opportunism' in the growth of Paris. The architect's solution was to apply his utopian plan to the city by demolishing districts and extending a large freeway through the City of Light. As he once noted, 'a city made for speed is made for success.' In his later years, Le Corbusier planned the city of Chandigarh, India, the new capital for the Punjab state. The architect based the master plan on careful observation of market demand and used a system of specialized roads. Overall, Le Corbusier's physical planning objectives are consistent with EPCOT's: de-congest the centers of cities, increase density, provide more transportation modes, and increase the area of green and open spaces. Le Corbusier was influenced by Tony Garnier's plans for the Industrial City (1901) for Lyon, France. This city would be oriented to workers and was based on Socialist principles. Prior to New York City's action in 1916, land uses would be zoned into districts by function.

Contemporary developments also influenced Disney and his planning team. For example, Disney was impressed by the plans for the new communities of Reston, Virginia (1962), and Columbia, Maryland (1963).[100] Developer Robert Simon Jr.'s original master plan for the 7,400-acre Reston property included an 85-acre, mixed-use town center consisting of office, retail, entertainment, and hotel space. Like EPCOT, Reston was designed to be a model alternative to suburbia. The urban core was planned to provide residents and visitors with a vital center.[101] Dwelling units were located in five residential villages, each with its own center. In addition, the Reston plan features a 1,000-acre business corridor.

Developer James Rouse's original plans for Columbia included 10 satellite villages for 100,000 residents, planned around a downtown. Rouse's four goals for the community were as follows: respect the land, build a real city as opposed to suburbia, promote growth of the individual and family, and make a profit. Rouse later stated that the third goal was most important.[102] This compares to Disney's most important goal for the experimental community called EPCOT: working with American industry to develop new technologies to meet the public need. As with Columbia, EPCOT's plan was opposed to suburbia and was dedicated to the public need and happiness of residents. Making a profit on EPCOT would be a completely different matter (see Chapter 6, Economic Analysis and Finance). Disney and Rouse actually toured East Coast developments together with their wives for three days.[103]

In the Radburn tradition, houses in the Columbia villages would be grouped in cul-de-sacs around public open spaces, meeting facilities, and elementary schools. Other prominent amenities included pathways, open space, and lakes. Using his own brand of social experimentation, Rouse would incorporate communal mailboxes to foster community and 'interfaith centers' in which people of all religions would mingle. Columbia's original plan also stressed toleration of racial differences in the community and the provision of a mix of housing at all price levels.

Another influence on EPCOT's physical planning, as previously noted, was Gruen's book *The Heart of Our Cities*, in which he proposed his own Metropolis of Tomorrow. The plan featured a metropolis based on a system of cellular clusters: the neighborhood (900 persons); the community (five neighborhoods; the town (four communities); the city (ten towns); and the metropolis (ten cities). Gruen's plan also included community, town, city, and metro centers. The Metropolis of Tomorrow also would feature various transportation modes, including travel by air, long-distance rail, inter-city high-speed transit, and a freeway system surrounding the cities. Gruen's plan for a typical city, including his 'petals' concept, is representative of the organic planning movement of that time and is clearly reflected in the EPCOT concept (see Figure 1.8).[104] Organic planning has its roots in the work of Howard, Geddes, landscape architect Frederick Law Olmsted, ecologist Artur Glikson, and others. Planning scholar Kevin Lynch emphasized that, like biological organisms, these plans must be understood as 'dynamic wholes' that repair themselves and regenerate.[105]

Gruen admired Howard's work. He explained that the differences between his diagrams and Howard's were 'due to the stormy development of technology and sociology in the intervening 60 years.'[106] EPCOT's radial plan seems to blend elements of the Garden City, Gruen's typical city organism, and the Maryland proposal for the planned 1964 World's Fair (see Figure 1.9).

Yet another influence could be Leonardo da Vinci. The da Vinci plates in Gruen's book show horse and cart traffic relegated to underground passageways but do not include plans. As previously noted, Lewis Mumford wrote that da Vinci proposed building a group of ten cities limited to 30,000 persons each, with gardens and separation of the pedestrian. Disney's younger daughter, Sharon Disney Lund, recalled that her father was fascinated by a large book he was given on da Vinci.[107] A da Vinci plan for a town is presented as Figure 1.10. Its circular plan, core, and radiating lines are reminiscent of EPCOT, along with the tunnels and central structure.[108]

Henry Ford and Thomas Edison, two giants of American technological progress, were also men Disney admired. It is impossible to identify specific influences they had on the EPCOT philosophy. Disney's whole life, from the end of the Victorian Age to the introduction of fiber optic telephone cables, was a 'state of becoming' and filled with extraordinary influences.

As mentioned, Henry Ford and Greenfield Village in Dearborn, Michigan, left lasting impressions on Disney and strongly influenced the creation of Disneyland. He visited there in 1940 and 1948 (once with Ward Kimball) and met Ford.[109] John Hench recalls that he visited Greenfield Village with Disney on one occasion as well.[110] As noted, technological progress through invention and free enterprise is readily observable there through its many

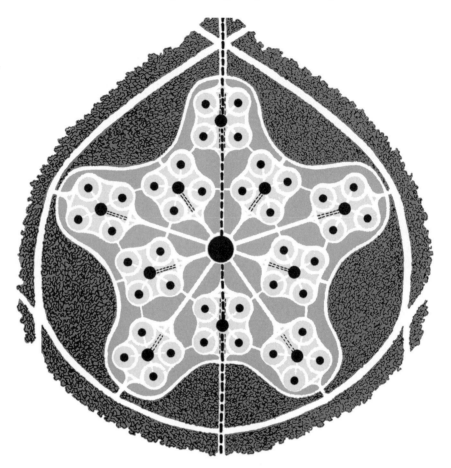

Figure 1.8 Victor Gruen's detail of a typical city, 1964. Disney also was influenced by the organic planning movement. Copyright Simon & Schuster

historical exhibits. Thomas Edison's Menlo Park and Florida laboratories also are preserved there. It is often said that Edison's greatest invention was one he didn't patent: the industrial research laboratory.[111]

In 1941, Disney made a goodwill and film-making tour of South America. In 1944, Walt Disney Productions produced *The Amazon Awakens*, which featured the 17,000-acre cleared jungle Ford Plantation at Fordlandia, Brazil, that Disney had visited during the 1941 tour. The plantation required facilities such as housing and schools for the workers and their children. Like EPCOT, it was a company town.

In some respects, EPCOT would be Disney's Florida laboratory for urban problems, carved out of the swamplands. Unfortunately, he did not live long

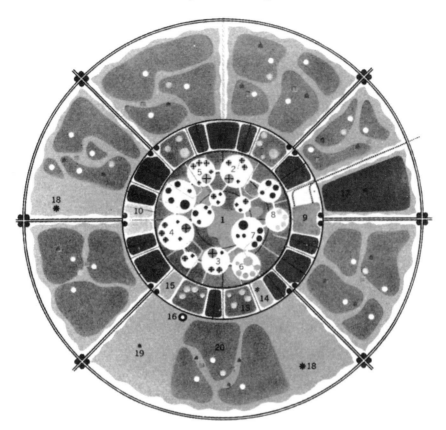

Figure 1.9   Washington Metropolitan Board of Trade's proposed plan for
the 1964 World's Fair. With its concentric rings and raised
platform for infrastructure, this plan strongly influenced
Disney's thinking about EPCOT. Copyright Simon & Schuster

enough to refine his final vision. But EPCOT would have to be more than a
scientific experiment. It would also have to satisfy the needs of visitors,
residents/employees, and part of its name: community. Again, these may not
have been compatible goals.

In addition to his adult influences, Disney's early life exhibits experiences that helped form the development of Disneyland and conceptualization
of EPCOT. For example, his father, Elias, was a carpenter at the World's
Columbian Exposition of 1893 in Chicago. In Disney's highly personal
film, *So Dear to My Heart*, Jeremiah's scrapbook features a souvenir from
the exposition. The White City of the exposition gave rise to the City
Beautiful Movement.[112]

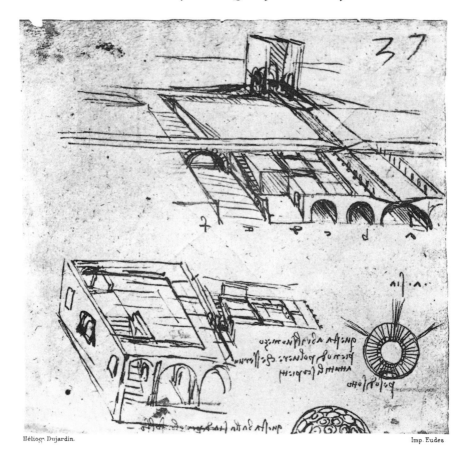

Héliog. Dujardin.   Imp. Eudes

Figure 1.10   Town plan by Leonardo da Vinci. Source: *Bibliotheque de L'Institut de France*

In addition, the exposition featured themed international villages and electric transportation conveyances, incorporating the work of George Westinghouse. Frederick Law Olmsted and Daniel Burnham were the two 'giants' behind the spectacular. As theme park historian Judith Adams notes about Disneyland, 'Walt Disney would embrace the unified ... planning concept, with its reliance on technology, that was so brilliantly incorporated by the World's Columbian Exposition.'[113]

It is important to ask again, what did the word *community* mean to Disney? Illustrative of his small town Midwestern roots, Disney made the following statement during a visit to his boyhood home in Marceline, Missouri: 'I feel so sorry for people who live in cities all their lives and don't have a little hometown. I do. I'm glad my dad picked out a little town where he could have a farm ... .'[114] Disney's recollections of a rural yesteryear would have to be reconciled with what he learned during visits to the laboratories of NASA and IBM to create a company town/visitor environment always in a state of becoming.

During the period 1918–19, Disney served as an ambulance driver in France. Both Disney and his architect friend, Welton Becket, enjoyed the radiant plan of Paris.[115] As John Hench is fond of saying, 'You get much more information by being on the spot and having this information as an experience.'[116] Disney had traveled and those experiences would also be applied to his planning process.

In 1972, architect Peter Blake, an authority on Le Corbusier, summed up his enthusiasm over EPCOT:

> [W]hat an extraordinarily imaginative idea to propose a vast, living, ever-changing laboratory of urban design! Not even Le Corbusier at his brashest ever proposed anything so daring … [I]t could become one of the most influential research tools yet devised for a rapidly urbanizing world.[117]

EPCOT would, like most of Disney's concepts, wait for its time and evolve.

Chapter 2

Transportation: The End of 'Autopia'

On the day before he died, Walt lay on the hospital bed staring at the ceiling.
It was squares of perforated acoustical tile, and Walt pictured them as a grid map
for Disney World ... Every four tiles represented a square mile and he said,
'Now there is where the highway will run ... There is the route for the monorail.'

Roy O. Disney[1]

EPCOT's transit orientation is one of its most distinctive planning features. Disney's fascination with transportation began early in life. Later, his model railroading hobby grew into a core element of Disneyland. After he added the monorail to Disneyland in 1959, Disney became a proponent of mass transit. EPCOT would include an underground transportation lobby beneath the downtown hotel with monorail service for inter-city trips and the WEDway PeopleMover for intra-city use. In addition, automobile and truck traffic was relegated to tunnels beneath the city. The EPCOT transportation plan is reminiscent of the postwar Stockholm satellite model as well as transit-oriented development theory of today.

Imagineer Richard Irvine noted that the way Disney moved people was the first expression of the EPCOT concept.[2] As mentioned, Disney moved large volumes of people at Disneyland and at the 1964–65 New York World's Fair. His California theme park was both a living museum of reproductions and a proving ground for new technology. Disneyland featured examples of various modes of transportation, including pedestrian, horse, sailing ship, steamboat, Santa Fe & Disneyland Railroad, horse-drawn streetcar, horseless carriage, Omnibus, Autopia, Skyway, monorail, Omnimover, and, ultimately, PeopleMover.

Disney's lifelong passion for steam trains started when he was a boy in Marceline, Missouri, a rural township on the Santa Fe Railroad's main line. In 1917, Disney spent the summer selling newspapers on the Santa Fe. By 1923, Disney had moved to Hollywood. There, he could board a Pacific Electric Red Car to travel to Santa Monica, downtown Los Angeles, or Orange County – the future home of Disneyland. By the time Disneyland opened 32 years later, a lot had changed. Only a few lines remained. By then, Sleeping Beauty's Castle rose above Interstate 5, surrounded by a sea of parking spaces, much like a Victor Gruen or Welton Becket shopping mall in suburbia. Los Angeles' rail system had lost the battle with the car and interstate highway system.

As the postwar popularity of the automobile reached a frenzy, Disney attended the Chicago Railroad Fair with animator Ward Kimball in 1948. Disney had been a postman in the Chicago area in 1918 and used the elevated trains to commute to his route.[3] Kimball recalls that Disney wanted to ride the 'el' during their visit 30 years later. According to Kimball, Disney said, "'Yeah, this is the one we take." We got on this thing, and it was unbelievable. Here we were roaring through the tenement districts, and you are three feet away from guys sitting on the bed reading the paper in their shorts. Walt said, "I remember this whole thing."'[4] Monorails and automobiles would enter EPCOT from a submerged roadway, similar to today's Alameda Corridor in Los Angeles.

By mid-1966, Disney prepared to unveil EPCOT's transportation plan. Only electric vehicles would be permitted to travel above the streets of the town center, separated from the pedestrian and similar to a concept in Victor Gruen's plan for Fort Worth, Texas. In addition, as with the plan for Radburn, New Jersey, where pedestrians were separated from traffic, the early project team wanted children to be able to get to school without crossing streets.[5]

As previously noted, each of the six proposed industrial complexes in Project Florida featured a central WEDway station hub. The six complexes were clustered around a monorail station that connected with EPCOT and the rest of the Florida property. Moreover, a semicircular access road linked each industrial complex with employee parking for non-EPCOT residents and with a truck loading area.[6]

Like Disneyland, EPCOT would also be a testing ground. In a letter to Vice President Richard Nixon in May 1959 inviting him to the televised monorail unveiling, Disney highlighted 'two Alweg Monorail Trains which are a prototype of a rapid transit system which may solve many of the traffic problems of our modern day.'[7] Thus, Disneyland's monorail, the first daily operating monorail in the United States, would be both a park attraction and demonstration to policy-makers. Disney's friend, author Ray Bradbury, notes that in 1964, Alweg Corporation offered to build and operate three demonstration monorail lines in Los Angeles using private funds, but the Metropolitan Transit Authority declined.[8] Disney was disappointed that the monorail had yet to be adopted in American cities. In retrospect, Florida Film writer Marty Sklar recalls of Disney:

> … how frustrated he was that he'd done this demonstration of the Monorail at Disneyland, and nobody picked up on it. He blamed the politics in L.A., and how it would never get done… All of these things were actually Walt setting an example, and that certainly culminated in his thinking about EPCOT. It was so much related to his experiences at Disneyland, of course, but also experiences he would have in his daily life.[9]

One of EPCOT's key purposes was to be a showcase. With control over the Florida property made possible by a special district, Disney appeared to hope that he could show the politicians how to plan, build, and operate a transportation system the right way.

EPCOT's transportation lobby was located directly beneath the hotel in the town center and is reminiscent of Le Corbusier's Contemporary City multi-level transportation lobby. It is also similar to concepts like the Archigram Group's 1963 Interchange that featured a transportation node with an interchange for monorails with guided vehicles and tracked railways.[10]

Disney's elevated WEDway PeopleMover was EPCOT's intermediate-range mass transit vehicle designed to transport commuters. With the monorail, the transportation lobby would be a bimodal mass transit station. The transportation plan was based on the hub and spoke layout. EPCOT's three-level transportation hierarchy is described as follows: the bottom level is for trucks; the middle level for automobile traffic and hotel parking, and the monorails and PeopleMovers use the top level.[11] Le Corbusier's transportation levels included mezzanine (fast motor), ground (railway lines), first underground (tubes), second underground (local and suburban lines), and third underground (main lines).[12] Architects during the 1960s designed megastructures incorporating basement levels that connected with underground streets. After the 1964–65 New York World's Fair, Disney returned to Anaheim to begin work with engineer Don Edgren on plans for two subterranean levels for the Pirates of the Caribbean attraction. High-capacity Arrow Development boats take visitors through animated, three-dimensional scenes, unaware that they travel underneath the berm and into an outside show building.[13] It was a revolution in the entertainment industry.

Disney and his planners, like many others during the 1960s, were trying to figure out how to minimize the impacts associated with the automobile in cities. Residents in the single-family 'radiential' areas of EPCOT would park their automobiles at home. Residential streets intersect a one-way road that circles the town center. This road, in turn, connects with an arterial that links EPCOT with other parts of Disney World and the nearby highway system. The new 'Autopia' hid automobile traffic underground and showcased the use of mass transit for residents and EPCOT visitors.

By the mid-1960s, Disney had not grown particularly fond of Southern California's freeway system. For example, he narrated 'Freewayphobia,' shown on television in 1967, which was a comic presentation of how motorists cope with modern freeways.[14] In contrast, a decade earlier, the studio's 'Magic Highway U.S.A.' extolled the importance of America's highways. Producers consulted traffic engineers and highway planners to present futuristic, suspended moving sidewalks.

Disney's Los Angeles, with its smog, noise, and accidents would have to be addressed with planning, engineering, and a future perspective. The EPCOT team was ready to consider all alternatives. These modes included vertical take-off and landing craft.[15] In retrospect, these craft appear as bold as the transportation schemes seen in the renderings of Le Corbusier, Frank Lloyd Wright, and some of the more progressive designers of the 1960s.

The primary identified modes of transportation in EPCOT were more than plans. WED Enterprises actually constructed prototypes of the two systems, the monorail and the PeopleMover. Disneyland's Tomorrowland featured a WEDway PeopleMover station, and had a monorail station in operation since 1959. A 'New Tomorrowland' opened at Disneyland during the summer of 1967. It was called 'World on the Move ... a whole network of totally new transportation systems.'[16] As previously noted, the PeopleMover took Tomorrowland visitors past the Progress City model, where they saw thousands of tiny moving electric vehicles. The narration tape stated that Progress City's transit system was controlled by computers.[17] After numerous tours of research and development facilities, this is the direction in which Disney saw urban transportation going in the computer age. Of course, it would be easier to achieve in a controlled environment compared to having to deal with the political maze surrounding urban transportation.

Disney visited research and development facilities to develop his transportation concept. Marvin Davis remembered one such visit during which Disney's focus on transportation was clear:

> In one plant, they were developing a photo-electric sensor device for blind people. His reaction was: 'Gee, this is exactly what we need for our streetcars. We'll have one little village that will have an underground trolley like they have in France. We won't have a motorman, except one of these devices. This device will detect somebody in front and it will either slow down or stop the trolley.'[18]

Disney typically appeared to be in search of new technologies to enhance story-telling, improve an attraction, or, in this case, develop the EPCOT concept.

One solution, the original Disneyland-Alweg Monorail System, developed by the Alweg Corporation in Cologne, Germany, debuted in Anaheim in 1959 after four years of research by WED Enterprises.[19] In 1958, Disney sent Roger Broggie and Admiral Joe Fowler to visit Alweg, which had developed a system using electric trains that ride on a beam constructed of steel-reinforced concrete. WED Enterprises had envisioned a monorail system for the park as early as 1954, when Herbert Ryman painted a suspended, experimental train that was loosely inspired by a French model vehicle.[20] By 1966, Disneyland's monorails had carried more than 22 million visitors.

The park's winding monorail line was laid out by Bill Martin, who remembers that Disney believed that the monorail would be a good 'medium' to use on the freeways.[21] In 1960, metropolitan transit officials, including those from the city and county of Los Angeles, inspected the Disneyland system.[22] While there was inspection, there was little imitation.

Figure 2.1 A Disneyland-Alweg monorail train is readied for unveiling in 1959. Imagineer/industrial designer Robert Gurr designed the futuristic exterior of the train. From the beginning, Disney viewed his monorails as prototypes with which to help solve modern transportation problems. Source: University of Southern California Regional History Collection

The automobile and interstate highway system were king outside Disneyland's berm.

The Anaheim park monorail system was a working prototype available to the EPCOT designers (see Figure 2.1). In 1961, the monorail was extended 2.5 miles to connect with the Disneyland Hotel, making it the first in the United States to cross a city street. Prior to that, the beamway length measured 0.8 miles. The original 'all-in' cost of the system was $1.4 million per mile. The two original 1959 trains (called Mark I) each had three cars, with an 82-passenger capacity per car.[23] They were powered by 55-horse-power, 600-volt electric motors.[24] Power and drive equipment was manufactured by Westinghouse Electric Company, a firm that would later express an interest in EPCOT. Westinghouse had its own Mass Transit Center at Westinghouse Air Brake and by 1967 was under contract with the Department of Housing and Urban Development (HUD) on projects like electronic highway surveillance devices.[25] The monorail supporting beams, still visible at the park, measure 32 feet to 60 feet in length. Moreover, more than six miles of wire feed the beamway. The beamway itself measures 20 inches wide and 35 inches deep. The supporting pylons measure up to 34 feet in height. In order to stop the trains, braking wheels are located on top of the beamway while rubber tires propel the trains. The Mark I monorail measured seven feet high from the top of the observation bubble to the top of the beam below. The original Mark I trains could achieve a top speed in excess of 80 miles per hour. For city transportation, as opposed to theme park use, larger trains and standing passengers would be required for profitable operation.[26]

As previously noted, in preparation for the 1964–65 New York World's Fair, Disney sent many of the WED Enterprises staff to the 1962 Seattle World's Fair. Participation in fairs gave WED Enterprises additional transportation experience. Although the Disney organization would not build a monorail for the Seattle fair, Disney negotiated with Robert Moses, president of the 1964–65 New York World's Fair, to build a monorail system at the Flushing Meadow site. The Seattle fair used an Alweg system. Harrison Price prepared a New York World's Fair monorail report in May 1962 proposing a system similar to Disneyland's. Ultimately, Moses purchased a less expensive, 'amusement class' system. Next, Disney proposed building a monorail to connect the fair's pavilions with its recreation areas. Moses insisted on using buses. John Hench and Price recall that Disney spent quite a bit of time with Moses, often discussing transportation and trying to separate buses and people.[27] The 'rail versus bus' battle in American communities continues today.

WED Enterprises developed the PeopleMover to be the intra-city transportation mode in EPCOT. The path of the WEDway within EPCOT began in the underground transportation lobby in the town center and radiated out above the downtown streets (see Figure 2.2).

The first stations would be located under office buildings, providing access to the town center and high-density apartments. The WEDway would then cross the greenbelt and enter the single-family neighborhoods.[28]

The EPCOT-prototype PeopleMover station located at Disneyland measured 16,600 square feet. Car doors and canopies opened and closed automatically, requiring a relatively small staff. In addition, a moving circular platform was synchronized to the speed of the vehicle.[29] As early as June 1964, Disney referred to something called a 'people mover.'[30] He later discovered a system at the Swiss National Exposition in 1964 and sent Bob Gurr to Geneva to study it.[31] By July 1967, Disneyland's WEDway station was in place and described as 'a hub and theme building for all of Tomorrowland.'[32] This place of prominence at Disneyland reflected the value Disney placed on this mode of transportation and was predictive of its future prominence in plans for EPCOT.

Disneyland's WEDway PeopleMover system was actually *designed specifically* for EPCOT by WED Enterprises and sponsored by Goodyear Tire

Figure 2.2 Late model PeopleMover vehicle based on the original
WEDway design by Robert Gurr. The Disneyland attraction
finally closed in 1995. Disneyland's WEDway system was
designed specifically for EPCOT. Source: author's photograph

and Rubber Company.[33] The Disneyland cars were approximately five-eighths
scale. They measured 5 feet 8 inches in height, and the combined concrete
pylon and guideway bed was 10 feet high. In addition, rubber wheels were
embedded in the WEDway steel guideway and rotated against a plate below
the cars to propel them. The cars were silent, electric, and ran continuously.
Moreover, power was supplied by a series of motors embedded in the track,
and a drive unit could be replaced while the system was running. Therefore,
as one WED Enterprises report noted, 'no single car can ever break down or

cause a rush-hour traffic jam.'[34] Cars in this intermediate transportation system could travel at speeds up to 12 miles per hour, with a capacity of 4,885 passengers per hour. The guideway measured 3,250 feet in length and there were 62 trains of four cars each.[35] Twenty passengers could be accommodated in each four-car coupling. Much of the system's original infrastructure still exists at the park in Tomorrowland, including the WEDway columns, created by WED Enterprises sculptor Mitsu. A Goodyear speedramp carried standing passengers up to the circular WEDway loading area. Disney, in his work with Dorothy Chandler on the Los Angeles Music Center, considered a similar moving sidewalk as a means of transporting theater patrons.[36]

In theory, unlike the freeway on-ramp, there would be no waiting in EPCOT for the WEDway; the next car would always be ready. Disney wanted cars to be available on demand, at the push of a button. As demand decreased, cars automatically went back into the 'roundhouse.' According to Imagineer Carl Bongiorno, 'Walt always said, "I want a car there within three minutes."'[37] In contrast, for the new town of Columbia, Maryland, which Disney admired, developer James Rouse envisioned a minibus system to pick up people at five-minute intervals and take them all over town.[38]

The WEDway also had its roots in the Disney organization's preparations for the Ford Wonder Rotunda at the 1964–65 New York World's Fair. Disney envisioned a system of stationary motors mounted along a track to propel Ford cars. John Hench recalls a trip to a Ford plant where pieces of steel were being pushed along an assembly line in a similar fashion, and WED Enterprises later 'set up the little version of the system where the driving force was a bunch of wheels … contacted … on the bottom of the car.'[39] By 1961, a test track had been installed at the Walt Disney Studios to develop the fair show for the Ford Motor Company. A motorized wheel was embedded in the track that contacted the bottom of the cars. In November of that year, the first test was performed, using Lincoln Continentals.[40] The system would be installed at the fair and visitors would ride in Ford cars and pass the dinosaurs that are now part of Disneyland's Primeval World.

When the Imagineers returned from the 1964–65 New York World's Fair, they had acquired a great deal of information about moving large volumes of people. Harrison Price refers to the fair as Disney's 'R&D crucible.'[41] It is ironic, however, that companies like Goodyear and Ford, representative of industries that helped bring about the demise of streetcars in Los Angeles, would assist Disney in his efforts to showcase the PeopleMover in EPCOT.

Similarly, an intermediate system called Carveyor, developed by Goodyear and Stevens-Adamson, is illustrated in Victor Gruen's book. Like the WEDway, it was elevated, but seats were mounted on platforms, which, in turn, were affixed to a moving belt.[42] Moving belts were first used at the Paris Exhibition of 1889. In addition, an electric moving sidewalk with benches was featured at the World's Columbian Exposition of 1893. This was the first such passenger-carrying platform. Perhaps Disney's father,

Elias, who worked as a carpenter at the exposition, spoke to him of its wonders.

In addition, Japan unveiled its bullet train in 1964. Along with their European counterparts, the trains display a competitive advantage over the airlines for trips under 300 miles and they support development concentrations at nodal points.[43] Population concentration and mass transit go hand-in-hand. Higher population densities at transit nodes were reflected in the EPCOT model and at Vällingby, Sweden, for example.

Despite the emphasis on mass transit, the automobile would still exist at EPCOT. The community of tomorrow would help generate automobile traffic that would impact the world beyond its radial plan. In 1966, Florida officials began to plan and design roads and interchanges to accommodate the new development.[44] Walt Disney Productions retained the engineering firm of De Leuw, Cather & Company to estimate traffic requirements on Interstate 4 and State Road 530. The engineers issued a report in July 1968 that offers examples of preliminary arterial connections.[45] Of special note is the inclusion of order-of-magnitude estimates of employees, residents, and hotel units for EPCOT and the industrial park at different points in time.[46] This suggests that Roy O. Disney was committed to his late brother's experimental community concept at this time.

Ray Watson, who advised Disney as the concept developed, emphasizes that EPCOT's transportation plan is very similar to Stockholm, Sweden's, with its already existing commercial core and new, 1960s residential communities linked by rail.[47] Perhaps it is no coincidence that Disney kept a booklet about Stockholm in his office.[48] Stockholm's plan consisted of four new satellite towns built during the period 1950 through 1970. A radial subway system and highways focused on the city center. In addition, satellite towns featured high development densities around central pedestrian shopping malls to maintain walking distances from transit. In the later developments, high-density apartment blocks were built near the town centers. These elements are featured in the EPCOT concept. However, both the British New Towns and the Stockholm satellites proved to be far more automobile dependent than planners in the late 1940s and early 1950s had envisioned. The EPCOT plan contains a certain irony. Even with its advanced transit modes, the concept features two automobile service areas for the projected high level of Disney World automobile traffic. The service uses are sited adjacent to single-family land uses. Although the plan shows a landscaped buffer, noise and fumes could have been negative externalities.

New Urbanists like Peter Calthorpe point to transit-oriented development (TOD) as a cure for many urban ills. Much like the EPCOT model, TODs include a transit stop and core commercial space in the center, surrounded by a band of public/open space and a band of residential land uses.[49] In his 1993 book *The Next American Metropolis*, Calthorpe writes that TODs should be 'located on or near existing or planned segments of a trunk transit line or feeder bus network.' The TODs should include a 2,000-foot average, 'comfortable' walking distance to the transit stop and core commercial area.

In order for TODs to succeed, communities must confront the high cost of transit systems and be strongly committed to maintaining high-density zoning around the transit stations. The state of Florida would grant Disney authority to establish land use regulations for the Florida property. He hoped that EPCOT would be a showcase of new ideas. However, it would be the responsibility of visitors to EPCOT to return home and implement change in their own communities.

In his later years, Disney and his associates attempted to interest cities in adopting the monorail as a viable mode of mass transit but did not succeed before Disney's death. For instance, Disney approached Las Vegas officials about running a monorail down the casino-lined Strip. The plan never materialized during his lifetime. Today, two monorail systems link hotels along the Strip. The system between the MGM Grand and Bally's uses trains purchased from The Walt Disney Company, courtesy of Bob Gurr and Michael Eisner. Gurr speculates that Disney would be 'tickled pink.'[50] A plan to expand the system along the east side of Las Vegas to link with downtown has recently been approved.

In Southern California, people continue to debate the virtues of monorails, buses, jitneys, magnetic levitation, light rail, heavy rail, and other forms of mass transportation. Light rail trains now run along the medians of certain freeways and a subway system is in operation. Disney introduced the first daily operating monorail to the United States in 1959. The EPCOT WEDway intermediate-range prototype appeared in Tomorrowland in 1967. Since then, Southern California has grown even more dispersed and freeway dependency more widespread. Low-density sprawl, made possible by the automobile, limits viable mass transit options. Both Victor Gruen and Peter Calthorpe were keenly aware of this problem, writing 30 years apart.

Gruen underscored the point when he quoted Disney's New York World's Fair acquaintance, planner Robert Moses, who said, 'It does not make any difference where one builds a freeway, it will fill up in any case.'[51] This stands in contrast to amusement park historian Judith Adams' assessment of the insulated Anaheim park: 'Disneyland's success in transporting enormous numbers of people ... [is] revolutionary and continue[s] to have substantial impact in the design of transportation systems in all venues.'[52] Because Disney was able to obtain nearly the same level of control over the Florida property that he had in his theme park, he would have been able to avoid the nemesis called the politics of urban transportation.

Although the EPCOT concept was never built, its prototype transportation systems continue to influence the way millions of people around the world think about mass transit of the future. Disney, Roger Broggie, Bob Gurr, and their associates brought the words 'monorail' and 'PeopleMover' into common usage. By the end of his life, Disney was an international cultural icon and in a unique position to lead his peers in American industry.

He could ask people to think about what the automobile had done to their communities. Frequently, freeways divided neighborhoods physically and socially. Freeways also tended to exceed their design capacities much sooner than anticipated. In the EPCOT concept, the automobile was banned from the dense commercial center, housing and employment were in close proximity, and electric mass transit systems were always within walking distance. In many respects, these elements endure today as the accepted form for transit-oriented development to follow in the future.

Chapter 3

Architecture and Construction

There's a green one and a pink one,
And a blue one and a yellow one,
And they're all made out of ticky tacky,
And they all look just the same

from the song, 'Little Boxes,' © 1962.
Words and music by Malvina Reynolds.
Used by permission. All rights reserved.

People don't walk out of the attraction whistling the architecture.

John Hench

Because the EPCOT planning process never got beyond the conceptual stage during Disney's lifetime, it is instructive to examine some of the company's other projects and contemporary influences. In light of today's high-tech developments and the functional obsolescence of buildings in many communities, the state of becoming takes on increasing relevance. Disney was familiar with obsolescence in Disneyland's Tomorrowland. Florida Film writer Marty Sklar outlined the other key elements relating to architecture and construction in EPCOT: 'encourage American industry ... to test and demonstrate new ideas, materials and systems emerging now and in the future ... ; and to provide an environment that will stimulate the best thinking of industry and the professions ... to meet the needs of people ... .'[1]

Disney's state of becoming is similar to ideas that emerged from the counterculture Archigram Group in the early 1960s. Their Plug-in City (1962–64), for example, was designed to 'investigate what happens if the whole urban environment can be programmed and structured for change.'[2] Thirty years later, designer Stewart Brand, trained as a biologist, reflected this philosophy in his 1994 book, *How Buildings Learn,* when he wrote: 'The design problem is to start a building which knows about the centuries yet adeptly meets the needs and employs the tools of decades.'[3]

The Disneys set up shop in Hollywood in 1923 and thereafter, their organization and its principals built residences, two motion picture studios, the world's first theme park, and four World's Fair pavilions. The nature of the entertainment industry itself, including its need for set design and construction, influenced the organization's real estate development projects. On any particular day during Disney's 40 years in Hollywood, 'munchkins' could skip off to the Emerald City or geosynchronous satellites could be developed. In other words, nearly anything seemed possible. A movie set could be struck and, like the animator, the art director and his crew could create the next illusion of reality. Ultimately, the line between the movie lot and the city blurred. For example, within the Los Angeles city limits there was the themed Grauman's Chinese (1927) theater and a host of movie set-looking retail buildings with odd shapes ranging from animals to the re-creation of international architectural themes. Following a long historical tradition, these themes eventually would appear in Disney's EPCOT concept. An earlier Los Angeles example, Abbot Kinney's west Los Angeles community of Venice, begun along the coast in 1904, was echoed by Harrison Price's early EPCOT description in 1966 of a modern-day Venice.[4] Price also wrote of the possibility of developing floating settlements, perhaps similar to the 1958–60 floating city concepts of Kiyonuri Kikutake, William Katavolos, Paul Maymont, and other designers.

Disney also was impressed by particular Los Angeles developments, especially the pedestrian-oriented, historically themed Farmers Market (1934) on Fairfax Avenue, and Hollywood's medieval European village/Streamline Moderne Style, pedestrian-oriented Crossroads of the World (1936) by Robert Derrah.[5] This latter project reflected elements of both yesteryear and tomorrow and originally was intended as a shopping mall.

Disney developed relationships with leaders of the Los Angeles architectural community, notably William Pereira, Charles Luckman, and Welton Becket. He also worked with the firm of Ladd & Kelsey. Pereira worked for the firm that planned the Chicago World's Fair of 1933 (site of the 1948 Railroad Fair). In addition, he has been credited with introducing modern architecture to Los Angeles, master planning the Orange County new town of Irvine and the Los Angeles International Airport (conceived as a 'Jet Airport of the Future'). Pereira's firm also designed the CBS Television City (1952) complex and the Los Angeles County Museum of Art (1964). Furthermore, he shared an Academy Award for motion picture set design.[6] Pereira's landmark Transamerica Building in San Francisco opened in 1972. Among Luckman's more important commissions were the design of the 1,620-acre Houston Manned Spacecraft Center (1961–67), NASA's space flight laboratory, and New York's new Madison Square Garden (1960). In addition, the firm of Pereira and Luckman designed the Disneyland Hotel for owner Jack Wrather.

Welton Becket was Disney's neighbor and closely associated with the early Project Florida years. Becket's commercial architecture firm, Welton Becket & Associates, designed the Los Angeles Music Center. Its Ahmanson Theater opened in 1964, followed by the Dorothy Chandler Pavilion (1965), and the Mark Taper Forum (1967). Culture had arrived in downtown Los Angeles. Becket also planned the 176-acre 'new-town-in-town' Century City (1957–61) on the former Twentieth Century Fox lot. The development includes hotel, office, entertainment, hospital, and retail land uses. In the film, *Conquest of the Planet of the Apes* (1972), Century City was used as a city of the future. The development is not quite self-contained, as it features the largest parking structure in the United States. Like Victor Gruen, Becket also was a pioneer in the design of large shopping centers. Becket maintained a client roster that included developer Del E. Webb Co., ALCOA, aerospace companies, and various public agencies. The architect also created a master plan for UCLA.[7] With relationships like these and his own staff at WED Enterprises, Disney could draw upon many resources to develop his concept for EPCOT.

Despite the architectural talent from which Disney could draw, EPCOT's conceptual design has not been without criticism. For example, over the years, the proposal to enclose EPCOT's town center has been the source of much confusion and even ridicule. One important argument against a dome, according to Reedy Creek Improvement District Administrator Tom Moses, is the issue of fire safety.[8] In addition to the futuristic aspect of the concept, there were logical reasons and design fantasy precedents behind Disney's concept to enclose the entire 50-acre town center with a dome. The Florida property is located in a subtropical climate in which plant-killing frosts occur and hurricanes strike. Moreover, the average rainfall is a hefty 50 inches per year.[9] To prevent toxic emissions within EPCOT's enclosure, all vehicles would be electrically powered.[10] The enclosure also would enable the architects to design simpler, less expensive structures for the town center and eliminate storm drains. The domed enclosure is one of the most striking features of the EPCOT concept. In the Florida Film, animation places a hemispherical top over the town center. However, the narration states only that the city center will be completely enclosed.[11] During June 1965, Disney initiated a one-week Planning Seminar Future for those who had been involved in the project. The construction of a dome-like structure may have been discussed.[12]

Later, in October 1965, *Orlando Sentinel* reporter Emily Bavar reported that Disney was 'profoundly impressed by Houston's great, domed stadium.'[13] The 1967 Progress City model on display at Disneyland did not, however, feature a dome.[14] Its town center buildings pierced through the roof enclosure of the international shopping area that featured large bubble skylights. As he had at his Burbank studio, Disney appeared to prefer natural lighting. Typical indoor lighting, wrote Christopher Alexander, 'destroys the social nature of space, and makes people feel disoriented and unbounded.'[15] This does not contribute to reassurance.

The dome concept was not new. In 1892, H.G. Wells wrote of a crystal dome 400 feet above a future city. In addition, Ebenezer Howard's Crystal Palace was derived from the immense glass structure of London's Great Exhibition of 1851. The exhibition was a showcase of technology in the Age of Progress. Approximately 6,500 exhibitors participated from nations around the world. Elements of this tradition also would carry over into the EPCOT concept. Moreover, architect and engineer Richard Buckminster Fuller, pro-posed a dome for Manhattan in about 1950 and constructed a geodesic sphere at the U.S. Pavilion at Expo '67 in Montreal.[16] Many of Fuller's ideas and philosophies would be expressed in his book, *Operating Manual for Spaceship Earth* (1969).

Similarly, Victor Gruen believed that 'all the regional shopping centers have created superior environmental qualities ... .'[17] Gruen designed Southdale Center near Minneapolis, the first covered, air-conditioned ped-estrian area in the United States, completed in 1955. This was the opening year of Disneyland. By the mid-1960s, large areas of space were being enclosed in mixed-use megastructures. Assessing the viability of Disney's domed enclosure, architect Jon Jerde concludes, 'The probability and the viability of that would be slim to none, actually. It covers a lot of acres. I don't know what the cost would be, but it would be pretty daunting.'[18] Jerde, also borrowing from Venice, Italy, designed Canal City in Fukuoka, Japan (1996) and Horton Plaza (1985), a regional mall with a 'canyon' that helped revitalize downtown San Diego, California.[19]

Unfortunately, the form of Disney's final EPCOT 'iteration' will never be known. While perhaps financially unfeasible, the 50-acre dome concept nonetheless is typical of the 'out of the box' thinking that doubtless contrib-uted to the Disney success story. Similar to his film-making experiences, if Disney had listened to the critics, Disneyland would never have been built. It is important to recall that even the greatest achievements in architecture, such as the Pantheon in Rome, with its 142-foot diameter hemispherical dome, was possibly called 'Hadrian's Folly' until it was completed. The EPCOT concept was still crystallizing at the time of Disney's death. While not all concepts come to fruition, innovations, as required by the Model Cities legislation, for example, rarely occur 'within the box.'

As previously mentioned, Disney was influenced by his travels. He was particularly fond of France, having served as an ambulance driver at the close of World War I. According to Disney, the EPCOT concept was 'not a sudden thing with me ... I happen to be an inquisitive guy and when I see things I don't like, I start thinking why do they have to be like this and how can I improve them?'[20] While world travel had a profound impact on Dis-ney, America's shopping mall phenomenon also captured his attention. Vic-tor Gruen echoed many of his contemporaries in 1964 when he wrote, 'The plaza has taken over the role formerly filled by the old town square.'[21] Gruen features his Midtown Plaza (1962) project in his book. The plaza was built in Rochester, New York, and has a three-story-high skylighted retail plaza, hotel, two major office buildings, and three underground levels. It looks similar to EPCOT's town center in cross-section. As he did with amusement parks years before, Disney visited new shopping centers in 1966, including developments in Rochester, Philadelphia, Washington, D.C., Baltimore, and Dallas. Disney was especially impressed by one mall in Dallas that incorporated a glass ceiling. This was possibly Exchange Park, which combines office buildings and hotels with the shopping mall.[22] Gruen's book also features a photograph of Cherry Hill, with a tropically landscaped main court, located outside of Philadelphia.

The shopping mall continues to stand as a symbol of the loss of town square and public space in the United States. EPCOT's surface level would incorporate design elements of a mall in the themed, naturally lit international retail area, which was quite unlike traditional shopping mall environments. Similarly, WED Enterprises designed the themed Blue Bayou restaurant building at Disneyland to be enclosed within the Pirates of the Caribbean attraction structure.[23]

Other themed areas mentioned in a 1967 brochure include Scandinavia, Asia, and South America.[24] It was Disneyland's Main Street, U.S.A., and New Orleans Square on a global scale.[25] The EPCOT renderings by Herbert Ryman and George McGinnis depict an international shopping area that is enclosed and not open to a dome. Moreover, in contrast to many downtowns, including Disney's Los Angeles, night-time as well as daytime activities are encouraged by the design (particularly with regard to lighting, public safety, and business occupancy – the major benefits of an owner-occupied shopping mall). Gruen's book features a conceptual rendering of a similar, skylighted retail pedestrian concourse with an elevated conveyance system and conventional 1960s retail elevations.[26]

EPCOT's high-density apartments encircle the urban core in a manner reminiscent of the Stockholm, Sweden satellite town designs. Some of the apartment buildings mitigate bulk by incorporating a step-back design. However, the size of the buildings could make it difficult to monitor the activity of children outside. According to a 1967 publication, the town center's wienie is a 600-room hotel.[27] EPCOT's 'final' sleek hotel design by George Rester, perhaps without the reflective glass, would not be an unusual addition to a skyline today. Disney visited John Portman's atrium hotel in Atlanta, the Plaza in New York, and Doral in Miami.[28] Once again, he displayed his belief in the usefulness of market analysis.

EPCOT's residential areas would be testing grounds as well as neighborhoods for residents. The potential incompatibility of these uses is the source of some of the strongest criticisms of the EPCOT concept. In 1966, artist Herbert Ryman produced watercolor paintings of single-family residential districts for the Progress City model. One Ryman watercolor shows a WEDway guideway behind an atrium house, with the Progress City hotel in the distance. Such renderings are merely concepts for the Progress City model and, at best, suggest potential low densities and building envelopes envisioned by Disney for EPCOT.

The company noted that 'Every element of the home, be it sewage system, [or] kitchen appliances … will serve as a practical proving ground … .'[29] According to EPCOT planner Marvin Davis, 'he'd [Disney] … talk for hours about the garbage disposal. He was really engrossed in it. And of course, we became engrossed, too.'[30] In the design and construction of other projects, such as Disneyland and its prefabricated Monsanto House, and the modular Contemporary Resort at Walt Disney World, Walt Disney Productions had already gained experience in testing new materials and systems. Similarly, the Archigram Group's Plug-in City concept also emphasized prefabricated units and exchangeable building components.

Clearly, EPCOT was a forward-looking concept for a forward-looking time. By 1967, a Florida state Senate resolution contained the design plan for the East Central Florida Region, in which the company's property is located. It included an artist's rendering of futuristic, hourglass-shaped towers with helicopters, jets, and palm trees, and it predicted that 'the architecture of the future will probably be even more daring.'[31] The prediction seemed to already be coming true because the transportation systems and radial plans of Disney's proposed industrial park were daring. Marvin Davis prepared a site plan for a typical industrial complex in October 1966 for the Florida Film. The plan includes five wedge-shaped buildings enclosing a total of 500,000 square feet.[32] Bubble skylights are used on these structures as well. While warehouse users would not prefer the irregular/inefficient plans of these buildings, research and development tenants might find the plans to be acceptable. Welton Becket & Associates, led by Disney's friend, designed a circular research and development facility for General Electric Tempo in Santa Barbara, California, although it was never built.[33] Like Disney's Burbank studio, the industrial complex plan includes recreational facilities for tennis, shuffleboard, and horseshoes.

Because Disney's original community concept never reached beyond the conceptual stage, it is instructive to examine some of his other projects that offer a window into what might have been, and that influenced the EPCOT philosophy. As previously noted, CalArts and the proposed Mineral King ski resort provided the Disney team with design experience. A set of CalArts blueprints was located in Disney's office.[34] Harrison Price paraphrases CalArts architect Thornton Ladd regarding the design: 'I will build a building where everything interrelates. Six schools are going to be jacked around and communicating with each other … .' Disney died one month after he saw the final model of CalArts.[35] The main building consists of the following functions: theater, art gallery, library, photo lab, ceramic and sculpture work room, practice and rehearsal rooms, and printing and lithography shops.[36] Directing the design of another campus environment helped Disney gain relevant experience for addressing EPCOT (see Figure 3.1). The Mineral King ski resort designs also were produced by outside architects Ladd & Kelsey.

Walt Disney World's Contemporary and Polynesian resorts were constructed in conjunction with U.S. Steel Realty Corporation and reflect several elements of the EPCOT philosophy.[37] Their modular room installation utilized systems that were advanced for the time. WED Enterprises engaged Welton Becket & Associates to design the hotels. According to Imagineer Richard Irvine, the firm was selected because WED Enterprises did not have

Figure 3.1 Oblique aerial photograph of the California Institute of the Arts campus, Valencia, California. Ladd & Kelsey, architects. Disney endowed and helped design this interdisciplinary school for the arts. Source: California Institute of the Arts

the expertise and because of Disney's good working relationship with Becket.[38]

Perhaps the most striking elements of the Contemporary Resort are the monorail beamways that the Imagineers added to extend through the hotel's 400-foot-long Grand Canyon Concourse. The structural engineering firm was Richard Bradshaw, Inc., and Don Edgren was the WED Enterprises engineer assigned to the project. Design of the hotel commenced prior to Disney's death and the facility opened in 1971.[39] Architect Marvin Davis worked with Becket principal Robert Tyler on the Contemporary's design. The hotel is a 14-story steel A-frame with 394 rooms in the main structure (see Figure 3.2).

A 1967 publication stated that the hotel would be based on a 'tomorrow' theme. Even the architect Le Corbusier named his city of tomorrow 'Contemporary' because 'to-morrow belongs to nobody.' Disney's Contemporary included parking for 1,250 automobiles in addition to the more futuristic monorails.[40] The 'unitized,' modular construction consisted of six-ton rooms (29 feet by 14 feet by 4 feet) with steel frames and interlocking plumbing and utilities' conduits hoisted into place and 'plugged in' to the A-frame.[41] The Contemporary room modules were constructed three miles from the site and construction was completed in only eleven

Figure 3.2   A monorail is visible in this view of the Contemporary
Resort's Grand Canyon Concourse. The large ceramic mural
is by Imagineer Mary Blair. Welton Becket & Associates,
architects. Source: author's photograph

months. The Grand Canyon Concourse is reminiscent of EPCOT's transportation lobby, located beneath the planned hotel megastructure. The Contemporary was the largest application of modular steel construction up to that time. The concourse also includes a 90-foot-high ceramic tile mural by Imagineer Mary Blair.[42]

Experience acquired during the 1964–65 New York World's Fair also contributed to the EPCOT philosophy. WED Enterprises created four pavilions for the fair at Flushing Meadow: the Ford Wonder Rotunda (Ford Motor Company), Progressland (General Electric), 'It's a Small World' (Pepsi-Cola/United Nations International Children's Emergency Fund), and Great Moments With Mr. Lincoln (State of Illinois). The fair opened on April 22, 1964. The architect of record for the Ford and G.E. pavilions was Welton Becket & Associates and the other two buildings were designed by WED Enterprises alone.[43] The fair's Unisphere was designed by Imagineer Harper Goff. As in Anaheim, Admiral Joe Fowler oversaw construction for WED Enterprises. Portions of the buildings were prefabricated in California.

The Ford Wonder Rotunda, with a 10-story domed entrance enclosing 275,000 square feet of building area, was the largest pavilion at the fair.[44] The pavilion featured an abstract 'Space City' at the end of the exhibit. Pepsi-Cola's structure was an unremarkable 'L-shaped box.' The uninspired design was due in large part to the pressure WED Enterprises was under to construct four pavilions in a short period of time.[45] Key 'It's a Small World' designers included Claude Coats, Rolly Crump, Mary Blair, Alice Davis, and Marc Davis.

Progressland originated in 1959, when General Electric asked Disney to create a show for the fair to educate, entertain, and show the role electricity has played in improving living conditions, and dramatize where use of electricity would take mankind in the future. This probably contributed to his thinking about a city of tomorrow during the same year the monorail was introduced at Disneyland. A Palm Beach, Florida development deal with RCA, including a city of tomorrow component, also was being considered at that time (see Chapter 4, Site and Technology). G.E.'s Progressland building at the World's Fair was circular, measured 194 feet in diameter, and was 40 feet high. According to Disney authority Paul F. Anderson, it was the first building to use offset hoops from which a suspended roof was hung.[46] At this point in his life, Disney seemed to be surrounded by domes.

The Progressland carousel consisted of six stationary stages for 32 Audio-Animatronics figures. The theater seats were on a ringed platform that rotated around the stages progressing from decade to decade. A 'City of Tomorrow' also was initially envisioned for the G.E. 'Sky Dome Spectacular Show' that was displayed on the interior of the dome.[47] A 1964 painting by John Hench shows a concept for the city, with elevated people movers evident.[48] During planning for the fair, Disney supposedly asked Hench, 'Johnny, how would you like to work on the city of the future?'[49] Much of this fair experience would be reflected in the EPCOT concept. In a 1968 interview, Welton Becket commented on the close involvement Disney had with the Progressland carousel, particularly with planning the exhibit and public space.[50] Perhaps the favorite co-star of the show was a lovable, Audio-Animatronics dog, wagging its tail as technology progressed.

Another forward-looking project, Disneyland's Monsanto House of the Future, had a direct impact on Disney's EPCOT conceptualization. 'I think that his [Disney's] Monsanto House was a reflection really of his eventual plans for EPCOT ... and why he never lost his enthusiasm for the work of large companies like General Electric and General Motors ... I don't know how many times he visited Bell Labs,' John Hench said.[51] In addition to plastics produced by Monsanto, house sponsors included Bell Telephone, the Kelvinator Division of American Motors, and Sylvania Electric Products Company.[52]

The Monsanto House was designed by faculty members of the Massachusetts Institute of Technology architecture department (Richard Hamilton and Marvin Goody) and building engineering and construction department (Albert G.H. Dietz).[53] The designers were asked to integrate plastics into the design in every feasible manner. The Monsanto Company's brochure, 'Monsanto House of the Future: an Experimental Design Demonstrating Structural Applications of Plastics,' foreshadowed the experimentation and demonstration elements of the EPCOT philosophy.[54] Construction of the Monsanto House began in January 1957 (see Figure 3.3).[55]

It is estimated that more than 20 million guests toured the house, which was redecorated twice before demolition in December 1967. The decor of the house of the future could remain futuristic only so long. Such episodes of obsolescence prompted Disney to say in 1965, 'the only problem with anything of tomorrow is that at the pace we're going right now, tomorrow would catch up with us before we got it built.'[56] The proposed solution would be the state of becoming.

While there were no plans for mass production, a Monsanto publication noted that the house was 'expected to have a strong impact on forward-thinking and progressive architects and builders.'[57] The house featured a children's bedroom, a kitchen open to the family/dining room, a parents' bedroom, and a core. The primary building materials were plastic reinforced with fiberglass. Thermopane windows were in multi-paneled sections. The 16-square-foot utility core consisted of baths, the kitchen, laundry, and heating. Moreover, to facilitate the dwelling's transport, four u-shaped modules (8 feet by 16 feet) were bolted to the concrete foundation and wood perimeter beam on-site.[58] As John Hench recalls, 'there was virtually no bad location for building it ... in a rocky location, or on a hillside, the ... pedestal would have been easy to work with.'[59]

Hench designed a revolving transparent screen for the house that would 'splash "various hues" across the room.'[60] The house's cross shape permitted sunlight to enter from all directions. Landscape architect Bill Evans

Figure 3.3 Photograph of the Monsanto House of the Future, Disneyland. Richard Hamilton and Marvin Goody, architects. Source: Charles Phoenix

53

designed the landscaping for the Monsanto House, including pools of water that fed the house's air conditioning system.

The total area of the Monsanto House was 1,280 square feet. Additional modules could be added to alter its configuration. The bathroom was designed by Henry Dreyfuss Company and included a sink that moved up and down to facilitate use by children. Other interesting features included microwave cooking (novel at that time), ultrasonic dishwashing, a push-button telephone with viewing screen, and a climate control center.

As architect Alan Hess concludes, 'most of the appliances and architectural ideas have gone the way of hula-hoops ... the structural plastic, the ultrasonic dishwasher, the movable bathroom sink.' Hess also believes that the building materials were no less expensive or more efficient than traditional materials.[61] Predictions of plastic houses of the future may have been proven wrong, but this Disneyland attraction did appear to contribute to Disney's EPCOT philosophy. Conceptually, the Monsanto House was similar to Richard Buckminster Fuller's Dymaxion House (1945), which had aluminum skin and received much media attention. Like the Monsanto House, the Dymaxion House was prefabricated and looked like an alien space vehicle. Architect Le Corbusier also was a strong proponent of mass-produced housing as early as the 1920s, well before 1947 and the appearance of developer William Levitt's suburban 'little boxes' on Long Island, New York.

Walt Disney Productions gained limited exposure to residential construction issues by virtue of planning Disneyland attractions, building motion picture sets, and constructing residences. For example, prior to planning for General Electric's participation in the 1964–65 New York World's Fair, WED Enterprises planned Edison Square, to be built at Disneyland. Act IV of the Edison Square show was to include a portable programmer that 'controls household operations' and 'appliances of the future.'[62] Moreover, Disney protégé Card Walker remembers that the studio constructed a house for the set of *The Parent Trap* (1961) that was well-received by the public.[63] Disney also designed a house for his daughter Diane and her husband, Ron Miller, former president of Walt Disney Productions.[64]

Another domestic facility, the Bathroom of the Future, opened at Disneyland in April 1956. The bathroom was sponsored by Crane, with fixtures styled by Henry Dreyfuss ('water controls of tomorrow'). The bathroom also featured Crane heating and air conditioning and 'a mural depicting man's primitive efforts at flow control.'[65] The exhibit reflected Disney's need to further develop Tomorrowland after the park opened, making the early exhibits more like county fair attractions.[66] From man's primitive habits to portable household programmers, the Disneyland attractions emphasized both the past and future – two recurring themes in the evolution of EPCOT design.

Beyond the Monsanto House and domestic facilities, Disneyland yielded much experience for the WED Enterprises design team. Disney initially considered using outside architects for the design of Disneyland. WED Enterprises originally retained the firm of Pereira and Luckman as architects. Some early city of tomorrow design concepts flowed to WED Enterprises from Welton Becket & Associates.[67] However, Disney and his in-house design team developed the EPCOT concept.

In EPCOT's town center internationally themed shopping mall, visitors would wander through 'canyons' in an environment similar to that of New Orleans Square at Disneyland (see Figure 3.4).

It was an idea that would become mainstream as the regional mall evolved into the themed 'mega-mall,' 'entertainment retail,' and Las Vegas casinos of today. John Hench echoed a belief held by architect Charles Moore and others when he said that Disneyland also attempted to create a missing sense of place in megalopolis. The key to creating this sense, according to Hench, was 'plenty of diversity [in design], but there isn't contradiction.'[68] Of course, this would always be easier to achieve in a privately-controlled environment than in the public realm.

Disney adopted a 'hands-on' approach to the construction of Disneyland. Construction commenced in August 1954 and Disney announced the park would be open in just eleven months (see Figure 3.5).

Disney visited the construction site almost daily and no detail was too insignificant for his attention.[69] Landscape architect Bill Evans recalls that Disney's Saturday morning walking tours of the park continued for 'some years' after Disneyland's opening.[70] Engineer Don Edgren adds that consultants, architects, civil engineers, structural engineers, mechanical engineers, and electrical engineers were all based at the Walt Disney Studios in Burbank during construction of the park. They worked under the art directors who worked under Disney.[71]

Approximately 2 million board feet of lumber, 1 million square feet of asphalt, and 5,000 cubic yards of concrete were used during construction and 350,000 cubic yards of earth were moved.[72] The buildings at the park must endure incredible wear from millions of visitors. The park became a laboratory for construction materials, with hundreds of items undergoing testing that was more rigorous than manufacturers' lab tests.[73] Testing new materials and systems would be a key element in the EPCOT philosophy. Disney learned almost every detail of the construction business.

Art historian Karal Ann Marling aptly notes that the buildings along Main Street, U.S.A. are essentially 1950s-style malls that extend deep beyond the street.[74] The few large retail structures were furnished with building façades at intervals of approximately 22 feet to maintain scale. This appears to be the strategy for EPCOT's town center. Disneyland also was designed at whatever scale the art directors, hired from the movie industry, determined was appropriate. For example, on Main Street, U.S.A., the first floor is approximately 90 percent of life-size, while the second floor is about 80 percent. This creates a 'forced perspective,' exaggerating vertical space as one looks north toward Sleeping Beauty's Castle.

Figure 3.4   Attention to architectural detail is evident in this photograph
of New Orleans Square, Disneyland. This photograph was
taken from the balcony of what would have been Disney's
private apartment. Source: author's photograph

Figure 3.5   Disney inspects his new park while under construction.
Sleeping Beauty's Castle would feature prefabricated
components. The design was refined by Imagineer/architect
Bill Martin based on original concepts by Disney and artist
Herbert Ryman. Source: University of Southern California
Regional History Collection

In addition to scale, another key to the 'architecture of reassurance' is the
impact of color coordination, one of John Hench's areas of expertise. The
uncoordinated buildings of Marceline, Missouri, Disney's boyhood home,
surely did not have a business improvement district with approved color
chart. Main Street, U.S.A. also includes recorded period music. Themed
Muzak might have resonated in EPCOT's international shopping districts.
This design element contributes to Disney's apparent objective of environmental reassurance.

Another critical element in Disneyland is its graphics. 'Walt looked at
every single graphic that went into the park,' recalled Imagineer Rudy
Lord.[75] Communication was a key word at WED Enterprises. Walt Disney
Productions had years of experience communicating graphically, and the
coordinated signage within the berm would stand in stark contrast to
Anaheim's neon jungle called Harbor Boulevard outside the park. Perhaps

the most important aspect of signage is providing orientation through use of universally understood symbols, a technique appreciated by Disneyland's millions of international visitors.

As has been discussed, Disney attempted to create a human-scaled and reassuring environment at the theme park. John Hench analyzes Disneyland's design in terms of psychology. He points to the child archetype in people and the park's ability to reach that. From this perspective, Disneyland provides a safe and readily comprehensible environment. It is scaled to the pedestrian, free of the automobile, and features the orienting hub and castle. Hench also states that the company has consulted 'a number of psychiatrists who've discovered that there's something beyond an amusement park there.'[76]

Hench concludes that an unsuccessful project is based on a designer's inability to communicate his vision to others.[77] Disney was familiar with universal symbols and human emotion. This is evident in his film work, particularly the animated features. Before computers, animators created the 'illusion of life' using an endless series of drawings and paintings on celluloid. Actually, animators Frank Thomas and Ollie Johnston point out that the representation of animal movement appeared 25,000 years ago in caves of southwestern Europe. It was not until the late nineteenth-century that film animation was born.[78]

The modern animator had to be expert in the observation of behavior, take total control over a two-dimensional universe, and, with a pencil, create characters with personalities to play credible roles. The ability to comprehend human emotions well enough to communicate them through moving drawings was astonishing and often taken for granted today. When the audience cried when Bambi's (1942) mother died, Disney and his team had reached the height of their powers to use universal symbols to touch the proverbial child.

Later, Disney and his team would apply these powerful communication skills in the three-dimensional setting at Disneyland. For example, animator Marc Davis made the transition to three-dimensional Audio-Animatronics at WED Enterprises. Using that highly technical medium, he helped to create the illusion of pirate mischief for millions of visitors.

Thus, Disney combined his intuitive sense of what touches the child in people with what is reassuring and animalistic. He drew upon a staff from an industry with a touch of theater to create an environment within the berm that drew upon universal symbols to make people happy. Happiness is a large part of the public need. However, catering to visitors in Anaheim and to residents in EPCOT posed two very different design challenges. And yet, as some planning theorists, such as Seymour Mandelbaum, point out, communication using images shared by a community is key to reaching 'consensual repair.'[79]

Pre-dating Disneyland as a construction experience was the Walt Disney Studios, a sophisticated complex of buildings for its time. It is The Walt

Disney Company's current headquarters and was originally designed specifically for producing animation. The 51-acre site in Burbank just northeast of Hollywood accommodates a campus-like, pedestrian atmosphere, with buildings and furniture designed by architect Kem Weber. The studios' original Streamline Moderne Style vocabulary, combined with building heights and massing, contribute to the overall campus feeling. Disney oversaw every stage of construction at the Burbank studios which were built to replace the Hyperion studio in the Silverlake district of Los Angeles. As Ward Kimball recalls, 'He'd been through the [development] business in the early days on Hyperion Avenue.'[80]

According to biographer Bob Thomas, Disney was 'determined to create the ideal animation workplace.'[81] Air conditioning custom-designed by General Electric would keep dust off camera lenses and film, control humidity (for paint drying), and fight the San Fernando Valley heat. This was a vast improvement over the sometimes sweaty conditions at the old Hyperion studio. In addition, water from a well at Burbank was used to pre-cool and pre-heat air. While Disney admired Henry Ford's assembly line, Kimball recalls that 'you didn't see anybody in there [Burbank] welding doors on cars.'[82]

The general move to Burbank occurred between December 1939 and January 1940. The cost of the new studios was approximately $3 million. The facilities for the following functions were planned, under construction, or completed by March 1940: animation (steel frame), cutting (steel), camera (steel), dialogue stage, orchestra stage, live-action stage, warehouse, central heating (steel), ink and paint (steel), process lab (steel), theater, restaurant, and administration. These structures enclosed approximately 295,000 square feet of space and were laid out to facilitate the animation production process.[83] The building systems are reflective of the growing sophistication of the animation process since the days of the black and white, silent 'shorts.'

The Animation Building, in the center of the campus, features eight separate wings (compared to a similar building at Hyperion, which had four) and a spine, constructed in two units in response to earthquake safety concerns. The Long Beach earthquake in 1933 caused significant damage in Southern California and affected building codes. The Animation, Ink and Paint, and Cutting (Editing) buildings also were designed to give artists rooms facing outside and maximize northern light exposure. Windows facing other directions were fitted with adjustable shutter awnings.

Anticipating EPCOT industrial complex recreation areas, the Burbank studios featured a rooftop gymnasium, and the Ink and Paint Building had a sundeck. Moreover, like EPCOT, the facility included the latest in technology. For example, decades before the invention of personal computer networks, Animation Building rooms featured electric bases with removable faces 'permitting the introduction at any time of extra telephone lines, small power lines, compressed air line [sic] or other equipment that might be required,' a company press release said.[84]

Disney also was involved in designing furniture with Kem Weber and with the 'undergrounding' of utilities, which was unusual at that time. An underground tunnel connected the Ink and Paint, Camera, and Cutting buildings. The most obvious benefit of the tunnel was to protect the animation cels, backgrounds, and film from the elements as they were transported to different locations.

Once again, the Walt Disney Studios reflected the growing sophistication of the animation process since the Disneys' tenancy on Kingswell Avenue in Silverlake where the restroom doubled as a darkroom (see Chapter 9, Operations and Management). At Burbank, water flowing to the process laboratory building was delivered at several different temperatures simultaneously. Air conditioning and fume-removal ducts were specially constructed to resist corrosion.

Other materials and systems designed for the animation process included an air-blasting, 'de-dusting' chamber in the Camera Building and extra insulation for sound stages (at the time, the noisy Lockheed airport was a neighbor). By 1945, work commenced on additional facilities, including film vaults and an administration building. Building the advanced Burbank studios must have influenced Disney's thinking about building materials and systems for EPCOT.

The studios' back lot featured sets used for live-action films. For example, sets for a downtown area were constructed in 1965. In addition, four original buildings on the 'residential street' were completed in 1960. In addition to Disneyland's façades, set building gave the company experience in creating the illusion of historical and contemporary development. Unlike in Anaheim and Burbank, however, EPCOT's 'sets' would be real houses where real people actually lived.

The earlier design and construction of the Hyperion studio also provided Disney with real estate development experience. In July 1925, the Disney brothers acquired the site for the Hyperion studio in Silverlake. The move from the Kingswell storefront was completed by the spring of 1926. By 1931, the Hyperion studio had grown from 1,600 square feet to 20,000 square feet.[85] A pattern of growth and need for expansion that began in the garage of Disney's uncle (see Figure 3.6) would continue until Disney's death.

The Hyperion's original one-story, white stucco building with grassy courtyard was expanded on three sides by 1931. In that year, a two-story, Spanish Revival animators' building and sound stage were added. All of the Hyperion structures were wood frame.

According to company archivist David R. Smith, in 1934, artists for *Snow White* were hired and another animators' building (11,200 square feet) was constructed. Prior to release of the film in December 1937, the Hyperion studio also added an ink and paint building, apprentice animators' building (across Hyperion Avenue), two apartment houses next door (used as offices), and a large feature building. By 1938, small bungalows, film vaults, shops, and labs filled all the available space. At this point, Disney convinced

Figure 3.6 Disney's first West Coast studio: Uncle Robert Disney's
garage. The humble structure was rescued and restored by the
Garden Grove Historical Society and is located in Heritage
Park, Garden Grove, California. Source: author's photograph

his brother to build a new studio. The aggregate Hyperion studio building
space was approximately 73,000 square feet by early 1940.[86]

As illustrated here, Disney's concept for EPCOT was the culmination of a
lifetime of experience and experimentation. Lessons were learned on the
personal level as well as the professional level. In 1926, for example, Disney and his brother Roy purchased two adjacent lots on Lyric Avenue near
Hyperion Avenue in Silverlake. The brothers paid $16,000 and built two
prefabricated houses.[87] In addition, they had a house constructed for their
parents. In 1938, their mother Flora died from carbon monoxide poisoning
associated with a closed furnace air intake. According to biographer Thomas, neither of the brothers could ever talk about it. Roy O. Disney ordered
an inspection of the furnace, and the findings indicated either 'a complete
lack of knowledge … or a flagrant disregard' of standards and 'poor and
cheap' installation.[88] Such an accident could easily have influenced Walt
Disney's thoughts on regulation and building codes for EPCOT.

Today, the company still receives telephone calls from small towns across the country asking for assistance in rehabilitating Main Streets. After World War II, the basic redevelopment strategy in the United States was the bulldozer. Arguably, the entertaining/reassuring values of Disneyland's nostalgia assisted in the growth of the historic preservation movement. Disneyland also impacted the design of shopping malls and possibly, a loss of 'authentic' space in the United States. In a 1997 interview in the *Los Angeles Times*, author Jane Jacobs stated, 'When I was a child, the worst thing you could say was that something was Victorian. Now Victorian is treasured again.'[89] Perhaps with its millions of visitors, Main Street, U.S.A. contributed to a greater appreciation of the past (or an idealized past that never really was).

It can be financially feasible to re-use the old buildings of America's Main Streets because they can provide opportunities for designers to breathe life back into once vibrant parts of communities. Examples of this trend in Southern California include the Third Street Promenade in Santa Monica and Old Town Pasadena. However, market demand and competition dictate that only so many rehabilitated, primarily retail districts in a particular region will succeed economically.

Disneyland's 1957 Monsanto House of the Future, demolished in 1967, showed a future that never really would be. This phenomenon led Disney to conclude that the built environment must be structured for change. Using designer Stewart Brand's term, the Southern California of the mid-1960s was often characterized as 'design for demolition.'[90] A common joke in the region held that local buildings were torn down after a few years to make way for what often became a visually contradicting state of becoming – Disneyland's external border, the 1960s Harbor Boulevard. It was characterized by uncontrolled signage, neon lights, motels, and honky tonks.

Disney's EPCOT concept identified two notions described by Brand: design for re-use and design for disassembly. The latter is reminiscent of the modules of Walt Disney World's Contemporary Resort, for example. If utilized on a scale to create efficiencies, this type of construction can reduce the owner/developer's investment. However, it requires a compatible building code. More than 35 years after Victor Gruen published his book, downtowns, including Los Angeles', are finding ways to utilize old buildings to earn a profit, revitalize the core, maintain character, and promote the health and safety of the citizenry. However, in many instances, the technological requirements of today's businesses often limit the number of uses to which old buildings can be put.

Although downtown Los Angeles' Bunker Hill lost a Victorian neighborhood during slum clearance in the early 1960s, the Community Redevelopment Agency of the City of Los Angeles' plans and financing mechanisms for the district have yielded some of the city's most prominent new buildings, art, and mixed residential and commercial land uses, located near a Metro Rail Red Line station. This underground system now extends to North Hollywood in the suburban San Fernando Valley. Those concerned with the built environment must find a balance between the need to preserve the past with the need to invent the future.

Brand also concludes that there is a 'shocking lack of data' about how buildings 'behave' over time.[91] In theory, EPCOT would be constantly learning as technology changed. As the Monsanto House of the Future indicated, change can come rapidly and in unpredictable ways. As the rate of technological change increases, EPCOT's structured-for-change environment becomes increasingly relevant in design and construction.

SITE

Chapter 4

Site and Technology

I would like a medium Vodka dry Martini – with a slice of lemon peel.
Shaken and not stirred.

Ian Fleming,
Dr. No, 1958

By technological utopianism … I mean a mode of thought and activity that
vaunts technology as the means of bringing about utopia.

Howard P. Segal, 1985[1]

Big Brother is watching you.

1984, George Orwell

The EPCOT site was part of the larger 27,443-acre master plan for Disney World in central Florida. As early as 1959, the Disney organization began looking for a site in the eastern United States where it could build another theme park. A joint venture opportunity to develop 12,000 acres with RCA and investor John D. MacArthur presented itself in Palm Beach in that year. Both economist Harrison Price and company attorney Robert Foster recall that the RCA deal 'contemplated the development of the "City of Tomorrow."'[2] This chapter presents an overview of the site selection and acquisition processes with emphasis on the EPCOT parcel as well as site engineering and technology.

In 1959, Economics Research Associates concluded that in order to achieve market penetration in the eastern United States that was comparable to that of the area west of the Mississippi, the company would have to establish a theme park on the other side of the river. RCA withdrew from the Palm Beach opportunity and Disney dropped out as well. WED Enterprises began focusing most of its attention on the 1964–65 New York World's Fair. By 1963, Disney was personally inspecting other Florida properties by air.

The Florida site selection and acquisition processes often have been described as a 'cloak and dagger' operation. A November 1965 headline in the *Orlando Sentinel* read, 'Disney Land Purchase Story Reads Like Bond Thriller.'[3] Residents of this region eagerly read the newspaper to learn the latest developments and speculation regarding a mystery buyer of 27,443 acres of land.

The subject property is situated in the East Central Florida region, which consists of the following counties: Brevard, Indian River, Lake, Orange, Osceola, Seminole, and Volusia. The company's property is located within two of these counties, Orange and Osceola. The largest private employer in the region was the Martin aerospace plant, which opened south of Orlando in the mid-1950s. In addition, the EPCOT site is situated approximately 60 miles west of the Kennedy Space Center at Cape Canaveral. In 1962, Cape Canaveral's technological complex accounted for approximately 53 percent of the region's personal income and employed about 36,000 persons.[4] There was also a new technology institute west of Orlando, which later became the University of Central Florida. The EPCOT property was well positioned for both tourism and technology (see Figure 4.1).

In November 1963, Disney and team members flew over the Reedy Creek Basin, the selected drainage shed. The Florida property generally could be characterized by pine forests, swamps, cattle ranches, and citrus groves.[6] Disney personally selected a relatively dry site for EPCOT.[7] The EPCOT site was approximately 1,100 acres in area.[8] By comparison, the site for the Epcot Center theme park, completed in 1982, was 400 acres.[9]

Marvin Davis recalled that he went to Florida with Disney 'quite a bit' and walked the property, flew over it in a plane a few times, and, at one point, rented a helicopter.[9] In fact, extensive studies were conducted by air to determine the most suitable locations for development. In November 1965, Disney told the *Orlando Sentinel* that he had looked at the land two or three times before.[10]

Disney had considered other east coast business opportunities. By early 1964, Disney expressed an interest in 'Interama,' sponsored by the state of Florida's Inter-American Center Authority and described as 'a permanent international exposition.'[11] This may also have influenced Disney's thinking about EPCOT's internationally themed town center. Interama, in Miami, would have featured international, industrial, cultural, and festival areas.

Robert Moses urged Disney to take over the 1964–65 New York World's Fair fairgrounds to build a new park. The fair site was not large enough to satisfy Disney's needs. He did not want to repeat the same mistake (lack of control over surrounding property) he made with Disneyland in Anaheim, due to a limited budget in the early 1950s. New York's winter climate was also a factor.

Other areas Disney considered for an eastern facility included the St. Louis redevelopment site, the Canadian side of the Niagara Falls, several projects for the Washington, D.C., area, and New Jersey. Disney outlined his own site selection parameters in late 1966: 'I don't like ocean sites because of the beach crowd, and also the ocean limits the approach. If you'll notice, Disneyland at Anaheim is like a hub with freeways converging on it from all sides. I like it better inland.'[12] The coasts could also generate too much natural competition for visitors. Furthermore, Disney initially wanted to

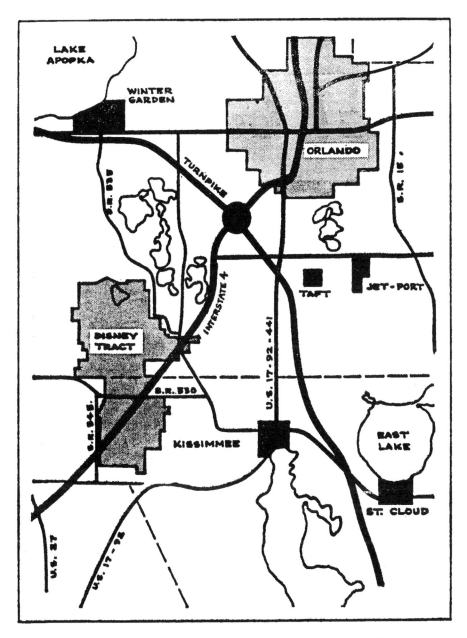

Figure 4.1 Map of the Florida property and vicinity, 1967. Like Disneyland, freeway proximity would be the major consideration in selecting a site for Disney World. Source: *Orlando Sentinel*, February 3, 1967

purchase between 5,000 and 10,000 acres of land. Roy O. Disney stressed that the land must be purchased at a sound real estate investment price.

The site selection and acquisition programs were supervised by company attorney Foster. The firm of Helliwell, Melrose & De Wolf was retained as local counsel. Paul Helliwell, who served in the World War II-era Office of Strategic Services (O.S.S.), worked with Foster. Phil Smith, initially a Helliwell attorney, also contributed to the processes. To add to the intrigue surrounding the selection and acquisition process, Helliwell's firm had been recommended by the company's New York counsel, Donovan, Leisure, Newton and Irvine. Along with President Truman, William Donovan is considered to be a founder of the Central Intelligence Agency. The confidentiality of the Disney transactions seemed assured. In addition, Roy Hawkins was retained as local real estate consultant and Bill Lund also worked on the location analyses for ERA.

ERA performed three studies for a Disney World location. The third study yielded three large sites and Foster evaluated those and others.[13] All told, approximately 30 tracts throughout central Florida were reviewed by Foster and 16 were inspected on-site.[14] Sites north of Orlando were determined to be too cold in the winter for tropical landscaping. Finally, the subject site was selected for its location near the intersection of Interstate 4 and the Sunshine State Parkway, major Florida highways. Therefore, EPCOT, a design opposed to the automobile, would be a demonstration site in the center of Disney World, whose location was chosen for its accessibility by the automobile. Another important consideration was that the Florida property's large Bay Lake could be privately owned under Florida law.

In general, the company's overall approach to land acquisition is aptly described by biographer Bob Thomas as 'a two-year cloak-and-dagger saga of deception, false identities, and dummy corporations.'[15] In addition to keeping the price of land low, Foster recalls that other reasons for secrecy included uncertainty about Project Florida's final plan, the potential exploitation of the company name, and securities law.[16] As a result, at least nine 'dummy corporations' with names ranging from Reedy Creek Ranch Co., Inc., to Latin-American Development and Management Corporation were used in the transactions.[17]

The Disney organization's strategy was to place the large tracts of the overall property under option first. In addition, in at least two of the land deals, accounting for 9,180 acres, the company was able to secure seller financing.[18] The EPCOT site is located on what was known as the Demetree property. Negotiations began in June 1964 and the buyer was confronted with a host of issues ranging from title questions raised by questionable subdivision maps to separate ownership of mineral rights. As of May 28, 1965, a total of 27,258 acres had closed.[19] The buyer remained a mystery and the total area of 27,443 acres would not be determined until surveyors could work their way around the snakes and swamps (see Figure 4.2).[20]

Figure 4.2 This 1998 satellite image shows that the overall layout of the Florida property is similar to Disney's 1966 Seventh Preliminary Master Plot Plan. Copyright Space Imaging

During the same month, the *Orlando Sentinel* ran a front-page editorial entitled, 'We KNOW We'll Get It, But We Don't Know WHAT.' It said in part, 'while unable to tell us for whom they were acting ... [the buyer's agents] asked us not to unduly publicize the purchases as this might overly inflate real estate prices and cause the principals to ... leave town.'[21] Clearly, the newspaper's publisher, Martin Andersen, was squarely in favor of economic development in the region.

On June 24, 1965, local counsel Helliwell spoke to the newspaper. The next day the headline read, '"Mystery" Site Deal Completed.'[22] The buyer, reported Helliwell, would now focus on planning and engineering. By late June 1965, the *Orlando Sentinel* speculated that Walt Disney Productions was the buyer and that it would team with other companies to build a 'city of the future, depicting what life will be like about the year 2050.'[23]

In summary, Walt Disney Productions purchased a total of 27,443 acres of land in central Florida prior to Disney's death for a price of approximately $5.1 million ($184 per acre). This area is roughly twice the size of Manhattan, or approximately 43 square miles. The company's 1965 annual report emphasized that the purchase did indeed represent a profitable investment simply as land speculation.[24] Just four years later, after a substantial investment by the company and with Phase One of Walt Disney World under construction, adjacent property sold for around $10,000 per acre.[25]

The mystery buyer that purchased the land ultimately was revealed. On October 21, 1965, after a visit to the Walt Disney Studios in Burbank with other Southeast entertainment journalists, *Orlando Sentinel* reporter Emily Bavar filed the story, 'Girl Reporter Convinced by Walt Disney.'[26] Although Disney attempted to convince Bavar that his was not the mystery industry, the reporter concluded that he was 'capable of building anything from a park to an entire city in a Central Florida pasture.'[27] Three days later, the newspaper finally declared, 'We Say: "Mystery" Industry Is Disney.' The article spoke of the possibility of two new incorporated cities on the property and added, 'From what The Sentinel has been able to piece together, the cities themselves will be part of the tourist attraction.'[28] Rumors were confirmed by Florida Governor Haydon Burns at a press conference the following day. Attorney Phil Smith became the first resident on the Disney World property, moving there in 1965 to look after the company's interests.

The ever-increasing need for space and Disney's ever-expanding imagination combined to give his organization experience in site selection and acquisition long before Project Florida. For example, after successfully participating in the Squaw Valley Winter Olympics in 1960, Disney engaged ERA to survey the skiing potential at San Gorgonio Mountain in Southern California's San Bernardino range and Mineral King Valley north of Fresno, California, near Sequoia National Park. Later, the company performed surveys of Aspen, Colorado, and Mammoth Mountain in California. Ultimately, in 1965, Retlaw Enterprises, Disney's family company (see Chapter 6, Economic Analysis and Finance), assembled and purchased approximately

26 acres along the Mineral King Valley floor, from the United States Forest Service. Environmental opposition eventually halted the project.

Land also would be required for another of Disney's last projects: CalArts. An original site near the Hollywood Bowl was deemed to be too small, had difficult terrain, and subject to government controls. In 1966, Disney donated 38 acres of the 728-acre Golden Oak Ranch in Placerita Canyon, the studio's location ranch in Santa Clarita, California, which was acquired in 1959 after a short leasehold.[29] However, seismic risk and other factors led Roy O. Disney to hire ERA to perform location studies of alternate sites and a 60-acre site near the location ranch was selected in 1967. The Newhall Land and Farming Company donated half of the land. The site enjoys easy access to Interstate 5. Disney endowed the interdisciplinary school for the arts with more than $40 million (1966 dollars).

The Disneyland site purchase in Anaheim was the company's first exercise in sophisticated location analysis and acquisition. In August 1953, Disney's economic consultant, Stanford Research Institute (SRI), issued its final report. C.V. Wood Jr. managed the engagement and Harrison Price was the project leader. Bill Cottrell, a WED Enterprises vice president, led the Disneyland site acquisition team. The company's general selection parameters included a site area of approximately 100 acres located in the Los Angeles metropolitan area. Just as he later would avoid the Florida shore, Disney passed on coastal locations like the Palos Verdes Peninsula both because of the land cost and the potential for a Coney Island environment.

Foreshadowing things to come in Florida, one disqualifying criterion was government control. Within its geographic district, Anaheim featured the lowest total tax rate.[30] It is ironic that in the future, ERA would study industrial development incentives in the Southeast to help the company to attract industry to EPCOT. In that capacity, Walt Disney Productions acted like a local government. As in Florida, the study also featured a search by air. Development of the Southern California region's freeway system also was an important factor. This would also be a critical factor in Florida. Also similar to Florida, the Anaheim land acquisition involved dealing with existing multiple ownerships. A portion of the preferred site also was put under option. 'Hold-outs' proved difficult, even with the assistance of real estate broker Coldwell Banker, and Disney selected a secondary site nearby.

The company also established another precedent: it kept its identity secret. It ended up purchasing only 160 acres initially due to a limited budget. Disney's first real exposure to the politics of boundaries and real estate began as Anaheim officials and the local chamber of commerce 'gerrymandered' to exclude those opposed to the incorporation of the Disneyland property.[31]

In addition to the Anaheim acquisition, the Disneys also had the experience of purchasing property for their studios. On July 6, 1925, the Disney brothers made a $400 deposit toward the purchase of a 60-foot by 40-foot vacant lot at 2719 Hyperion Avenue near Griffith Park Boulevard, in the

Silverlake district of Los Angeles.[32] Construction of a new studio began shortly thereafter. As noted, it was not long before the studio's needs out-grew the Hyperion Avenue space. On August 31, 1938, the Disneys put money down on the 51-acre parcel in Burbank located at the northeast corner of Buena Vista Street and Riverside Drive. The purchase price for the land was $101,897.[33] Land on the southern border of the Burbank property, separated by Riverside Drive and located north of the Los Angeles Flood Control Channel, was planned as a potential amusement park in 1951.

Due to space constraints at the Burbank studios, WED Enterprises moved into a small building on Sonora Avenue in neighboring Glendale in August 1961. Between 1961 and 1965, the WED Enterprises staff grew from ap-proximately 100 to 300 persons. In June 1965, WED Enterprises moved into a nearby office park in Glendale and would then take over several nearby buildings at the former site of the Glendale Airport.

With a track record of complex property acquisitions behind it, Walt Disney Productions would be confronted with an even greater challenge: site engineering for the 27,443 acres of generally untamed wilderness it purchased in central Florida.

Site engineering and technology in EPCOT would be more closely re-lated than in a normal residential community. In 1968, Admiral Joe Fowler summarized Disney's view of technology in EPCOT, envisioning houses with individual power plants, fuel cells, and pipes for trash collection.[34] Still, technology would not be limited to power or trash. WED Enterprises engineer Don Edgren recalls that Disney said 'that he wanted EPCOT to be the leader in as many of the technical fields as possible.'[35] In addition, the ecology movement was beginning to bloom and the team was moving in that direction as well. Unlike the Monsanto House of the Future at Disney-land, for example, EPCOT would incorporate change continuously. Through tours of the research and development laboratories of American industry, Disney and his team appeared to hope that the 'Great Big Beautiful Tomor-row' might just merge with the Great Society.

Site engineering would be a serious challenge in developing the Florida property. As previously noted, the EPCOT site was one of the largest areas of dry land located within the Florida property.[36] The land is virtually flat and naturally poorly drained, with an average slope of 0.0004.[37] The 27,443-acre tract had more elevated terrain on the west, north, and east and is drained by surface streams flowing south, primarily Reedy and Bonnet creeks.[38] Most of the Florida property was 75 feet to 95 feet above sea level and covered by large swamps.[39]

General Joe Potter was assigned to supervise site engineering in Septem-ber 1965. His aide, Colonel Tom Jones, recalls that draining the Florida property was merely a 'neat little trick for him.' In military terms, Jones reflects, 'between Joe Potter and Joe Fowler, they ramrodded the building of Florida.'[40] Disney retained the Florida engineering firm of Gee and Jenson to develop a plan for the reclamation of the drainage area. In October 1965, experimental site clearing and grading began in the northwest corner of the property and the consultants began their water control and drainage studies.[41] One Gee and Jenson report, 'Plan of Reclamation for Reedy Creek Drainage District,' dated June 1966, was located in Disney's office.[42] Gee and Jenson engineers Herb Gee, Ted Jenson, and Fred Green were knowledgeable about drainage districts and relevant Florida laws.[43] The firm would be a valuable resource during the formulation of a special district for the property. By 1972, Walt Disney Productions had constructed 50 miles of canals, levees, and 30 automatic gated control structures, the largest privately funded project of its type up to that time.[44] The EPCOT team also sought creative ways to utilize water in planning and design.[45]

Although the EPCOT site was relatively dry, it was 'riddled with sinkholes,' the largest being 1,500 feet in diameter.[46] A limestone base beginning at about 100 feet beneath the Reedy Creek area lay below sandy sediments, clay, and silt.[47] This porous limestone and its underground caverns can collapse to create surficial sinkholes. Therefore, site engineering for EPCOT would entail: (1) draining the swamp water, (2) dredging muck, (3) compressing stable material, and (4) shaping the final contours. Although Epcot Center, at 400 acres, is smaller than EPCOT might have been, it still offers a glimpse of the magnitude of work required to prepare the site. To prepare the Epcot Center site, work crews removed 5 million cubic yards of earth, 1 million cubic yards of muck, and 500,000 cubic yards of sand.[48] As many as 4,500 construction workers were required to prepare the site, which was alive with crocodiles and dangerous snakes.[49]

Such geologic conditions prompted the engineering firm of Dames & Moore and civil designer Ken Klug to pour concrete into a large cavity beneath what is now the Transportation and Ticket Center at Walt Disney World.[50] During construction of the Contemporary Resort, piles up to 150 feet or longer were used, whereas a pile under more typical conditions would measure 40 feet to 60 feet in length.[51] Such piles, or caissons, create friction along their sides, contribute to support of the load, and often are used in clays. Appropriately perhaps, EPCOT's site engineering was as challenging as the concept itself.

Florida Film writer Marty Sklar emphasizes that much of the EPCOT concept grew out of Disney's own personal experiences. For example, like many, Disney was not pleased when garbage trucks woke him up. This led to a search for a new trash collection system.[52] Ecology also appeared to be on Disney's mind. WED Enterprises researched a self-contained sewage plant that would yield no effluent. As John Hench remembers, 'He [Disney] set up all kinds of things. We had waste water experiments all over the place at first … .'[53] On a 1966 research trip, Disney flew to St. Petersburg, Florida, to view a new type of composting system. These and similar concepts at the time were building toward the ecology movement and are precursors to today's concept of sustainable communities. Of course, even Ebenezer Howard planned to use refuse in his garden cities to fertilize agricultural areas at the beginning of the twentieth century. Disney also insisted on underground utilities. As previously noted, utilities were placed below ground at the Burbank studios and the company also paid to have high-tension power lines buried in Anaheim. Other conceptual power sources under consideration included fuel cells, solar energy, and nuclear power.[54]

Utilidors, the underground basements beneath the Magic Kingdom in Florida, were planned prior to Disney's death. As architect Bill Martin recalls, 'Walt had "greased the wheels" for a lot of things that we were doing after he passed away, but he had always worked that way.'[55] The 'urban basement,' 9 acres in area, contains sewer and other pipes, cables, conduits, and the American introduction of the Swedish AVAC (Automatic Vacuum Collection) trash disposal system. The AVAC system (designed in conjunction with Aerojet-General Corporation and installed by Fluor) funnels trash underground in pneumatic tubes and is a system directly connected to Disney's objectives for EPCOT.[56] Garbage moves at approximately 60 miles per hour to a central compacting plant.

Walt Disney Production's version of the underground passageway was Disney's idea; he first used it under Disneyland's New Orleans Square. Architect Le Corbusier believed that service mains should be accessible throughout their length. Similarly, Ebenezer Howard's plan included underground utilities and postal pneumatic tubes. The company's utilidor system is also reminiscent of the Washington Metropolitan Board of Trade proposal for a raised platform for the 1964–65 New York World's Fair. Utilidors allow expansion and flexibility of facilities above the surface. The utilidors beneath the Magic Kingdom are approximately 22 feet wide and 11 feet high.[57]

The property's high water table posed another engineering challenge for the company that would have to be solved to make utilidors and EPCOT possible. Martin developed the idea of draining Bay Lake and using the fill to elevate the Magic Kingdom site. Due to the high water table, the site had to be raised an average of 14 feet and water continues to be pumped almost continuously. Some sections are approximately 10 feet below the water table.

In addition to being hidden storage spaces for utilities, utilidors enable servicing of restaurants, shops, and attractions to proceed without interrupting the 'show,' or illusion in the park. An employee dressed for Tomorrowland need not walk through Town Square in public view. Instead, signs in the utilidor guide personnel to the appropriate elevators below the Magic Kingdom's 'lands.' The utilidor also includes elements of the Digital Animation Control System, which centrally runs all of the park's Audio-Animatronics figures. This system of central control, similar to Progress City's centrally operated, computerized transportation system, is another example of the potential magnitude of control in Disney's EPCOT concept.

By 1971, Donn Tatum, then president of Walt Disney Productions, stated that 'the new systems, the new devices, the new techniques which have been

found feasible during years of investigation will provide a body of knowledge and experience as we move into … EPCOT.'[58] However, the concept's
underground transportation hierarchy would be a more difficult and expensive engineering challenge than the utilidors of the Magic Kingdom. For
example, Reedy Creek Improvement District Administrator Tom Moses
believes that ventilation technology for Disney's proposed tunnel system
did not exist in 1966.[59]

Disney planned to meet many of the challenges facing EPCOT by imple-
menting advances in technology. Although his company had produced its
own significant technological achievements, Disney wanted to develop partnerships with the technology leaders of American industry. Toward this end,
EPCOT planner Marvin Davis traveled with Disney to research and development laboratories operated by corporations such as RCA, Xerox, and
IBM. Davis recalled, 'We got to see products and concepts that wouldn't be
on the market for five or ten years.'[60] John Hench also traveled with Disney,
stopping at NASA and 'different industrial complexes he loved to visit so
much.'[61] In addition, General Joe Potter and Card Walker traveled with
Disney. Walker recalls that the technology at RCA and AT&T was 'really
way out' (see Chapter 6, Economic Analysis and Finance).[62]

While Disney and his staff traveled around the country to develop the
EPCOT concept, Walt Disney Productions had already produced technological milestones in the entertainment industry. For example, Audio-
Animatronics debuted in Disneyland's Enchanted Tiki Room attraction in
1963. Movements were recorded on reel-to-reel magnetic audio tape which
triggered the bird mechanisms that were part of the show. Technology had
indeed come a long way. In 1949, Disney and his staff had produced a 9-
inch-tall 'dancing man' operated by a complicated set of mechanical cams
below a miniature stage. Disney explained the new Audio-Animatronics
technology as follows:

> It's sound and animation through electronics. It's opened a whole new door for
> us. We can program whole shows on tape. The tape sends signals and the little
> figures go to work and they sing and act and move according to the impulse that
> comes from the tape. And this is all possible because of this big drive we've had
> on the space age development, the electronic age.[63]

One of Disney's most important skills was the ability to associate himself
with some of the best people in the industry. For example, Ub Iwerks began
working with Disney in 1920, eventually following his friend to Hollywood
in 1924. He worked on *Steamboat Willie* (1928), the first animated film with
synchronized sound, and invented the multihead optical printer, used in the
combination of live action and animation. Iwerks also designed a modification of the Haloid Company's Xerox process, which eliminated the need for
hand inking in animation, and he was instrumental in the development of
the Circle-Vision/Circarama 360-degree photographic process.

Another company technological wizard was Roger Broggie, who joined Walt Disney Productions in 1939 and established the studio's machine shop. Broggie helped devise the multiplane camera. This mid-1930s development provided greater sense of depth and movement in animated film by vertically separating animation cels and backgrounds. The multiplane was completed in time for limited use in *Snow White*. This followed the short film, *Flowers and Trees* (1932), in which Disney employed the Technicolor process in animation for the first time. Broggie also was involved with most aspects of Imagineering, including most Disneyland attractions and the development of Audio-Animatronics.

The 1964–65 New York World's Fair featured the Audio-Animatronics Abraham Lincoln, which also opened at Disneyland in 1965. Imagineer Wathel Rogers recalled that Mr. Lincoln's mechanisms included '16 air lines to the Lincoln head, 10 air lines to the hands and wrists, 14 hydraulic lines to control the body, and two pairs of wires for every line.'[64] Sculptor Blaine Gibson used an actual Lincoln face mask to sculpt the features of the sixteenth president. Imagineer Bob Gurr designed the Lincoln figure's heavy structural frame. Finally, John Hench recalls the difficulty the team had in getting Mr. Lincoln to perform, 'To me it was just like Walt had willed him to [work],' Hench said.[65]

General Electric's 1964–65 New York World's Fair Progressland carousel was Disney's version of a history of technology and featured an Audio-Animatronics cast. Disney was personally involved in developing even the minutiae of the show. The show's theme song, 'There's a Great Big Beautiful Tomorrow,' was written by Robert B. Sherman and Richard M. Sherman and is said to reflect Disney's optimism.[66] Perhaps revealingly, the theme song was changed to '[Now is] The Best Time of Your Life' to reflect the 'now'-oriented 1970s. Approximately 16 million people saw the show at the fair. The Carousel of Progress (the Disneyland version) highlights what Disney and General Electric believed were many of the significant technological innovations of the century. The future is depicted in a rendering of Progress City by Collin Campbell that could be seen outside the stage 'window' in Act Four. The narration from the Disneyland version of the show was written by Larry Clemmons. Act One begins with the pre-electric 1880s and Act Four closes with General Electric's Medallion Home of the 1960s.[67] The carousel was a staged, animated example of Disney's state of becoming.

The studio also developed Fantasound, an early experimental stereo system. Disney developed it in conjunction with RCA for the 'visualization' of classical music through animation, known as *Fantasia* (1940). Conductor Leopold Stokowski convinced Disney and his chief engineer, Bill Garity, to develop a system that would ultimately use 33 microphones and 420,000 feet of film (18,000 feet were used in the final print). Oscillators were purchased from William Hewlett and David Packard, still working in a Palo Alto garage.

Additionally, Walt Disney Productions learned a great deal about technology during World War II. By the end of the war, Disney estimated that his company had produced approximately 300,000 feet of film per year for the government. According to Disney, 'We learned a great deal during the war years when we were making instruction and technological films in which abstract and obscure things had to be made plain and quickly and exactly applicable to the men in the military services.'[68] This skill is evident in the animated sequences of the Florida Film, for example. During the period 1941 through 1945, the studio's educational and military training films included the following subjects: environmental sanitation, protection against chemical warfare, aircraft maintenance and repair, and simplex and phantom circuits.[69] Work on these 'state-of-the-art' subjects, interaction with the defense industry, and topics like environmental sanitation, must have contributed to Disney's background in conceptualizing a technological community. The company also began a short-lived Educational and Industrial Film Division in 1944. Customers included giants of American industry: General Motors, Firestone, AT&T, Westinghouse, and the Steel Institute. These early relationships created contacts who Disney could call upon when he began his technical and market research for EPCOT in the mid-1960s.

America's space program, particularly advanced environmental planning for space stations, influenced the thinking of urban designers in the mid-1960s. The Disney organization has had a long-standing relationship with NASA and its predecessors. It began in full force in 1954 when Ward Kimball prepared storyboards for a three-part television series. The first program was 'Man in Space' (1955), the second was 'Man and the Moon' (1955), and the third was 'Mars and Beyond' (1957). Because Disney was busy with the construction of Disneyland, he gave full control of the series to Kimball, who contacted scientists Willy Ley, Heinz Haber, Ernst Stuhlinger, and Wernher von Braun to assist in the production of the shows (see Figure 4.3).[70]

President Eisenhower watched the first show, 'Man in Space,' and was impressed. He requested a copy of the film and, paraphrased by Kimball, 'He told Walt, "I want to show some of our stuffed-shirt generals that don't believe in this stuff how it's going to be."'[71]

The 'Mars and Beyond' program featured von Braun and Stuhlinger discussing futuristic, EPCOT-like topics such as recycling waste products to produce drinking water and air, and the growth of vegetables.[72] Marty Sklar recalls that living systems and new ways of growing food were 'absolutely the kind of things that Walt was trying to do with EPCOT.'[73] The studio also produced 13 nature films for the *True-Life Adventures* series, produced between 1948 and 1960, which received eight Academy Awards. The topics of the future of agriculture and ecosystems also were contained in the book, *Our Margin of Life* (1964), a copy of which was located in Disney's office.[74]

Even with the company's contacts with research and development facilities and its own technological achievements in the entertainment industry,

Figure 4.3   Disney, shown with Wernher von Braun, visits the Army
Ballistic Missile Agency in Alabama in 1954. Von Braun and
other scientists advised producer Ward Kimball during the
creation of a television space series. Source: NASA Imaging
Branch

EPCOT would require new solutions. As Imagineer Carl Bongiorno recalls, 'a lot of the technology was not available to even get a number on. The technology, much of it, had to be developed.'[75] But if von Braun could build a Saturn V rocket, then why couldn't American industry and possibly the Model Cities program address the nation's urban crisis using EPCOT as an experimental venue? This appeared to be at the core of Disney's bold proposal for the Florida property. The experimental community, however, would be both a showcase of American technology and an ongoing urban scientific experiment. While participation in such an endeavor might have been exciting for EPCOT residents, they also would have wanted to live relatively normal lives. This was a critical issue that Disney did not have much time to address before his death.

Chapter 5

Landscaping

The collection of images has included something to please almost everybody,
and the arrangement has juxtaposed the pieces so closely, then joined them
with thick, real foliage so successfully, that the visit, whatever path
you choose, has very tightly choreographed itself.

William J. Mitchell,
Charles W. Moore, and
William Turnbull Jr.,
The Poetics of Gardens[1]

Based on the landscape designs at the Burbank studio campus, Disney's Holmby Hills residence, and the topiary, islands, and mock jungles of Disneyland, it is a safe assumption that landscaping would have been a key component in EPCOT. While Marvin Davis' conceptual EPCOT plans feature lakes, trees, and turf in the greenbelt, industrial park, and 'radiential' areas, detailed landscaping remained for a later stage in the planning process. In addition, Herbert Ryman's Progress City paintings, early expressions of Disney's thinking about EPCOT, include lakes, trees, and abundant green space, although they are highly conceptual. The Progress City narration states that landscaping was used to make industrial areas more like parks.[2]

Landscaping did not start out as a formal discipline at WED Enterprises. Sometimes, as was the case with landscaping the Monsanto House, Imagineers like John Hench and Bill Evans would complete a 'seat-of-the-pants' landscaping plan on-site, with plenty of arm waving during actual construction.[3] This was the way landscaping could be done during the early days of Disneyland. It is significant that, after Disney's death, the WED Enterprises team placed 22,000 miniature trees and shrubs in the Progress City model.[4] Clearly, it was the team's understanding that landscaping would be a major element in EPCOT.

The evolution of the role landscaping has played in community planning is reflected in The Urban Land Institute's 1968 *Community Builders Handbook*. It included only two pages in its 'Landscape Planting' section. The following is a representative, vague excerpt: '[a] well-designed planting scheme will contribute to the beauty of a development and will serve a useful purpose as well.'[5] By 1990, landscape elements warranted a subchapter of their own and covered topics ranging from entrance gateways to lake management.[6] Judging from the handbooks, community developers have placed a greater emphasis on landscaping since the 1960s, learning that it can contribute to economic, aesthetic, and other values.

While the emphasis on water in the early EPCOT concept is a partial reflection of the abundance of water on or below the property, Christopher Alexander wrote that the need people have for water as a community design element is profound.[7] The preliminary work of the EPCOT team embodies this theory. Perhaps it was reinforced along the Rivers of America at Disneyland, which front New Orleans Square. Disney's own drawing of the plot plan shows residential water frontage along portions of the 'petals' in the west, north, and east.

When Disney was ready to prepare a landscaping plan for EPCOT, he would have turned to Morgan 'Bill' Evans. Evans and his brother, Jack, met Disney in 1950. Jack Evans designed the landscaping for the Holmby Hills house and Bill Evans assisted in the planting. The process became a typical landscape formula for Disney in enhancing atypical design elements such as trestles, bridges, berms, and tunnels. After grading, the largest trees were planted, followed by the smaller ones and shrubs. Finally, an irrigation system was installed and turf planted.[8] Disney turned to the Evanses again when he was planning the park in Anaheim in 1954.[9]

On Evans Road, just north of Sunset Boulevard in Pacific Palisades' Rustic Canyon, the Evans family owned 22 acres and used their property to test new plant material. The brothers constantly searched the world for new material and, with their father, introduced well over twenty species of plants into the United States. Their houses in Rustic Canyon featured themed landscaping, including tropical, magnolias, and 'formal.'[10] Bamboo stalks still thrive there. Disney toured the canyon and developed landscaping options for Disneyland.

Disney also was influenced by Tivoli Gardens in Copenhagen, with its many shade trees and flowers. And he gained limited exposure to landscaping by overseeing the site preparation, planting, and irrigation processes at the Burbank studios. The studios feature more traditional campus landscaping components: turf, coral trees, and eucalyptus trees.

Disneyland, on the other hand, was anything but traditional. One of Disneyland's landscaping achievements is the Jungle Cruise attraction, which takes visitors on a boat cruise through a simulated jungle river environment. As Karal Ann Marling comments, 'in many ways, the Jungle Cruise defined what Disneyland was all about. It was a cinematic experience, an art director's pipe dream … .'[11] Imagineer Harper Goff developed much of the attraction's concept. The landscaping of the Jungle Cruise is still viable today, as mature bamboo canopies create a jungle illusion. Overall, 90 percent of the plants at Disneyland are non-indigenous to California and there are more than 800 plant species (see Figure 1.2). Today, approximately 1 million annuals are planted at the park each year.[12]

As previously noted, the scale of Disneyland's environment is critically important to keeping the visitor involved in the 'show.' Therefore, trees cannot become too mature for their surroundings. Many trees are maintained in buried pots, with their root systems confined. This might be termed the 'landscaping of reassurance.' A tree along Main Street, U.S.A. that is the size of the enormous Swiss Family (now Tarzan's) Treehouse would destroy the illusion created by the designers. Control in the Disneyland design extends beyond the built environment to the green environment as well.

The earthen berm that surrounds Disneyland was also an essential element in the design of Disney's backyard in Holmby Hills. Its purpose is to prevent visual intrusion and to exclude sound. As Evans notes, 'Trees alone won't do that. It takes about a hundred feet of dense trees to block sound, but you can do that with about twenty feet of earth.'[13] Disneyland's landscaping team also pioneered methods of moving large trees for Disney, including the placement of metal pins in trunks, wrapping roots, and lifting by crane.

WED Enterprises created environments ranging from a jungle, to Tom Sawyer Island, to Tomorrowland. Perhaps EPCOT's landscaping might have incorporated some of the experience acquired in Tomorrowland. As Evans remembers, 'We felt that the architecture of Tomorrowland was very bold and very prominent, very conspicuous, so we tried to use equally assertive plant choices, plant species that made a statement on their own.'[14]

The company sometimes looked to the past as a source for trees. For example, in 1962, mature trees from Pershing Square in downtown Los Angeles were acquired for New Orleans Square at Disneyland. The trees were being displaced by a parking garage construction project. Evans also had contacts in various communities to let him know when 'good specimen trees' were about to be removed from city streets.

As early as January 1967, a tree farm was started in Florida for the property's future needs.[15] In landscaping EPCOT, Evans would have been confronted with many of the same problems he solved in work on other Florida projects, ranging from the Magic Kingdom to the Animal Kingdom.

Most important, unlike Anaheim, central Florida has periods of freezing weather because of the jet stream. The only broadleaf evergreen trees – required for shade and shelter for frost-tender plant material – are live oaks and magnolias and 'that's the end of the list in central Florida.'[16] In contrast, there are approximately 30 or 40 different choices of evergreen trees that will thrive in Anaheim. In addition, central Florida's growing season is virtually year-round. Therefore, plants grow quickly and much effort is required to maintain the intended design scale and landscape plans; much of the plant material must be constrained.[17]

While working in Florida, Evans had frequent contact with EPCOT planner Marvin Davis, based in Glendale, California. '[I]f it turned out that one of the proposals for the hotel or something coincided with a particularly bad piece of swamp,' Evans recalled, 'I'd relay word back to him.'[18] Evans also oversaw the initial landscaping for the CalArts project, and due to a very small budget, the overall effect was sparse at opening. The landscaping has matured since 1971.

Despite the traditional and nostalgic forms of landscaping found at the Burbank studios, Disneyland's Town Square and hub (the Plaza), and even his own backyard, Disney ultimately might have been tempted to select 'assertive' plant material more along the lines of Tomorrowland for EPCOT. Or, alternatively, EPCOT's landscaping might have been similar to landscape architect and planner Anne Whiston Spirn's description of Epcot Center, which 'with its swirling bands of brilliant blooms, is meant to reassure the visitor that the future will be a happy place.'[19] Whatever the final choices in plant materials, it is evident that Disney would have used water elements, shade, and extensive landscaping in EPCOT.

ECONOMICS
AND MARKETING

Chapter 6

Economic Analysis and Finance

Our society will never be great until our cities are great. In the next forty years we must rebuild the entire urban United States ... There is decay of the centers and the despoiling of the suburbs.

Lyndon Johnson, 1964

Money – or rather the lack of it to carry out my ideas – may worry me, but it does not excite me. Ideas excite me.

Walt Disney

Roy has a mission which he, better than anyone else, recognizes – and that's not to check Walt, but to see to it that he has the freedom.

William Pereira[1]

Disney's EPCOT philosophy says little about the cost of building a community of tomorrow. However, he did turn to the economic consulting firm of Economics Research Associates for order-of-magnitude estimates of costs and revenues associated with the concept. Preliminary real estate economic estimates for the EPCOT concept were presented to Disney in July 1966, prepared by Harrison Price with the assistance of associate Tom Ashley.

Unfortunately, Disney was unable to provide Price with any substantial feedback related to the ERA economic estimates for EPCOT before he died.[2] Today, Price says of Disney, 'He had a seed idea, attempting a Walt idea – "I want to do this." And if he'd lived another decade, he would have done it.'[3] Nevertheless, after years of working closely with Disney, Price had a good sense of his client's and the team's general direction.

Unlike many new towns, EPCOT's economy would have been able to draw upon immense visitor expenditures and related employment. Anaheim's city coffers had reflected the economic benefits of the Disneyland theme park. In 1964, ERA completed a report entitled, 'The Economic Impact of the Disneyland Recreation Complex on the City of Anaheim.' During the period 1955 through 1964, when more than 49 million people had visited Disneyland, the economic impact on the city of Anaheim alone was estimated at $556.2 million (current dollars).[4] This figure included in-park sales, retail sales outside the park, wholesale sales, construction, property taxes, and sales tax. Moreover, ERA's 1967 estimate of the economic impact of Walt Disney World was in excess of $6.65 billion during the first ten years.[5] This estimate included new visitor expenditures, new payrolls, and construction materials and equipment.

In 1959, a company project on the east coast was still far from certain. It was Price who concluded that Disneyland would never penetrate two-thirds of the population in the eastern one-third of the United States.[6] During the 1964–65 New York World's Fair, the company learned that it could 'play well' to the population east of the Mississippi.[7] Disney believed another Magic Kingdom and recreation complex, along with an industrial park, would generate visitor and resident/employee demand for housing, lodging, shopping, office space, entertainment, recreation, and services in EPCOT.

According to Price, former planner Ray Watson 'was a bellwether on how you plan large acreages. I told Walt he needed somebody like that, so I brought him out … That was a big influence.'[8] Watson critiqued EPCOT twice with Disney in 1966.[9] He remembers that 'I had a hunch he'd [Disney] have to pay people or subsidize them to live there, and he asked me about that.'[10] Price doesn't believe subsidization would have been necessary and points to The Walt Disney Company's recent residential development of Celebration, Florida: 'If you look at the way it's selling down there now by lottery – he [Disney] would have been able to carry it off his way,' Price says.[11] Nevertheless, Watson asks, 'could anyone have built the Monsanto House economically and sold it … ?'[12] This question presumes that EPCOT housing would have been comparable to Disneyland's Monsanto House of the Future. Still, Disney's last iteration of the EPCOT concept appeared to be a community of renters in a living laboratory rather than a standard community development.

Looking back, Watson now stresses that the EPCOT concept, even more than other new towns, would have entailed tremendous up-front costs, especially the transportation systems and the multilevel transportation lobby. EPCOT's international shopping area, says Watson, 'is … the commercial center of the community but it's so large it will have to attract more than the people who live there.'[13] EPCOT would be both an experimental community and a tourist attraction. The millions who would visit the Magic Kingdom at the northern end of the Florida property would enter through the entrance complex in the south, board a monorail, and travel through the heart of the industrial park and EPCOT before arriving at the theme park. This was not a typical planned community.

While EPCOT would have its experimental and prototype functions, it could only house 20,000 company and industrial park employees. In its 1967 report entitled, 'Economic Impact of Disneyworld, Florida,' ERA stated that a large amount of the generated housing demand would be met in the greater Orlando area and in the surrounding counties.[14] The impact of the Disney World development on surrounding communities would become an issue of much public debate in central Florida after the Magic Kingdom's opening in 1971.

Price and Ashley also established rough dwelling unit and housing acreage estimates for the EPCOT concept.[15] The overall density is 6.6 dwelling units per gross residential acre. Estimated prices for single-family dwellings (attached and detached) ranged from $8,000 to $50,000 (in 1966 dollars), or $42,480 to $265,500 (in 2000 dollars).[16] By comparison, a typical new house in James Rouse's new community of Columbia, Maryland, cost $30,000 (in1967 dollars).[17]

Based on the housing unit mix and densities, ERA estimated a land requirement of 779 acres for housing in EPCOT.[18] Using the same overall household size, a community of 20,000 persons would require approximately 1,045 gross acres for residential land uses. Again, 1,100 acres is a reasonable estimate of the size of the EPCOT site selected by Disney. Adding 50 acres for the town center to 1,045 acres for residential uses yields a subtotal of 1,095 acres. This does not include the greenbelt ring. These estimates help support the EPCOT site area estimate of approximately 1,100 acres. By comparison, Ebenezer Howard's recommended Garden City area was 1,000 acres. At 1,100 acres, the gross population density for EPCOT would be 18.2 persons per acre. This compares to new town figures published by Real Estate Research Corporation in 1971, ranging from 7.2 to 28.9, with an average of 14.9 persons per acre.[19] By this measure at least, EPCOT was near the average.

While no formal cost estimates were prepared for Disney's concept, ERA used simple industry cost indices to present Disney with per room hotel and per square foot regional mall construction costs.[20] These basic measures clearly demonstrate that EPCOT was at a very preliminary stage of planning. For example, the ERA figures do not address the inclusion of the planned hotel's recreation deck, special convention facilities, or extraordinary costs associated with the subterranean transportation lobby beneath the hotel. In addition, the retail estimates do not consider the additional cost of custom international theming in the retail center.

ERA's economic base analysis yielded an estimate of town center retail sales in Year 10 of $110.3 million (1966 dollars).[21] Today, typical total operating expenses, including cost of goods sold, property taxes, and replacement reserves, can approximate 65 percent of total sales in a theme park.[22] Thus, a rough estimate of $38.6 million (1966 dollars) can be obtained for net income accruing from the town center retail space. With an appropriate capitalization rate, this stabilized income could yield a value well in excess of $1 billion (2000 dollars).[23] This approaches the cost of a company theme park like today's California Adventure located across from Disneyland and reflects another reason why the team included so much themed retail space in EPCOT's core: added value. Based on the Disneyland experience, ERA's retail sales estimates were based on the upper end of national industry figures for regional malls published by the Urban Land Institute.[24]

In addition to retail sales, EPCOT could have featured other revenue sources, including sponsorship by American industry, recreation fees, admission, non-retail space in the town center, neighborhood commercial centers, lodging and convention activities, and apartment/house rentals. However, accounting for revenues and costs in EPCOT would test even the most capable valuation firm. For example, the typical planned community would not include structures in a state of becoming.

However, with or without the hard numbers, some Imagineers apparently put faith in Disney's ideas simply because they were his ideas. In 1997, Marvin Davis reflected on the overall feasibility of EPCOT: 'When we first worked on Disneyland,' he said, 'I didn't think it would work, but by this time I was a believer. I knew that if Disneyland could work, anything Walt did would work.'[25] Still, it is important to clarify that EPCOT would be an experimental and showcase community because, as Ray Watson observes, 'it's not a prototype of what some community developer would follow because they would go bankrupt doing it.'[26]

Facing the expensive challenges of cavernous limestone and a high water table beneath the surface, a multilevel transportation system, a dome to enclose 50 acres, intra- and interurban electric transit, experimental construction materials and methods, and all the other up-front costs associated with a more traditional community development, the Disney 'magic' that creatively financed Disneyland would now turn to American industry and possibly HUD to finance EPCOT.

In addition to economic estimates, Economics Research Associates furnished Disney with a summary analysis of various real estate development financing sources for EPCOT. Disney also considered approaching the newly formed Department of Housing and Urban Development (HUD) to determine if federal funds were available for the project. It was 1966 and Walt and Roy O. Disney were running a company that had finally earned the admiration of Wall Street. A May 1966 article in *Fortune* was entitled, 'Now the Bankers Come to Disney.'[27] The Disney organization had begun to contact American corporations with preliminary information about participation in the EPCOT concept. With corporate successes like the film *Mary Poppins* (1964) and Disneyland, and the potential of a new Magic Kingdom in Florida, financing for EPCOT might have been somewhat easier to negotiate than the $500 the brothers borrowed from their uncle to start the partnership in 1923. Still, as Imagineer John Hench recalls, Roy O. Disney 'hated to be in debt.'[28]

The two brothers began as partners and incorporated as Walt Disney Productions in 1929. Stock was issued to the public for the first time in 1940. Interestingly, Henry Ford had counseled Disney not to sell public stock in order to avoid loss of control.[29] Section (h) of the 1940 amended Articles of Incorporation, adopted after the construction of the Burbank studios, gave the Disney organization authority to become community developers: 'to subdivide properties; to construct ... buildings, houses, warehouses, public or private roads, streets, alleys, reservoirs, irrigation ditches, wharves, tunnels, conduits, subways, and structures of all kinds ... .'[30] Little did the Disneys know then that in 25 years they would control thousands of acres in central Florida.

As mentioned, Walt Disney Productions had developed contacts with other American corporations over time. Very important to corporate relationship building were the Disneyland sponsors. According to Imagineer Randy Bright, 'A kind of symbiotic relationship developed between Disney and American Motors, Kodak, Richfield, Kaiser Aluminum, TWA, Monsanto, and many other sponsors that would be there for the Park's grand opening … .'[31] By 1961, six years after Disneyland opened, other corporations were represented at the park as well. These included Bank of America, AT&T, Coca-Cola, General Dynamics, National Lead Company, and The Upjohn Company.[32] Similar to the future EPCOT concept, Disneyland became an international showcase of American industry.

Disney's participation in the 1964–65 New York World's Fair helped to solidify industry relationships and in various other ways, helped the company's bottom line. Portions of the four shows Disney produced, 'It's a Small World,' 'Great Moments With Mr. Lincoln,' General Electric's Progressland carousel, and the Ford Wonder Rotunda's Primeval World, would find their way to Disneyland in some form. In addition, Disney's association with General Joe Potter, executive vice president of the fair, proved useful because Potter had many contacts in American industry and government.[33]

Marty Sklar, who worked on Ford Motor Company's pavilion, recalls, 'It seems clear in retrospect … that Walt used the … fair … as a stepping-stone toward EPCOT. Certainly we didn't need the extra work at the time, but it gave Walt access to the chief executives of GE and other companies he would want to deal with in the future.'[34] General Electric, for example, was the fifth largest industrial concern in the world at the time of the fair.

Disney's Florida Film was made in large part to attract industry participation in the EPCOT project. Not only did the concept include a showcase of industry in the form of an industrial park, but the constantly changing EPCOT would require a steady stream of new technology from industry. By January 1966, Disney was ready to approach industry with the EPCOT concept. Disney, Potter, Admiral Joe Fowler, Roger Broggie, Lee Adams, Marvin Davis, and Bob Gurr visited Westinghouse Research Center in Pittsburgh, Pennsylvania, and other companies during this early trip. Adams was responsible for the central plant at the Burbank studios and was familiar with high-voltage power transmission. The program for the Westinghouse event was entitled, 'City of Tomorrow.'[35] Disney worked with a roll of Davis' brown-line drawings during the flight back east, which Gurr later referred to as 'one of the first official go-out-and-sell-it junkets.'[36] Disney met with Westinghouse Chairman Don Burnham on the trip.[37] Card Walker remembers that 'it was a good meeting.'[38] Broggie and Gurr discussed monorails and propulsion with personnel at General Electric during the same trip. Today, Gurr recalls seeing his very first laser demonstration.[39]

Because of Disney's status as an international celebrity, Gurr remembers, 'You had to wait for the Westinghouse guys to calm down' before settling into a meeting.[40] This status apparently was being put to work in selling the EPCOT concept. In a sentimental moment, Gurr says, Disney 'pointed to this one spot on a big oval shaped drawing and said, "This is where the park bench will be where Lilly and I are gonna sit at night and watch all the people … ."'[41] Later, Potter recalled that Disney was very interested in Westinghouse.[42] Disney did a lot more traveling in the company plane during 1966.

Potter and Jack Sayers (head of Disneyland lessee relations) met with senior representatives of more than 65 American industries in 1966 'to inform them of potential areas of participation.'[43] As Potter recalled, he visited a hundred companies, including food-packing concerns, IBM, AT&T, U.S. Steel, Du Pont, Bell Laboratories, Honeywell, and Allied Chemical.[44] He also stated that 'in many cases [we] got into their research laboratories.' Such contacts continued after Disney's death.[45] Visits were made at the request of Disney to help develop the EPCOT concept.[46] Traveling under the auspices of Walt Disney did not hurt. Potter recalled, 'When I first started out, I said, "Walt, how am I going to get in?" And he said, "Tell them I sent you! … " [A]nd I never got turned down once … .'[47] A May 1966 letter from Southern Bell stated, 'The "City of Tomorrow" … will indeed present a challenge …. Our people will be ready to draw freely from … the Bell Laboratories … .'[48]

The idea of industry cooperation in EPCOT was not without potential problems. In an interesting observation regarding the proprietary nature of product prototypes, John Hench recalls that Disney 'didn't understand … how jealous people are of keeping it [secret] and not exposing it.'[49] Similarly, investments of private industry in prototype products on display in EPCOT would have to be protected. Disney, however, appeared to have little patience for legal matters. Hench raises a critical question about the concept: at what stage of development would American industry have been willing to display its secrets to visitors, residents, and competitors in EPCOT?

Prior to Disney's death, his brother Roy believed that Project Florida might be too expensive for the company to fund alone. According to Disney's nephew, Roy E. Disney, the two brothers did have arguments concerning the wisdom of developing a city of tomorrow as might be expected based on their years of working together.[50] General Electric proposed a merger but Walt Disney did not want to relinquish control. The possibility of a merger with Westinghouse also was discussed. In the end, Walt Disney Productions would proceed on its own. Financial structuring for a project like EPCOT would require creativity. In January 1967, Roy O. Disney announced that EPCOT could cost as much as $75 million.[51] However, no detailed cost estimates were made for Disney's original EPCOT concept during his lifetime. According to former WED Enterprises treasurer Carl Bongiorno, 'It [the plan] was moving so much that nobody really took the time.'[52] Phase One, the Magic Kingdom and adjacent area, would help generate the cash flow required to help finance later phases of the Disney World development, including EPCOT.[53] In general, Disney did not like to make sequels (that is, another theme park). However, he agreed with his brother who said, 'We believe if we get eight to 12 million customers there it will be a lot easier to attract industry.'[54] Similarly, Marvin Davis recalled, 'He [Walt Disney] knew where money was and how to get it. The Magic Kingdom was a given for that reason alone, but it was always just a part of the project … His attitude was, "I want to do EPCOT!"'[55] Moreover, the sheer size of the Florida tract would permit Disney to capture additional expenditures lost to outside establishments that cropped up around the smaller Disneyland property.

Harrison Price prepared a summary of potential financing sources for EPCOT in July 1966.[56] This summary provided information regarding traditional forms of financing, loan-to-value ratios, terms, and interest rate 'spreads.' ERA provided Disney with a lesson in real estate development finance. The question is: would the insurance companies listed under regional shopping centers have expressed an interest in placing a mortgage on EPCOT's international shopping area? Without an operating history for the project, they probably would have looked to other collateral (like the Magic Kingdom). After all, what is riskier than retail space in the community of tomorrow? The net income from the Magic Kingdom would go a long way toward servicing debt.

As previously noted, ERA prepared a presentation outline seeking HUD support for EPCOT for Disney. Harrison Price recalls that 'HUD was exploding' in 1966.[57] The growth of the new department was staggering. By 1967 – two years after its creation – HUD's annual programs had reached $12 billion for private and public investments. Price remembers that Disney did not have an opportunity to discuss the August 1966 outline with him in any detail.[58] Its contents, however, reflect the thinking of Disney and his team. ERA's work continued after Disney's death. Between 1969 and 1971, ERA prepared HUD incentive studies for Walt Disney Productions. In addition, the firm was engaged to analyze industrial development incentives in the Southeast during the period 1969 through 1973 because, as Price put it, Walt Disney Productions was 'looking for ways to get help on building this city.'

In 1965, the year HUD was established, the Johnson Administration's Task Force on Urban Problems recommended a 'demonstration cities program' and flexible building regulations.[59] On November 3, 1966, President Johnson signed the Demonstration Cities and Metropolitan Development Act of 1966 and changed the name to Model Cities. Most relevant to EPCOT were the provisions relating to technology. Section 1010(a)(2) states, 'promote the … application of new and improved techniques and methods of constructing, rehabilitating, and maintaining housing, and the application of advances in technology to urban development activities.'[60] Title II (Planned

Metropolitan Development) grants required project review by the regional planning agency, and special districts would have to submit plans to the local county government.[61] These review requirements would have run counter to Disney's desire for control over the special district where he hoped to build EPCOT. In hindsight, the Model Cities program proved vulnerable to numerous problems, including political tampering, inappropriate funding, administrative complexity, and impractical perspective. In addition, federal home mortgage programs continued to subsidize flight to the suburbs, ignoring the growing problems of the inner cities.

In retrospect, it is difficult to believe that Disney ultimately would have relinquished much control over EPCOT to the administrative complexities of the federal government at the same time his staff was busy setting up a 'hands off' special district to govern the Florida property (see Chapter 8, Regulation and Community Governance/Social Planning). While the company could easily have mobilized Florida politicians in support of a HUD application, any funds probably would have come with too many strings for the Disneys.

Still, with the magnitude of resources available to HUD, it certainly was worth the company's investigation. As part of that process, Disney's Florida Film was screened for HUD representatives. In May 1968, Florida Governor Claude Kirk met with HUD Secretary Robert Weaver, who expressed his desire to view Disney's film. In correspondence dated that same month, Kirk wrote to Roy O. Disney, 'If their budget allows they [HUD] are going to initiate money in your projects in cooperation with private enterprise in the area of housing and urban development.'[62] Apparently, Disney's EPCOT concept had been 'sold' to Secretary Weaver. However, Roy O. Disney made it clear that 'right now we are so busy working on the first phase that we have not had an opportunity to develop any detailed thinking with regard to EPCOT.' He added, 'Some of our people have shown the EPCOT film to people in Mr. Weaver's department ... We will make contact again and make sure Mr. Weaver does have the chance to see the film ... .'[63]

In terms of private financing sources, Disney may have liked bankers even less than he cared for big government. Still, the Disneys had a long-term relationship with Bank of America, dating back to the 1930s and A.P. Giannini. While Roy O. Disney was the finance and administration side of the partnership, John Hench emphasizes that 'Walt was a good businessman, too.'[64] Similarly, former WED Enterprises treasurer Carl Bongiorno recalls, 'I could never stay ahead of Walt. As I was making a presentation to him, he was always on the next board.'[65] Disney was a graduate of the hard knocks school of finance, however. His early Laugh-O-Grams studio, which produced silent Alice comedies, had gone bankrupt. Walt Disney was a credit risk at the age of 21.

As mentioned, *Snow White*, the first full-length animated feature, was known as 'Disney's Folly' during production. With the film far exceeding budget, the Disneys showed several early sequences to concerned banker

Joe Rosenberg of Bank of America, who left quite satisfied that the film would be financially successful. With the profits from the film, the Disneys built the Burbank studios. While Disney forged ahead with ideas, his brother ultimately found ways to finance them.

During the period 1952 to 1966, Walt Disney Production's net income (in current dollars) increased from $452,000 to $12.4 million.[66] Stock ownership in 1966 was allocated as follows: 38 percent, Disney family; 13 percent, investment trusts; and 49 percent, public (widely dispersed ownership).[67] EPCOT's development could have benefited from the tax-exempt financing status of the Reedy Creek Improvement District and City of Bay Lake.

Disney established WED Enterprises, Inc. (for Walter Elias Disney), in December 1952. It was an independent contractor to Walt Disney Productions and controlled by Disney. Disney would assign his share of profits from films and other property to WED Enterprises to help keep it going. The entity owned Disneyland's railroad and monorail. Due to changes in securities laws, Disney sold his interest back to Walt Disney Productions in February 1965. It would be renamed Walt Disney Imagineering in 1986. Assets not taken over by the company in 1965 were transferred to Retlaw Enterprises (Walter spelled backwards). In addition, MAPO, Inc., the Imagineers' research and development group, was incorporated in 1965. MAPO was named for the film, *Mary Poppins*.

The best example of Disney's belief in a project and creative financing for it is Disneyland in Anaheim. Equity sources included the brothers' borrowing against life insurance policies, loans from friends, savings, and the sale of Walt and Lillian Disney's vacation home at Smoke Tree Ranch in Palm Springs. The theme park concept was new and, therefore, a risky investment. During a legendary rushed weekend in September 1953, Disney and artist Herbert Ryman conceptualized the first rendering of the park for potential financiers in New York. Roy O. Disney and Imagineer Richard Irvine 'pitched' the lenders, using the rendering and a park narrative by Bill Walsh. With so much risk, the Disneys were turned down for loans. In a bold stroke, Disney presented his concept to all three television networks during a period when the movie studios were wary of the new medium of television. While two declined, the new ABC-Paramount network contributed $500,000 and guaranteed loans up to $4.5 million. In return, the network received a 34.48 percent interest in Disneyland and a one-hour weekly program from the Walt Disney Studios. In keeping with the Disneys' philosophy of always controlling 'the deal,' Walt Disney Productions bought out ABC and the other owners in 1959. The development cost of Disneyland at opening day in July 1955 was $17 million. By mid-1967, the total investment had reached $92 million.[68]

The total required investment for EPCOT will never be known. EPCOT would be an urban laboratory with a large dome in its center and a good deal of unique infrastructure to build up-front. It could not be the prototype community development for real estate finance. However, with potential industry participation, public sources, and a new Magic Kingdom and hotels to possibly service debt, the Disney brothers' creative financing talents were now taken very seriously in New York.

Chapter 7

Marketing

Fellas, I want this deal. If necessary, I'll stand on my head in Macy's window to get it.

Walt Disney

Disney's WED Enterprises would be a community developer like no other because it had the marketing power of Walt Disney Productions behind it. In the early 1930s, Kay Kamen linked studio films with international merchandising. Integration became a cornerstone of the company's marketing philosophy. In the instance of EPCOT, the company was not selling a film linked with products or a theme park attraction. Still, the concept did integrate community and attraction. Its residents would be a 'captive audience' because they would be company or industrial park employees. EPCOT's retail core and hotel would largely be dependent upon tourism. In addition, office tenants would be corporate. During Disney's tenure, EPCOT's marketing primarily would focus on American industry and the people of Florida.

Marketing the unusual EPCOT concept no doubt would be a challenge, but the company certainly had prior experience in this area. After all, a decade earlier it had successfully marketed another unique development: Disneyland. The Anaheim theme park was marketed like no other real estate development. In 1950, Disney commissioned a study of the company's potential involvement in the new medium of television and the first special was broadcasted on NBC. After the success of the special, Disney was in a position to leverage a weekly television series into a marketing and real estate finance vehicle. Four years later, the ABC television show called *Disneyland* reached 40 million viewers weekly. Not many community developers can access a market of this size. The first show, 'The Disneyland Story,' aired on October 27, 1954. Disney, who hosted the show himself, appeared holding a pencil in front of a bird's-eye view painting of the park by Peter Ellenshaw. Construction progress reports were shown throughout the first season. On opening day, July 17, 1955, 22 cameras broadcasted live coverage of Disneyland nationwide, with Disney, then-actor and future President Ronald Reagan, television host Art Linkletter, and actor Bob Cummings serving as hosts. Soon, Disney would be known as 'Uncle Walt' across the country and television gave him a stature never known before in American culture.

In addition to television, other early Disneyland marketing efforts included targeting conventions and special groups, promoting on a regional basis, working with park lessees, and using the *Disneyland News*, a publication distributed to park visitors.[1] All of this was happening as babies 'boomed,' suburbs spread, shopping malls opened, and domestic consumption soared; it appeared the stars were aligned in Disney's universe.

Learning from its past experiences, the Disney organization used various media to market the EPCOT concept. Not surprisingly, Disney would turn to the powerful medium of film to promote his ideas. This follows in the tradition of architect Le Corbusier, who presented his city plans on film in 1929. Disney was able to call upon company veterans like Ham Luske and Max Stewart to create the promotional production known as the Florida Film. Both men were part of the television team that had produced the Disneyland and 1964–65 New York World's Fair programs. Luske had been director of the studio's highly technical military training films beginning in 1943. In addition, he animated an important character in the company's history, Snow White. Stewart produced all of the storyboards for the Florida Film. The Florida Film reflects experience in presenting technical information through animation art.

Disney's unusual presentation also would require a script. As previously noted, Marty Sklar wrote the script with Disney. Sklar was a former editor of the *Daily Bruin* student newspaper at UCLA. He began working for the company in 1955, starting in Disneyland Public Relations and writing for the *Disneyland News*. Sklar began to work directly with Disney almost immediately. As Harrison Price recalls, Sklar became the 'word man' for the Florida Film. Working with Disney, Sklar was able to distill all of the EPCOT team's concepts into one script.[2] Card Walker, who was vice president of marketing, also was involved in the film's production.

Disney's segments of the Florida Film were shot on October 27, 1966. The film features maps, renderings, and animation, and runs about 25 minutes. The setting for the film was a reproduction of the EPCOT team's secret room at WED Enterprises in Glendale, California. Disney filmed two different endings: one for the Florida Legislature and the other tailored for leaders of American industry. The Florida Film was completed after Disney's death. He did, however, see some of the film segments.

In a recent interview, Sklar described the process of writing for Disney:

> Over the years I had the opportunity to write things for Walt ... including the quotes done for Walt. I didn't do the writing without first talking with Walt. They were always his ideas, and after awhile, I got to understand what he wanted to say and how he wanted to communicate. He trusted me enough to let me write the first draft. Then he would red-pencil his notes back to me.[3]

No matter how much autonomy Sklar enjoyed, there reportedly never appeared to be any question about who was in charge. Sklar remembers one incident that illustrates that point: 'I had just finished the script. I ran into General Joe Potter ... and gave him a copy. When I got to the meeting with

Walt – of course, Joe had already gone into Walt's office and told him how much he liked the script – Walt was furious! He demanded, "Don't I deserve to get the script before anyone else?"'[4]

Disney would take it upon himself to communicate his final concept to the public. After more than a decade of hosting his television show, he, too, had become a polished showman. Exactly twelve years earlier, on October 27, 1954, a younger Disney had appeared on camera before a national audience and had enthusiastically pointed to areas on Ellenshaw's painting of Disneyland. On October 27, 1966, an ailing but equally enthusiastic Disney stood before a camera and pointed to Marvin Davis' classical looking site plan of EPCOT. This was not the typical community developer 'pitching' a project to a local planning commission. In addition to the film, EPCOT would have been on display to millions of visitors annually.

The Florida Film is Disney's own encapsulation of the general direction in which he hoped his final dream of EPCOT and Project Florida would go. The film also was a powerful marketing tool that drew upon the experience of an innovative studio. In addition to the film, Walt Disney Productions also sought newspaper coverage to promote Project Florida, for example, when Florida Governor Haydon Burns held a press conference on October 24, 1965, to formally disclose the identity of the secret buyer of the central Florida property. The next day, a front page article in the *Orlando Sentinel* announced, 'It's Official: This is Disney's Land.'[5] The secrecy that surrounded the company's land acquisition also served its public relations interests. The sense of anticipation created by the secrecy made it a story the local media could not ignore, generating free publicity throughout most of the acquisition process.

Disney's marketing effort also benefited from the support Project Florida received from *Orlando Sentinel* publisher Martin Andersen. An editorial from the paper on October 24, 1966, stated in part:

> What area can hope to compete with the Moonport at Cape Kennedy backed up by the crowning creation of Walt Disney who will turn 30,000 acres into a land of fun and fantasy as much out of this world as the astronauts zooming among the stars of a distant galaxy. The magic of this modern Merlin will touch us all here in this promised land of prosperity.[6]

Perhaps Camelot, as interpreted by Walt Disney and an unlikely potential partner, HUD Secretary Robert Weaver, would live on just west of the Cape.

Thus, the company received free publicity as a function of the region's desire for economic development and because the 'Disney image' was an attention magnet. This image of American family wholesomeness and happy childhood memories had been carefully crafted by the company for more than forty years. To the counterculture of the 1960s, it could symbolize other, often negative things, about American culture.

On November 15, 1965, the company held its first official press confer-ence to discuss Project Florida following the announcement of the land-owner.[7] The Disney brothers appeared at the press conference with Governor Burns. In addition to Disney's introduction of early concepts for communi-ties called 'Yesterday' and 'Tomorrow,' the company presented *The Disney Image* promotional film and *The Economic Impact of Disneyland* slide presentation.[8] Both presented the company in a favorable light, highlighting the economic benefits the world's first theme park had brought to Southern California.

The marketing power of Walt Disney Productions reached a print mile-stone on February 3, 1967 – just weeks after Disney's death – when the entire first section of the *Orlando Sentinel*, printed in full color, was dubbed the 'Disney World Souvenir Edition' and carried the banner headline, 'Flori-da's Disney World Unveiled: "Supercalifragilisticexpialidocious."'[9] One half of the front page featured George Rester's 'cut away' rendering of the EPCOT core, painted and modified by Herbert Ryman.

On February 2, 1967, another press conference had been held in Winter Haven, Florida. There were 908 invited guests, including state cabinet mem-bers, legislators, the governor, and representatives from Wall Street.[10] The late Walt Disney's Florida Film, with its special ending for Florida, was shown to the invitees. The images of the enthusiastic Disney, explaining his last concept, moved the audience. Company-related attendees included Roy O. Disney, Card Walker, Paul Helliwell, Donn Tatum, Richard Morrow, and Jack Sayers. During the press conference, Governor Burns' successor, Gov-ernor Claude Kirk, highlighted the $6.65 billion in economic benefits the state stood to gain, according to Economics Research Associates estimates.[11] In addition, Tatum outlined the company's legislative proposals. That evening, the Florida Film was shown to the public via statewide, color television broadcast, with prerecorded comments by Kirk and Roy O. Disney. Later, on April 17, 1967, the Florida Film was screened before both houses of the Legislature. Needless to say, the scope of this marketing campaign was unprecedented in the history of private development in the United States.

When Disney spoke at his company's first press conference in November 1965, a whole generation had grown up with Mickey Mouse. The company already had proven it was a pioneer in using film, product line integration, and television in marketing campaigns. Less than two years later, on swampy terrain, Walt Disney Productions sold EPCOT and the promise of economic growth to the state of Florida using the internationally familiar Disney image as a calling card. Combined with the ERA economic estimates, the company's message was difficult for a region desirous of growth to ignore. Today, Florida Film writer Marty Sklar reflects on the content of Disney's final promotional film. 'It was not just a sales job … [EPCOT] was his blueprint, coming out of his head … a blueprint of what was on his mind.'[12]

REGULATION
AND GOVERNANCE

Chapter 8

Regulation and
Community Governance/Social Planning

In this new era that we're goin' in, we can't forget the things that happened, oh, such as, I mean, the Founding Fathers and that Constitution, which is such a vital thing to what we're doing today ...

Walt Disney

And you've got to indicate to the people who run it, the people who own it, that unless you're free, the machine will be prevented from working at all.

Mario Savio, 1964
University of California,
Berkeley

Walt Disney Productions sought and was granted special legislation from the state of Florida establishing the Reedy Creek Improvement District and two municipalities on the Florida property. Reflecting Disney's original goals for EPCOT, the preamble of the district statute identifies one of the district's purposes as, 'the utilization of the many technological advances achieved by American industry in developing new concepts in community living ... .'[1] Furthermore, the law authorizes 'enterprises conducted within the district to undertake a broad and flexible program of experimentation ... .'[2] This chapter presents an overview of the enabling statutes, with particular emphasis on their relevance to Disney's preliminary goals for EPCOT. In addition, the chapter outlines some of Disney's early thinking about community governance and social planning for the experimental community.

Florida Governor Claude Kirk signed the three bills into law on May 12, 1967, after Disney's death, but a legislative public hearing had already been scheduled prior to December 1966.[3] A memorandum on the 'Establishment of Special Taxing Districts and Municipalities on the Walt Disney Productions Property' was prepared by the law firm of Helliwell, Melrose & DeWolf.[4] Paul Helliwell, active in the land acquisition program, also would be an advocate on behalf of Walt Disney Productions in the negotiations with Florida legislators. The origins of the municipalities apparently trace to a conversation attorney Robert Foster had with Disney. Disney related how at a cocktail party Jules Stein had told him about all of the trouble he was having with the city and county of Los Angeles in operating Universal City. Foster convinced Disney, however, that many authorities, or 'civil rights functions,' such as law enforcement, could not fall under the jurisdiction of a special district. Disney decided that the municipalities would 'be the repositories for all the civil rights functions that could not be incorporated into the district.'[5]

Foster, who oversaw the property acquisition, also led the efforts to secure passage of the legislation. Foster reported to company General Counsel Richard Morrow. Attorney Phil Smith also assisted in the effort. In addition, company tax expert George Sullivan worked on those issues. Other resources included local counsel Tom DeWolf and the New York law firm of Donovan, Leisure, Newton and Irvine. Today, Foster emphasizes that the district legislation was essentially a 'bare bones enabling statute.'[6] As the EPCOT concept evolved into Epcot Center, more specific regulations for an experimental community were never drafted. It could also be expressed that the special district would interfere with creation of a participatory form of government for EPCOT residents that would also satisfy Disney's desire to maintain control over planning, development, and operation of the entire Disney World property.

Even though it was bare bones, several clauses in the district statute make indirect reference to EPCOT. For example, Section 23.7(b) states, 'the standards and requirements set out in the regulations may be modified by the Board in case of a plan and program for a new town … .' Another section provides for transportation 'whether now or hereafter invented or developed including without limitation novel and experimental facilities such as moving platforms and sidewalks … .'[7] Moreover, authority to 'develop and operate such new and experimental public utilities … , closed-circuit television systems, and computer service and facilities … ' also is included in the statute.[8] Finally, the Legislature granted the new district the right to generate power by nuclear fission.[9]

In essence, the Florida legislation created a multifunction, multicity, multicounty special district.[10] One of the main reasons the district was established, according to the statute, was that the property spanned two counties – Orange and Osceola – and that created a need for a new quasi-governmental structure.[11] Other primary reasons for the legislation offered by the company included its desire to pay for its own internal infrastructure and the need to defend the property against potential annexation by other jurisdictions.[12] Robert Foster remembers that the attorneys used the *California Community Services Act* as a starting point during the preparation of what would be very different legislation in Florida.[13]

According to General Joe Potter, 'it [the district statute] merely combines all these authorities [types of special districts] into one package.'[14] Potter had worked on the passage of the legislation and became the first district manager. Florida engineer Herb Gee also assisted in preparation of the legislation. Florida was familiar with single-purpose districts at the time but the Reedy Creek Improvement District would be multipurpose and unique. By 1962, Florida had 159 special districts, the most of any state. By comparison, California had 55.[15] Significantly, the legislation passed both houses of the Legislature with only one dissenting vote.

While the district does not have its own police force, it does enjoy a host of governmental powers, prompting some to call it the 'Vatican City of leisure and entertainment.'[16] The Reedy Creek Improvement District's powers include sovereignty over its own roads,[17] the right to condemn private property,[18] the right to impose penalties for non-compliance,[19] exemption from eminent domain by other bodies,[20] operation of airport facilities,[21] provision of fire protection,[22] the right to levy taxes, the right to issue bonds, the right to drain the property, the right to oversee planning and building and safety functions,[23] and the right to provide public transportation.[24]

In addition, the Florida Legislature granted the district an array of financial powers that are considered to be comparable to those of a county. First, the district may assess the following taxes: ad valorem, maintenance, utility, and drainage. The district's liens are on a par with those of the state and county governments and may be foreclosed.[25] Other revenue sources include gasoline taxes or other fuel tax funds available for road construction,[26] flood control/water management districts and navigation districts eligible for funds from the state,[27] and mosquito and pest control funds from the state.[28] The statute requires that all rates, fees, rentals, tolls, fares, and charges shall be 'just and equitable' and uniform for users of the same class.[28]

The district also may borrow money through general obligation bonds,[30] revenue bonds,[31] utility service tax bonds,[32] special assessments,[33] assessment bonds,[34] and short-term borrowings.[35] District projects are public property and its assets, bonds, and other revenues are exempt from taxes levied by the state and its political subdivisions. In addition, authorization of bonds requires a majority vote of the district's Board of Supervisors. The board is elected by the landowners within the district. Each landowner receives one vote for every acre of land and parcels in excess of a half-acre. All board members must be owners of land within the district.[36] New municipalities within the district may be created by majority vote of the landowners. Two incorporated cities exist within the district's boundaries: the city of Bay Lake and the city of Lake Buena Vista (formerly city of Reedy Creek). The EPCOT site is located in the city of Bay Lake.[37] The district provides staff to both cities.

Within the regulatory environment of EPCOT itself, however, one might expect tensions to develop among the various jurisdictions (the district, city of Bay Lake, city of Reedy Creek) and the Disney organization as well. These jurisdictions might have served as instruments in the kind of institutional design laboratory Disney mentioned toward the end of his life. The legal complexities posed by the interaction of these entities and potential residents, however, would prove to be daunting.

Attorney Foster recalls that he viewed an early screening of the Florida Film during the summer of 1966. It was at this time that Disney disclosed to the lawyers 'that he was actually thinking about people living in the place … That's when I realized what we were really getting into.'[38] Passage of the Florida statutes would be the first priority of Foster and Disney's legal team as opposed to governance of the EPCOT residents.

The municipal enabling statutes make indirect reference to an experimental community. The statute establishing the city of Bay Lake, in which the EPCOT site is located, provides for a council-manager form of government,[39] experimental public utilities,[40] police,[41] 'new concepts' in community living,[42] bond issuance,[43] a municipal court,[44] and common contracts and agreements with the special district.[45] Once again, this was essentially a bare bones enabling statute in 1967 and still under negotiation at the end of Disney's life.

The district has not been without its critics over the years. Reflecting back, real estate economist Harrison Price says, 'It was really done to be efficient, to be able to do the quality job that he [Disney] wanted to do with that huge tract of land.' Price stresses that the district was not established to avoid 'civic responsibility,' a charge commonly leveled against special districts.[46] Responding to criticism related to levels of accountability within special districts, a 1964 study found that 'They are quasi-public and, therefore, take on some aspects of both government and business and thus, in many respects, are exempt from many public controls exercised over both business and government.'[47]

District Administrator Tom Moses has heard many arguments against special districts during his tenure. While some people believe that a special district is a needless level of government, others see it as self-government. Another measure of special districts, cited by the Congressional Advisory Commission on Intergovernmental Relations in 1964, is the '[d]egree to which the district permits or hinders the exercise of effective control of government by the people.'[48] This would become an issue in EPCOT community governance planning. In contrast, Moses' response is that the district brings government closer to those paying taxes and it has executed mutual assistance agreements with outside agencies regarding highways and other issues. Moreover, the landowner (The Walt Disney Company) pays property taxes to the counties in which the district is located without receiving services from them.[49]

After his experience with Disneyland, Disney understood that his concepts for EPCOT would not fit within existing Florida building codes. The experience gained in building the Anaheim park would lead Disney to recognize the desirability of flexible regulations in Florida. Many materials and systems utilized in the construction of Disneyland were not covered by existing building codes. ERA's HUD outline argued that Disney's vision for an experimental community would require innovative regulations in the areas of planning and building approvals, citing British New Town development corporations as precedent.[50] The EPCOT team also argued for the right to use performance standards in planning and development. This was consistent with the code innovation envisioned by the Model Cities legislation. Performance zoning was first used in the early 1950s to regulate noise, smoke, and dust associated with industry. It was based on development performance standards as opposed to traditional zoning by land use. The statute creating the Reedy Creek Improvement District as adopted by the Florida Legislature requires development to conform to a comprehensive plan and provide 'adequate public spaces and improvements for the circulation, recreation, light, air, and service needs of the tract … .'[51] The board also establishes a Planning and Zoning Commission and a Zoning Board of Adjustment. The district's Comprehensive Plan and Land Development Regulations are used by the district and municipalities by joint agreement. In summary, the district is exempt from county regulation relating to zoning, building, subdivision, safety, sanitation, and from state law relating to land use and building codes.[52] The district legislation continues to raise a classic public health and safety question: how much authority can be delegated to a landowner while still maintaining the public's well being?

A year after the district was created the board began to develop the first *EPCOT Building Code* set, and it was adopted by the district in 1970. Its preface, written by Marty Sklar, states as a goal of the code, 'To provide the flexibility that will encourage American industry, through free enterprise, to introduce, test and demonstrate new ideas, materials and systems emerging now and in the future from the creative centers of industry.'[53] This language mirrors that of the Florida Film script. According to Sklar, 'EPCOT was always the underlying aim – the building codes were written with that in mind.'[54]

The district building code committee included General Joe Potter, Robert Foster, Tom Moses (a former technical director of the *Southern Building Code* Congress), John Degenkolb (a building code expert), various engineering firms, engineer Don Edgren, and others from WED Enterprises.[55] The committee soon realized that amusement rides were not covered in the existing Florida code, nor were several applications of plastics and fiberglass. The group performed research by visiting Underwriters Laboratory. The *Uniform Building Code* and *Southern Building Code* served as starting points for the committee's work. Stephen Fjellman, usually critical of Walt Disney World, wrote, 'Disney has always claimed, with justification, that its building codes are significantly stronger than state and local codes.'[56] By 1974, the *EPCOT Building Code* set was approved for use throughout the state of Florida. Building code innovation continues to be an important issue in community development in the United States. For example, historian Kenneth Jackson writes, 'restrictive building codes continue to retard the introduction of most prefabricated techniques in the United States, which is now less advanced than Europe in developing inexpensive construction methods.'[57]

As previously noted, before the Anaheim site was purchased for Disney-land, Disney considered constructing an amusement park on property the company owned across the street from the Burbank studios. In 1952, Disney approached the Burbank City Council with a preliminary set of plans. He was rejected out of concern that an undesirable Coney Island-type environment might potentially develop in the city. The preliminary plan included linkage of Disney's park with the Travel Town trains in nearby Griffith Park. In addition to Burbank (zoning and permits), Disney encountered the layers of government he hoped to avoid later in central Florida, including the United States Army Corps of Engineers (flood control); the Los Angeles Parks and Recreation Department (Griffith Park); and the California Department of Transportation (proposed Ventura Freeway, State Route 134). Disney would soon discover that negotiating with public officials would be different from running the studio.

Eventually, with the assistance of Stanford Research Institute, the Anaheim site was selected as the future home of Disneyland. Disney, accustomed to building motion picture sets, soon struggled with the realities of occupancy regulations and building codes.[58] As his art directors discovered that millions of guests would actually *walk through* the Main Street, U.S.A. façades, Disney would soon face a new problem: the lack of control over land uses beyond the park's borders.

However, Disney learned the lesson of controlling the built environment in 1964, when he headed off a hotel project under consideration by the Anaheim City Council. Sheraton wanted to construct an 18- to 22-story hotel near the park. As counsel for Disneyland, Robert Foster had spent many days before the Planning Commission and City Council in Anaheim speaking on behalf of the park's interests. The Disney organization argued that the hotel tower would be visible from within the park and thus objectionable because Disneyland's main attraction was 'visual illusions.'[59] In 1966, the city denied Sheraton's request and a lower building eventually was built. The next year, an ordinance passed restricting building heights around the park.[60] Obviously, during the later years of his life, Disney the film maker learned a great deal about land use regulation and local politics (see Figure 8.1).

Disney did not live long enough to see the environmental movement gain full momentum. In 1955, he received a citation from the Sierra Club in honor of the studio's wildlife films. Ironically, three years after Disney's death, the same organization obtained an injunction against the federal government to halt the proposed Mineral King ski resort. In December 1965, Disney obtained a three-year United States Forest Service preliminary permit to build on up to 80 acres. As late as September 1966, Disney participated in ceremonies at Mineral King Valley with California Governor Edmund G. Brown to announce state and federal support for a highway into the valley. In November 1966, just prior to Disney's death, preservationists opposed an access road into the valley during a public hearing. Disney

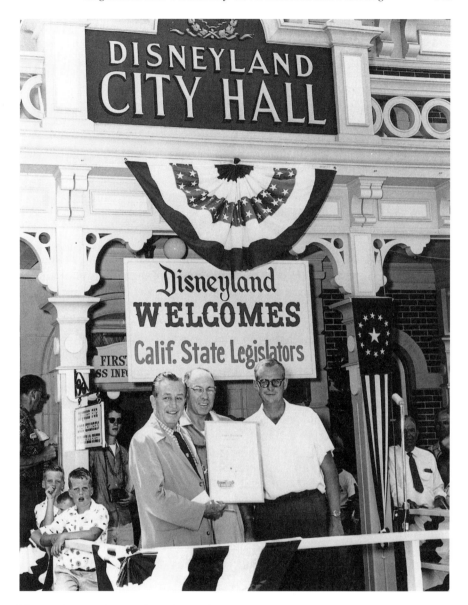

Figure 8.1 Disney, the 'king' of the Magic Kingdom, entertained legislators long before the advent of Project Florida. Here, he accepts a California State Senate Resolution honoring Disneyland from Senators John Murdy and John McCarthy in 1957. A delegation of 135 legislators was hosted at the park. Source: University of Southern California Regional History Collection

stated that development of Mineral King represented both a challenge and an obligation to preserve the natural beauty of the valley. The environmental dispute continued and as a result the project was never built.

The years since 1966 witnessed a revolution in the adoption of regulations designed to protect the environment. Of these, the most important to community developers is the Environmental Impact Report (EIR). Industrial designer Bob Gurr reflects on the changes in the project approval process:

> There's a lot more thoroughness now in showing 'proof of compliance' with regulatory agencies. You can't just go 'do it' anymore … [Y]ou have to go file [an] E.I.R. … and wait a year for a government agency … Now companies have to file advance reports and once that's done, surrounding groups lobby against them. We have to deal with that today, but Walt Disney didn't have much of that in the '50s and '60s.[61]

Ironically, Disney's Reedy Creek Improvement District was granted the authority to 'adopt regulations to prohibit or control the pollution of air and water.'[62] This provision placed a great obligation on the district.

As previously mentioned, President Johnson had declared war on America's urban crisis. In 1966, the Model Cities legislation cited a problem in urban development around the country, namely: '[T]he multiplicity of political jurisdictions and agencies involved, and the inadequacy of the operational and administrative arrangements available for cooperation among them.'[63] Similarly, Harrison Price wrote that new ways must be found to create effective regional planning.[64]

Today, many Americans appear to approve of the concepts of greenbelts and smart growth often associated with regional planning, but continue to value private property rights. In a recent poll, 57 percent of respondents favored the establishment of a protected greenbelt around their communities. However, 69 percent believed it was more important for individuals to do what they want with land they own, versus 29 percent who said it was more important for the government to have the ability to regulate development for the common good.[65] Disney, with 27,443 acres and a legislative package, could put a greenbelt anywhere he wanted one as a demonstration to visitors. In theory, if they liked the idea, they could take it back to their own communities. Disney's lessons in local politics, however, must have taught him that changes in land use policy are rarely easy matters, particularly outside the berm.

While Disneyland may have included some of the physical features of a community, it lacked community politics. EPCOT would launch Disney into a different, but perhaps not altogether unfamiliar realm: public policy. Attorney Robert Foster reflects that Disney 'was moving [into] that next level into dealing with the ills of inner cities and was becoming a sociologist as he was doing it.'[66] It was the period of the Great Society's managerial liberalism and, again, it is difficult to imagine that Disney's track record of maintaining control over his projects could have easily intersected with a growing federal bureaucracy. This record, contemporary systems-based planning practice, and American democratic tradition would all compete for Disney's attention during EPCOT conceptualization.

The EPCOT concept drew criticism from community planner Ray Watson in 1966. He remembers telling Disney, 'You need to decide whether you are indeed building a community that is a natural community where people will come, raise their families, form their own city government, grow and so forth … But if you're doing this as a place for an exhibit, then you need to separate that.'[67] This, of course, would be the ultimate governance tension in the original EPCOT concept: laboratory attraction or natural community. However, Disney's preference for control did have its limits as he stated, 'the first duty of culture is to defend freedom and resist all tyranny.'[68]

Unfortunately, Disney had even less time at the end of his life to refine his governance and social planning ideas than he did EPCOT's physical plan. As architectural critic Paul Goldberger noted, 'Disney never quite got around to explaining exactly what that life was that he wanted to see lived in EPCOT … .'[69] Still, Disney and his team communicated several notions worthy of examination. It is important to note that these ideas were changing as quickly as EPCOT's physical plan toward the end of Disney's life. For example, during an interview in October 1966, Disney stated, 'There'll be no landowners, and therefore no voting control. People will rent homes instead of buying them, and at market rentals. There will be no retirees. Everyone must be employed. One of our requirements is that people who live in EPCOT must help keep it alive.'[70]

He added, 'In EPCOT there will be no slum areas because we won't let them develop.'[71] All of this might be possible in a controlled, privately owned community, but to be a true model city, EPCOT's social experimentation would also have to yield lessons for communities outside its radial plan.

Disney also noted in October 1966 that he planned to create a second city in Florida that would be an experimental laboratory for administering municipal governments. The second city also would accommodate retirees or people who wished to purchase property.[72] Davis and Disney discussed the need to have a sufficient number of managerial professionals living in EPCOT to administer the community.[73] In addition, Disney had developed a concept called 'the cashless society,' presumably made possible by computers.[74]

Disney's voting control and landownership statements illustrate the plans he had to create the special district to help administer Project Florida. While Disney would only begin to scratch the surface of these legal complexities before his death, he did wrestle with them. If the company sold EPCOT land parcels to residents, it would dilute development control over the Florida property. Disney reasoned that EPCOT would have to be a community of tenants. However, many experts believe that home ownership helps prevent the formation of slums by creating stakeholders in a community. Plus, a community of renters does not necessarily guarantee landowner control. In

New York City, for example, rent control legislation eventually resulted in tenant control of land economics.[75] Recently, however, attorney Foster stated that later developments in condominium ownership law and air rights transfers could possibly have given Disney more legal options than he had in the 1960s.[76]

Nonetheless, the EPCOT concept hinged upon tenants. For example, EPCOT planner Davis believed that 'as long as it is all leased out, no property sold to anybody, then that control can be maintained. And that's the only way you can do it.'[77] Furthermore, Davis emphasized what seems to many to be the 'guinea pig' aspect of the concept, because employees would be part of the experiment.[78]

A consistent theme throughout Disney's projects was the desire to create an ordered environment. As Imagineer John Hench reflects, 'Walt hated to not have control of the thing.'[79] By design, however, the state of becoming in EPCOT would be beyond even Disney's control, as Imagineer Carl Bongiorno remembers:

> Even prior to his death, everyone knew that you couldn't have 25,000 [sic] people living in a community … and constantly change, upgrade, move, innovate, go into people's homes, take out appliances, put new ones in, control everything about the project when you have a one-man, one-vote democracy.[80]

Although Bongiorno was not a member of the original EPCOT planning team, his statement reflects contemporary Supreme Court rulings mandating one-person, one-vote. These decisions would apply to both special districts and municipalities and were based on the equal protection clause of the U.S. Constitution. Landownership could not be a prerequisite to voter participation in a body exercising general governmental powers. Landownership would be required to vote in special district elections.

Toward the end of his life, Disney appeared to recognize that the issues of landownership and voting control in the planned special district would necessitate the need for a temporary status for EPCOT residents. For instance, industrial designer Bob Gurr, who traveled with Disney to various companies, remembers that Disney told executives that EPCOT residents might be on a sabbatical and live there for a year to a year and a half.[81] In this scenario, a natural sense of community stability would have been difficult to achieve.

ERA's HUD presentation outline also proposed a two-tier system of government for EPCOT to permit developer authority over new town planning approvals and democratic control over other civil functions by residents. As noted, this proposal had its roots in British New Town development practice. The British development corporations had wide-ranging authority over land management, infrastructure, building, and generally anything else deemed necessary. This often resulted in strained partnerships with the local authorities which retained planning powers. Harrison Price noted that a bifurcated form of government would have to be studied and tested in American courts. Reflecting the existence of the proposed special district, Price also wrote that the experimental community must not include elected public officials.[82] As of August 1966, the proposed special district appeared to preclude provision of traditional elected officials due to the landowner-ship requirement. Still, the so-called bifurcated form of government was to include democratic control over the non-planning and building aspects of the lives of EPCOT residents. Could the special district board controlled by the company have coexisted with direct democratic participation of EPCOT residents? These preliminary concepts would have put Disney's administrative laboratory and state and federal laws to new tests indeed. In the area of community governance, Disney ultimately might have had to learn a new art form: compromise.

At some point, Disney also considered the possibility of establishing some form of representative government for EPCOT including an elected board of control with representation from industry, merchants, residents, and Walt Disney Productions. In addition, an executive committee, city manager, and resident and business advisory committees also were considered prior to Disney's death.[83] It should be reiterated that Disney did not have much time to devote to issues concerning EPCOT's potential residents before his death. Robert Foster recalls that Disney informed his attorneys in June 1965 that he wanted to use innovative systems in Florida but he had not yet mentioned residents to the legal staff.[84] In addition, Foster remembers that during the period 1965 through 1966, potential residents at the Florida property were not a 'burning issue' with the legal team.[85] Passage of the 'bare bones' special district and municipalities statutes was the first priority. Disney would not live to witness the signing of those statutes.

As Disney mentioned, the second city he proposed would be home to senior citizens. Florida was the retirement capital of the United States and in the 1960s, retirement new towns were springing up across the country. The narration tape for Disneyland's Carousel of Progress stated that there was a community for senior citizens.[86] As Card Walker recalls,

> There was a lot of talk there at the end about a community. I think the prototype would have been Leisure World [a retirement community south of Disneyland]. We all made a trip down ... and studied what they were doing and how it worked ... I think Walt had in mind: why not ... have a community there designed for the benefit of older people ... [with] medical and also close to the parks where they would have something to do ... Yes, he was well into that.[87]

While retirement communities and assisted living facilities proliferate to-day, many argue that senior citizens offer rich experience to a mixed community, particularly as life spans increase.

The EPCOT concept also addressed families and the teenage population. As Davis recalled, 'Walt had great hopes of using this community as a model form of treating the teenage problem. And his idea was to devise a system by which youths would judge their peers ... monitoring their behavior.'[88] The crime rate among teens in the 1960s escalated dramatically. The plans for the Mineral King ski resort included a teen center. As a youth, Disney joined the DeMolay young men's organization, with its seven precepts: filial love, reverence for sacred things, courtesy, comradeship, fidelity, cleanness, and patriotism. Later, he reflected, 'Its precepts have been invaluable in making decisions, facing dilemmas and crises.'[89] Members monitor peer behavior.

By the mid-1960s, however, the Vietnam War jolted this sense of family by dividing the country and its youth. In addition, a drug culture developed among teens. In 1972, General Joe Potter simply stated, 'Walt Disney developed a plan for the family' at EPCOT.[90] This would have been difficult to achieve under a corporate sabbatical scenario. With family stability, increasing numbers of women in the workforce, and even the nature of the family unit itself undergoing dramatic and rapid change, meeting the public need in this regard might have been EPCOT's greatest challenge.[91]

Reflecting this social change, government Professor Robert Putnam has identified four factors responsible for the decline of civic engagement and social capital in the United States since 1965: pressures of time and money, including two-career families; suburbanization and commuting; electronic entertainment, particularly television; and, most important, generational succession.[92] These changes are a far cry from Disney's rural yesteryear and point to a continued need for community innovation in the Information Age. Changing values also appear to affect urban poverty, as government scholars Christopher Jencks and Paul E. Peterson noted in 1991:

> The most powerful force contributing to the formation of the urban underclass, perversely enough, may be the changing values of mainstream American society, in which the virtues of family stability, mutual support, and religiously based commitment to the marriage vow no longer command the deference they once did.[93]

If only Disney's nostalgic Carousel of Progress could have featured the true American families of the future.

Similarly, Disney also considered the issue of education, but did not get very far in conceptualizing the kind of schools he wanted to establish in EPCOT. He did appear to be enthusiastic about the idea, however. He was quoted as saying, 'I'd love to be part of building up a school of tomorrow ... This might become a pilot operation for the teaching age ... .'[94] In addition, Disney has been credited with creating 'edutainment,' saying, '[T]he normal gap between what is generally regarded as 'entertainment' and what is defined 'educational' represents an old and untenable viewpoint.'[95] He took an active role in the education of his artists and, ultimately, the establishment of the interdisciplinary CalArts. The schools of EPCOT, likely to combine education and entertainment in the curricula, were never fully articulated, however. By 1968, Admiral Joe Fowler stated simply that Disney expected the development of educational facilities that would be twenty years ahead of their time.[96]

Although Disney never graduated from high school, he displayed an interest in learning throughout his lifetime. For example, civil designer Ken Klug recalls something Roy O. Disney told him on an airplane: 'So he came walking down the aisle and says, "Ken, is that a correspondence book?" And I said, "Yeah, it is." And he said, "Yeah, we guys that didn't graduate from college, Walt and I have been taking correspondence books all our lives."'[97]

Along with education, the EPCOT planning team began to address the issue of resident participation at the neighborhood level. Neighborhood participation in local government, recently introduced in Los Angeles, was a feature of Section 103(a)(2) of the Model Cities legislation, which required 'widespread citizen opportunity in the program.'[98] A 1967 report, *Strategies for Shaping Model Cities*, by Arthur D. Little, Inc., concluded, 'There is no complete substitute for some direct citizen involvement in policy formulation.'[99] Similarly, General Joe Potter quoted his old boss, Robert Moses, as saying, 'surely megalopolis will simply remove government further away from people … .'[100] This was another criticism of suburbanization and the loss of a town commons in the automobile city.

Disney believed that, unlike the small railroad towns of his youth, the bigness of cities kept people from knowing one another.[101] Disney's yesteryear featured an agricultural community, not suburbia. In 1906, a young Disney and his family moved to a 48-acre farm outside Marceline, Missouri. Diane Disney Miller speaks of the 'spirit of community at threshing time' that her father experienced as a youth.[102] However, as biographer Steven Watts emphasizes, Disney 'paid homage to community cohesion in his historical [film] productions, but he also included affirmations of personal character.'[103] The sprawl of the suburbs and the horrors of the inner cities of America in the 1960s were far removed from Disney's yesteryear.

Disney's experimentation also had its limits in the area of social planning. For example, unlike community developer James Rouse's Columbia, Maryland, 'interfaith centers,' EPCOT would feature separate places of worship. Apparently, EPCOT would not be a 'dry' community. Although Disney did not permit the public sale of alcohol within Disneyland's berm, he was a social drinker and liquor stores were included in the ERA retail sales estimates.

The need for people to assume responsibility was a recurring theme in the evolution of the EPCOT concept.[104] Similarly, the narration tape for the Carousel of Progress described progress as something not to be taken for granted and requiring effort.[105] A key question about company towns is who will hold the residents accountable for the level of responsibility required to maintain it? Many would argue that social responsibility is inherent in a

democracy, otherwise democracy would perish. For example, political scientist James March and organizational scientist Johan Olsen conclude that
'to be a democratic citizen is to accept responsibility for crafting the practices, rules, forms, capabilities, structures, procedures, accounts, and identities that construct democratic political life.'[106] However, as previously noted,
Professor Putnam has found that civic engagement has been on the decline
in the United States since 1965.

During the period 1964 through 1965, two of the most important pieces
of civil rights legislation in the nation's history were signed into law by
President Johnson: the *Civil Rights Act of 1964* and the *Voting Rights Act of
1965*. ERA's HUD presentation outline stated that EPCOT would promote
fair housing practices.[107] The country was in the midst of a period of civil
unrest. For example, during the summer of 1965, 34 people were killed,
1,032 injured, 3,952 arrested, and 6,000 buildings were damaged during the
Watts riots in Los Angeles. A little more than a year earlier, while the
Audio-Animatronics Great Emancipator spoke to packed audiences at the
New York World's Fair, civil rights demonstrations were raging outside.

In the areas of community governance and social planning, Disney's
death left his team with several significant questions to be answered. These
included legal complexities, such as voting rights within the special district.
Because of the turbulence of the 1960s, society would not be readily amenable to a 'quick fix.' Disney had assumed the most difficult challenge of his
career – EPCOT. Company employees might have helped him experiment
with new forms of community governance within EPCOT's radial plan. It is
difficult to know if these social innovations would have been applicable to
often restless and angry citizens living in urban centers beyond the boundaries of the special district.

Judging by his personal Midwestern experience, it is likely that Disney
would have desired to create a natural community for EPCOT's residents
just as he had attempted to make the Burbank studios plan something of a
'workers' paradise' earlier. However, the experimental community would be
on exhibit in a tightly controlled environment. Disney, never a fan of centralized control over his own rights, would have had to be extremely careful
with the rights of the company and industrial park employees living in
EPCOT. Attorney Foster, who originally advised Disney on municipalities,
recently reflected on the experimental community:

> It was pretty on film and pictures. We had to take care of the problem of what
> was going to happen when the guy who wanted to have a pet dog and walk it
> down the street ... whether they were going to be a lessee or going to be an
> employee or independent citizen and all that stuff. Unfortunately, Walt died
> before we ever got into those issues. A good 75 percent were legal things ... .[108]

Unlike the dozens of 'urban confections of philosophers' throughout history
– as urban historian Spiro Kostof called them – EPCOT was backed by

1,100 acres of land, three state statutes, a model marketing machine, a financially sound corporation, a charismatic leader, and a team of talented professionals that crossed many disciplines. Its scope, though, was as broad and complex as American society and its legal system themselves. Its sketchy social components were no more ambitious or idealistic than those of the Model Cities program in the days of the Great Society and the Great Big Beautiful Tomorrow. EPCOT was an imaginative proposal.

Chapter 9

Operations and Management

All the world's a stage,
And all the men and women merely players:
They have their exits and their entrances

William Shakespeare

At the end of 1966, there were no blueprints for EPCOT, let alone facilities to operate and manage. However, the Disney brothers' long careers as managers of studios and the world's first theme park created operations and management traditions that surely would have been adapted for application in EPCOT. Imagineer Richard Irvine believed that EPCOT was an extension of Disneyland ideas and philosophies toward people. Disney's state of becoming also was reflected in the words of Van France, founder of the University of Disneyland, who said Disney 'designed a park and created an organization that would accept change.'[1] The University of Disneyland was established in 1962 to train park employees.

Regarding matters outside the berm, Disney had his opinions about municipal management. In October 1966, he let his feelings be known about city government: 'We pay a lot of taxes and still have streets that aren't paved or are full of holes. And city street cleaners and garbage collectors who don't do their jobs. And property owners who let dirt accumulate and help create slums. Why?'[2] As previously noted, he was just beginning to explore these issues with his EPCOT team toward the end of his life. While the questions appear somewhat naive, the problem-solving process within WED Enterprises would have placed them squarely in the *tabula rasa*, or 'blue sky' stage.

At Disneyland, the Disney organization 'found that cleanliness breeds cleanliness' and officials insisted on a spotless environment.[3] Along the same lines, many communities have found that measures such as mural painting help reduce graffiti. In fact, in 1967, WED Enterprises installed exterior ceramic murals in Tomorrowland that were resistant to graffiti and pollution. Still, Disneyland was a theme park – a sanctuary from the outside world. But with features such as the monorail, PeopleMover, and murals, Tomorrowland could be utilized as a demonstration site for the real world as well as a place for entertainment. EPCOT, on the other hand, was to be a living community. Its core focused on a massive themed shopping center, not an idealized Town Square. The constantly changing residential areas were to be on display to visitors via the PeopleMover. Without further refinement, the original concept was closer to what architect Michael Sorkin has termed, 'city as theme park.'[4] While an urban laboratory in the midst of Disney World could very well have yielded new technologies and systems to help American communities, its operations and management would be unique to say the least.

In many respects, however, Disney did operate a community of sorts at the Anaheim park. Lacking experience in the beginning, the Disney organization attempted to obtain the best outside operators it could locate for functions like parking, security, janitorial services, and crowd control. In addition, outside contractors ran food and merchandise services. This arrangement assisted the park's cash flow in the early years. Predictably, the loss of full control over these operations ultimately did not appeal to Disney. For example, the company learned that contractors could not be depended upon to open their establishments every day. Finally, Disney told the WED Enterprises staff, 'You guys have got to go out and find out something about food ... .'[5] In 1959, the company bought out the concessionaires.

Cleanliness, reflected in the EPCOT research into waste disposal, was critical in Disneyland's operations. During the late 1960s, the Disneyland Maintenance Division employed approximately 1,000 persons. To this day, employees maintain the park 24 hours a day, seven days a week. In addition, the Disneyland Building and Grounds Department, with its 'midnight warriors,' oversaw the following functions: hosing and steam-cleaning of approximately 45 acres of asphalt and concrete; parking lot sweeping; cleaning, dusting, waxing, and vacuuming; disposing of litter; gum chipping and scraping; and cleaning 150 restrooms every 15 minutes.[6] With millions of guests each year, the park endures more physical wear and tear than most communities.

Disneyland's other divisions might have provided Disney with relevant experience for operating EPCOT. These departments included: Retlaw (train) maintenance, engineering, electrical, and various other maintenance trades. Landscape maintenance is of particular interest in community development and at Disneyland, the landscaping department was responsible for approximately 5,000 sprinkler heads. The air-conditioning department oversaw high-quality heating, ventilation, and air conditioning (HVAC) systems designed for large crowds. The paint department worked with 4,000 shades in a master color book and had 20,000 signs to maintain.[7] Again, landscaping, color, and signage remain critical elements in the success of Disneyland's design.

Physical maintenance of Disneyland was critical to Disney. He once was quoted as saying, 'And those sharp pencil guys tell you, "Walt, if we cut down on maintenance, we'd sure save a lot of money." But I don't believe in that – it's like any other show on the road; it must be kept clean and fresh.'[8] In EPCOT, Disney would have been challenged to develop new ways to encourage residents to keep the world within the radial plan clean. This might have included use of the AVAC trash collection system in residences.

As the head of a studio, Disney was familiar with organizational structures and in the final months of his life he would begin to wrestle with an organizational chart for the governance of EPCOT. The organizational structure at Disneyland included administration, construction, entertainment, finance, food operations, general services, lessee relations, maintenance, marketing, merchandise, and operations. Disneyland's organization included 4,900 park employees during the summer season of 1968.[9] Park management also included an executive committee.

Employee training is an essential component of Disneyland operations. Disney emphasized that Disneyland is a 'show.' Therefore, employees are called 'cast members.' The University of Disneyland employee training program concept, developed by Van France, has gained popularity in the service industry. The original university curriculum included supervision, communications, management, mathematics, park history, policies, and public speaking. Richard Nunis, former Disneyland director of operations, noted, 'They [park employees] have to be able to learn a script and stick to it' like actors.[10]

In explaining Disney's training philosophy, France noted that Disney 'had established his own unique school for training his animators, and he could understand why a new breed of "show people" had to be developed.'[11] Employees were taught the official Disneyland terms, such as guests, hosts/hostesses, audience, attractions, security officers, and costume. The following terms did not exist within the berm: customer, employee, crowd, rides, guard, and uniform. When dealing with the public, a cast member was 'onstage' and playing a 'role.'[12] Disney also insisted that the organization operate on a first-name basis.

EPCOT, on the other hand, would be both a show and a place for company and industrial park employees to reside. EPCOT's show might have included cast members performing roles in the international shopping area in the town center, in transit areas, or even neighborhood commercial centers. Using Michael Sorkin's term, would EPCOT have been a real city designed and operated with prominent theme park features like cast members? This is one area of the concept where reality and fantasy become uncomfortably closely related.

There would also have been a very fine line between being a cast member and a resident in EPCOT because of its availability to visitors. It is not clear how Disney planned to separate the functions of a community from those of a model-city attraction. There also is no evidence to suggest that Disney planned to utilize Audio-Animatronics figures in EPCOT as he had at Disneyland. Disney once stated, 'We're not going to replace the human being, believe me on that.'[13]

A 1955 booklet titled 'Your Disneyland: A Guide for Hosts and Hostesses' outlines many of the original park guidelines. For example, 'The Disneyland Look' consisted of natural-looking cosmetics, neat hair, clean hands and nails, shined shoes, a clean costume, and a fresh shave for men.

Moreover, employees were instructed to 'try a smile,' use courtesy words, and 'treat any question as if it were the most important thing in the world … .' There were also 'Disneyland Taboos,' like on-the-job consumption of alcoholic beverages. Finally, the guide states that teamwork is 'essential.'[14]

Therefore, it is likely that under Disney's management EPCOT would have been clean and well-maintained. Parts of the community available to visitors likely would have been staffed by cast members schooled at Disney's university. (For issues related to community governance – far less amenable to individual management – see Chapter 8, Regulation and Community Governance/Social Planning).

With only 300 employees at WED Enterprises in 1965, Disney's management style could be very hands-on. Architect Bill Martin recalls, 'Walt was in on everything. Nothing was really consummated until he gave the okay.'[15] Disney could also be a taskmaster, especially at construction sites. In Imagineering terms, Disney was usually 'plussing,' or, as Harrison Price recalls, 'making things work better.'[16] Disney seemed to believe that if he could build the 'ideal animation workplace,' master his toy train layout, build a miniature railroad in his backyard, and install a monorail at Disneyland, a real model city was not beyond reach.

Architect Charles Moore wrote that at Disneyland, 'everything works, the way it doesn't seem to any more [sic] in the world outside.'[17] In Anaheim, Disney had the luxury of control within the berm. With the Florida legislation, the Disney organization also set the stage for control within EPCOT's radial plan. The experimental community would be insulated like Disneyland. Most likely, its residents would be better behaved than in the average American city since they would be company or industrial park employees. As the pace of urban life quickens and the quality of life deteriorates in many American cities, the notion of interacting with employees trained in customer service when venturing to the crowded discount 'big box' store just might be a reassuring thought.

Throughout their careers, the Disneys had not always owned and operated their own facilities – they had been lessees as well. In 1919, Disney launched a commercial art business with friend Ub Iwerks and rented desk space at the *Restaurant News* offices in Kansas City. Prior to that, Disney operated a studio in the garage of the family house on Bellefontaine Avenue in Kansas City. In May 1922, Disney established Laugh-O-Gram Films, Inc., and rented a suite on the second floor of the McConahay Building in Kansas City. The building now is listed on the National Register of Historic Places. As previously noted, in 1923, this enterprise went bankrupt, and Disney moved to Los Angeles.

In October 1923, after outgrowing his uncle's garage at 4406 Kingswell Avenue in the Silverlake community of Los Angeles, Disney rented three rooms at the rear of a storefront occupied by Holly-Vermont Realty.[18] By February 1924, with a staff of seven, Disney and his brother Roy leased the adjoining store at 4649 Kingswell Avenue. The sign on the window read

'Disney Bros. Studio.' By 1925, the operation had outgrown the Kingswell space, and the Disneys began construction of their own Hyperion studio.

The future Walt Disney Productions also gained operations and management experience at the Celebrity Sports Center in Denver, Colorado. The center was constructed by a group of celebrity investors, including Disney and his friend Art Linkletter. Amenities included 80 bowling lanes, an Olympic-sized pool, an arcade, restaurants, a nursery for young children, and a slot car raceway.[19] Walt Disney Productions later purchased the center and it was used to train Walt Disney World employees in resort operations.

In the entertainment and construction industries, labor and management disputes often come to the forefront. While it is futile to speculate about the nature of labor relations in EPCOT the company town, certain background information about Disney and the company is useful and would have influenced the way he viewed EPCOT's residents. For instance, in 1941, there was a strike at the new Burbank studios. Biographer Bob Thomas notes that it had a profound effect on Disney and that 'he suffered disillusion … .'[20] Disney's disillusion may have stemmed from what his daughter Diane Disney Miller believes was a sense of paternalism.[21] In 1947, Disney appeared before the House Un-American Activities Committee to discuss what he believed were Communist influences behind the studio strike. Later, the construction of Disneyland was affected by last-minute strikes by plumbers and asphalt plants in Orange County. Despite Disney's negative experiences with and feelings about labor unions, by the late 1960s, 34 labor unions were represented at Disneyland.[22] In EPCOT, Disney would be faced with an extraordinarily delicate and perhaps impossible balancing act: his intense belief in the rights of the individual versus the high level of control he believed was necessary to achieve the goals of the experimental community. As Harrison Price remembers, 'he was talking about a company town.'[23]

Chapter 10

EPCOT After Disney

If you want to view paradise
Simply look around and view it
Anything you want to, do it
Want to change the world, there's nothing to it

From 'Pure Imagination,'
© 1970. Used by permission.
Paradam Music, Inc.

That magnification of all the dimensions of life, through emotional communion,
rational communication, technological mastery, and above all, dramatic
representation, has been the supreme office of the city in history.

Lewis Mumford, 1961

The year 1966 saw the passing of entertainment industry pioneer Walt Disney, who died on December 15, following unsuccessful lung surgery in November. It would now be up to his older brother, 73-year-old Roy O. Disney, to run the company. Instead of selling the land in Florida, he decided to continue pursuing his brother's dream.[1] In 1967, employees of a number of major corporations were assigned to task forces to work with WED Enterprises on new systems and materials for EPCOT.[2] The company's new management team was relatively unfamiliar with WED Enterprises, which had long been Disney's own private company. Marty Sklar remembers that 'people within WED, like Dick Irvine and John Hench, had to persuade management that some version of Walt's vision was still possible.'[3] Irvine and Hench were the vice presidents leading WED Enterprises at the time.

Also in 1967, Roy O. Disney decided to change the name of Disney World in Florida to Walt Disney World as a tribute to his brother. Biographer Bob Thomas explained Roy O. Disney's motivation: 'Everyone knew Ford cars, he reasoned, but not all people remembered that Henry Ford had built the company.'[4] By mid-May 1967, the company had secured its legislative package and could move forward with development of the Magic Kingdom in Florida. The following year witnessed the assassinations of Martin Luther King Jr. and Robert F. Kennedy, and in its coverage of the Vietnam War and its related protests, television brought bloodshed into every American living room. In the midst of this turbulent period in the nation's history,

Roy O. Disney appeared to be committed to carrying out his brother's wishes for their swampland purchase in Florida. Already the company was developing an advanced communications system for the property called WEDCOMM. Florida Telephone Company and RCA were partners in the venture. In 1970, Roy O. Disney made the following statement regarding the plans for EPCOT:

> The agreements which our company has reached with U.S. Steel, RCA, and Aerojet-General are but the first ... The research carried out and the experience gained in the construction and operation of Phase One will provide immense knowledge for our organization as it assumes the challenge of creating the Experimental Prototype Community of Tomorrow in future years.[5]

Florida's Magic Kingdom opened on October 1, 1971, and Roy O. Disney died two months later. By the middle of 1972, General Joe Potter was speaking of 'mini-EPCOT planning,' which involved 'examples of new things that can be used by other cities for the benefit of our society.'[6] Later that year, company planning consultant Bill Stubee observed that, 'the Disney organization is fascinated by technical experimentation, but scared to death of social concerns.'[7] Student protests at CalArts and throughout the country no doubt contributed to reluctance to enter the field of social planning at the time. With Disney's 'teen-age problem' ever increasing, development of EPCOT, a demonstration to the world, could pose risks to both the Disney image as well as the value of the company stock. In hindsight, it is difficult to imagine Disney's reaction to such things as spray-painted peace signs on his monorail cars in EPCOT.

Planning statistics for a living community called EPCOT appeared in architect Peter Blake's June 1972 article in *The Architectural Forum*.[8] In 1973, the Progress City model, that was so similar to the EPCOT concept was removed from the Carousel of Progress building at Disneyland. By early 1974, Sklar had convened an EPCOT planning group consisting of many of the original EPCOT team members, among them, Bob Gurr. 'And so we literally started in where we all thought Walt left us with ideas,' Gurr recalls. It soon became apparent to most group members that they could not move forward with the original EPCOT concept without Disney's leadership to help them refine his ideas.[9] EPCOT planner Marvin Davis later reflected, 'This "community" thing would have worked only so far, without Walt's guidance. And God knows, there's nothing that we need more in our world today than what Walt was trying to do.'[10] Michael Eisner, now chairman of Walt Disney Imagineering, agrees. 'What he [Disney] left behind,' Eisner said, 'is just the first expression of an idea that he didn't have time to follow through on.'[11] WED Enterprises and the EPCOT team underwent a major transition during the period 1972 through 1975, when five key employees retired: Admiral Joe Fowler, Richard Irvine, General Joe Potter, Marvin Davis, and Roger Broggie.

It is true that Disney's own vision as well as his stature among the world's business leaders were critical to the success of EPCOT, as the planning group concluded. In addition, a variety of issues confronted the planning group, including EPCOT's engineering challenges, cost, voting rights and administrative complexities, and legal protection of prototype products.[12] Disney left the planning team with ideas but those ideas remained at a conceptual stage and often in Disney's own mind. Moreover, external factors also entered into the planning group's decision process. Another federal community-oriented statute, the *Urban Growth and New Community Act of 1970*, had yielded discouraging results for the future of model communities. Twelve of the thirteen new communities built under the Act went bankrupt in the early 1970s. As Disney advisor Ray Watson noted recently, most of the failures were the result of developers having to carry too heavy a debt burden to finance up-front infrastructure costs.[13]

EPCOT would have entailed an even higher debt burden for a community developer and Walt Disney Productions. The average developer would not, for example, be able to finance PeopleMovers, monorails, and other costly infrastructure based on house sales and community shopping center revenue alone. In naming EPCOT, Watson concludes, 'I think experimental community would be the right term. I don't think it's the community of tomorrow.'[14] Using this perspective, EPCOT would have been more of an urban model and showcase than a prototype for community developers.

While John Hench is a proponent of an ordered environment, he also understands that even gifted professionals do not possess crystal balls.[15] Many dreams of visionaries have failed. EPCOT became a concept without the visionary in December 1966. In a 1974 interview conducted during a period in which the EPCOT planning group was wrestling with Disney's ideas, Hench said, 'Take Brasilia as the perfect example of perfect planning that doesn't work … .'[16] The elegant bird-like form of Lucio Costa's Pilot Plan for Brasilia (1957) was accompanied by ambitious social planning concepts and rapidly developed unforeseen shantytowns at its periphery after it was built. In addition, Hench cites Paolo Soleri's Arcosanti (1970), an experimental community located north of Phoenix, Arizona, which is architecture merged with ecology and a social agenda. Visitors' fees would become the main source of income as the community evolved into an attraction.[17] Skilled artists and wordsmiths can make most any plan appealing. Many plans end up collecting dust on shelves, others fail miserably in execution; some do succeed. Urban historian Spiro Kostof concluded that the so-called artistic plans like Brasilia's 'often remain on a theoretical plane … Or else they struggle, in the absence of centralized resources and political power … .'[18] Few would argue that Marvin Davis' EPCOT plans lacked artistic merit.

Still, Walt Disney Productions did not lack resources or political power following Disney's death. In 1966, the company was a newly emerged 'Wall Street darling,' would possibly obtain funding from HUD, was supported by millions of loyal consumers, and had a strong reputation for combining creativity and technical skill. The company's political power was impressive. The Reedy Creek Improvement District in Florida essentially enjoyed the powers of a county government. Despite all of these strengths, EPCOT's progress was seriously weakened by the loss of Disney's personal leadership and vision. As planning group member Bob Gurr recalls, 'The EPCOT that we all talked about, we saw Walt talk about, I think we didn't understand it at the time … But you've got to also remember that the things that Walt would send people off to do almost always worked.'[19] Perhaps with more refinement, EPCOT would have evolved into another one of Disney's big gambles that paid off, this time for the benefit of both the company shareholders and American communities.

The seeds for Epcot Center were sown by the end of 1974. Walt Disney Production's annual report that year introduced a preliminary model of World Showcase, a satellite center planned to accompany the original EPCOT.[20] In addition, a series of other EPCOT satellites was planned, including facilities to showcase industrial research, energy, the environment, the arts, sciences, health, a computer center, and 'experimental prototype living environments.'

The following year, the company formally announced that EPCOT, Disney's living community in a state of becoming, was unworkable. Speaking on behalf of the management team of Donn Tatum and Card Walker, Walker wrote:

> Consumed by the need to find solutions to the problems of our cities, Walt devoted the last years of his life to developing his initial concepts for EPCOT … [We] must avoid building a huge, traditional 'brick and mortar' community which might possibly become obsolete … We believe we must develop a community system oriented to the communication of new ideas, rather than to serving the day-to-day needs of a limited number of permanent residents.[21]

At this stage, the company announced conceptual plans developed by WED Enterprises for a nonprofit Future World Theme Center consisting of the following units: science and technology, community, and communication and the arts. In addition, a hospital and EPCOT Institute (administrative) were also part of the WED Enterprises plans. Finally, a 'world city' model would be constructed to depict a future community in the process of 'growth and adaptation.'[22]

Ultimately, the experimental community of EPCOT evolved into the $800 million Epcot Center, with its Future World and World Showcase, a 'permanent world's fair' at Walt Disney World (see Figures 10.1 and 10.2).

In October 1976, Walker outlined the basic philosophy behind Epcot Center. He said it would be 1) a 'demonstration and proving ground for prototype concepts,' 2) an 'ongoing forum of the future,' 3) a 'communicator to the world,' and 4) 'a permanent, international people-to-people

Figure 10.1 Spaceship Earth, Future World, Epcot Center. The world's largest geodesic sphere was designed after Imagineer John Hench's consultation with Richard Buckminster Fuller. Source: author's photograph

Figure 10.2   Italy pavilion, World Showcase, Epcot Center. Source:
                   author's photograph

exchange.'[23] Similar to the original EPCOT concept, the 1976 conceptual
plans for Epcot Center placed greater emphasis on prototype product testing
and development than would be found in the final plans.[24]

Epcot Center opened at Walt Disney World on October 23, 1982, incorporating WED Enterprises' International Street concept. Unlike EPCOT, the
eleven 'nations' of Epcot Center are not enclosed. Early concepts show
enclosed wedges, similar to those seen in Disney's EPCOT international
shopping core. The open, themed structures of Epcot Center are grouped
around the World Showcase Lagoon. The nations represented include Canada,
the United Kingdom, France, Morocco, Japan, United States, Italy, Germany, China, Norway, and Mexico.

Early in the conceptual process, Future World and World Showcase were
separate parks and then merged. Similar to Disneyland and the EPCOT
concept, Future World shows are sponsored by industry. Spaceship Earth
(sponsored by AT&T) is the park's primary wienie and at 180 feet in
diameter, is the world's largest geodesic sphere. The sphere, mounted on
legs, was conceived by John Hench after conferring with Richard Buckminster
Fuller. Referred to as the 'golf ball,' Spaceship Earth is the evolution of
Disney's city dome in EPCOT and appears to be named in honor of Fuller.
Disney's friend, author Ray Bradbury, helped outline the script about the
story of communications that was recorded and is played to visitors in
Spaceship Earth.

Future World reflects other elements of Disney's original EPCOT concept. For example, The Land (sponsored by Nestlé) features advanced agricultural methods and growing areas developed in association with NASA and the U.S. Department of Agriculture. As previously noted, agriculture and ecosystems were of special interest and concern to Disney. It was expected that EPCOT would have drawn upon expertise from several sectors, including academia. This also has been the case with Epcot Center. WED Enterprises worked with experts like Carl Hodges of the University of Arizona's Environmental Research Laboratory, who later went on to help develop the Biosphere 2 experimental laboratory.[25] Drawing from the EPCOT concept, the Horizons pavilion displayed cities of the future and robot food harvesters before it was removed. The Universe of Energy (ExxonMobil) features alternatives to the use of fossil fuels. Other Future World pavilions include Wonders of Life (MetLife), The Living Seas, Imagination (Kodak), and Innoventions (formerly CommuniCore). To bring the story full-circle, Disney's amateur railroading friend and television space series producer, Ward Kimball, assisted in the development of the World of Motion pavilion (General Motors, now Test Track).

John Hench and Florida Film writer Marty Sklar led the development of Epcot Center for WED Enterprises. John Decuir Jr. was the lead in-house designer. Construction management was contracted to Tishman Construction Company. Epcot Center touches upon all of the elements of Disney's original EPCOT philosophy to varying degrees except one: it is not a living community of people. That would come later and not in the form of a radial plan.

In describing the Epcot Center philosophy, Walker emphasized the word 'communicator.' That word had helped the company grow for more than 50 years at that point. In 1998, United Nations Secretary-General Kofi Annan, in an address at Epcot Center, stated, 'Modern communications mean that whether we like it or not, we are connected, inextricably and irrevocably. I think Walt Disney saw this coming. His special way of communicating with people all over the world was a foretaste of what we know today.'[26]

International communication was nothing new to the Disney organization. In Disney's day, the world's only theme park was in Anaheim and world leaders as well as ordinary people from around the globe rushed to experience it. In addition, the studio's films and merchandise were distributed internationally. The secretary-general's statement relates to Seymour Mandelbaum's theory of communication using images shared by a community to reach consensual repair. Many of the company's graphic images cross cultural boundaries in ways that spoken language does not. Some believe that this phenomenon can result in cultural imperialism destined to result in the loss of national identity. Others see it as an opportunity to reach shared understanding and promote free enterprise. Whatever the answer, technology now binds us irrevocably together and shared images remain as important as they have ever been, whether they are Disney's characters, computer icons, or paintings on a cave wall.

The EPCOT philosophy continued in other ways. Disney's favorite community topic was transportation, be it model railroading or promoting the monorail. It should come as no surprise that the EPCOT concept's most lasting influence would be in the area of public transportation. Community Transportation Services was formed as a subsidiary of Walt Disney Productions in 1974.[27] In July 1979, the Houston Intercontinental Airport selected Disney-Turner to install a WEDway system.[28] The company had teamed with Turner Construction to link three terminals. The system opened in August 1981. The new WEDway cars were powered by the linear induction motor system, in which a magnetic field pushes the vehicles along. This was an advancement over the original rubber wheels and plates underneath the cars. The new system debuted at Walt Disney World in Florida in 1975 and received a commendation for design achievement by the National Endowment for the Arts and the United States Department of Transportation.[29] In addition, in 1976, it met the requirements of the Urban Mass Transportation Administration for use as a downtown people mover.

The company's monorails are now designated Mark VI, with cars designed to permit passengers to stand in a more urban configuration. There are now 14.7 miles of monorail beamway at Walt Disney World. In 1986, the installation was named a National Historic Mechanical Engineering Landmark by the American Society of Mechanical Engineers.[30] As successful as the monorail has been at Disneyland and in Walt Disney World, it cannot solve the urban transportation problem on its own. In fact, there is no single 'fix.' As urban transportation expert Martin Wachs notes,

> The complexity of the urban area, of individual decision making about residential and work location and travel, and of American politics makes it difficult to conceive of a single policy or technology that can promise an immediate increase in mobility while decreasing the negative impacts of the transportation system.[31]

One alternative to the use of fossil fuels today is the fuel cell, developed for the space program in the 1960s. In 1968, Admiral Joe Fowler worked with General Electric to develop a fuel cell.[32] This was another example of the continuance of the EPCOT philosophy after Disney.

Still, there was more to EPCOT than transportation. According to Marty Sklar, 'Walt's original ideas are still very much alive. We never really forgot about them. It was just a question of saving them for the right moment.'[33] For example, Roosevelt Island in New York adopted the Swedish AVAC trash disposal system after it was seen in use at Walt Disney World.[34] This is an example of the showcase aspect of Disney's original EPCOT concept.

Florida's Reedy Creek Improvement District has applied its code criteria to a variety of new materials, systems, and designs, particularly during construction of Epcot Center. The district also has used a variety of new techniques to provide energy to the property.[35] John Hench believes that an

Figure 10.3　Lake and town center, Celebration, Florida. Source: author's
photograph

industrial facility may one day be developed on the Florida property, echo-
ing the original industrial park concept in Disney's plan.[36] As Marty Sklar
suggests, the EPCOT ideas have awaited their time and are coming in
pieces.

One of the most recent pieces is a planned, living community called
Celebration, Florida. Comparing aspects of the original EPCOT concept and
the town of Celebration yields insights into each plan, although the two
concepts are vastly different. Original EPCOT team member Bob Gurr
believes that Celebration is 'the last little tiny speck of the [EPCOT] idea.'[37]
In a memorandum to company chief Michael Eisner, Peter Rummell, former
president of Disney Development Company, wrote, 'It will have fiber optics
and Smart Houses, but the feel will be closer to Main Street than to Future
World.'[38] The Florida property would finally have a city of 'Yesterday.'

In March 1994, The Walt Disney Company broke ground on a portion of
approximately 9,600 acres of unincorporated land in Osceola County. The
initial Celebration plan collaborators included Robert A. M. Stern, Charles
Gwathemy, Robert Siegel, Andres Duany, and Elizabeth Plater-Zyberk.
Skidmore, Owings & Merrill and Charles Moore also contributed to the
plan. Jacquelin Robertson and Stern were the final plan collaborators (see
Figures 10.3 and 10.4).

Prominent Celebration architects included Robert Venturi, Denise Scott
Brown, Philip Johnson, Cesar Pelli, William Rawn, Michael Graves, and

Figure 10.4   Single family houses, Celebration, Florida. The design
places porches near sidewalks in an attempt to promote
'neighboring.' Source: author's photograph

Charles Moore. Wing Chao, executive vice president of master planning,
architecture, and design at Walt Disney Imagineering is the company's chief
in-house architect. House architectural styles in Celebration are varied and
include Colonial Revival, Classical, French Country, Coastal Mediterra-
nean, and Victorian. Celebration also features amenities such as a public
golf course, nature trails, and a downtown lake. The first residents arrived in
June 1996, almost 30 years after Disney's death.

The most obvious similarity between EPCOT and Celebration is the
targeted population of 20,000 persons. Disney's original EPCOT concept,
however, was an experimental community and themed shopping experience
driven by technological change and operated in conjunction with American
industry. PeopleMovers would traverse the residential areas to showcase
new innovations. Celebration is a New Urbanist community. Technology is
only one and not the paramount cornerstone. The other cornerstones are
education, health, place, and community.

The company did partner with American industry and experts to develop
infrastructure for the community. For example, in conjunction with AT&T,
Celebration Company, a subsidiary of The Walt Disney Company, developed a community intranet with bulletin boards and chat rooms. This is
similar to Disney's 1966 plan to incorporate a two-way closed circuit televi-

sion system into EPCOT.[39] While EPCOT could have included a small hospital, Celebration features Celebration Health. This 60-acre campus was planned with leading national medical experts. The community-integrated health system is designed to link communications technology with data regarding patients' blood pressure and other measures.

Like EPCOT, Celebration has become something of a showcase. Due to its proximity to Walt Disney World and national media attention, the town attracts many visitors. Unlike the EPCOT concept, Celebration residents can own property. The land used for the development was taken out of the Reedy Creek Improvement District. The Celebration Company established two community development districts to provide infrastructure and two community associations.

Builders in Celebration must follow adopted design guidelines published in a pattern book. Planners hoped to avoid the 'little boxes' effect with a fairly wide range of architectural styles. In addition, each house must include a bay window or balcony, a cornice, or a columned porch. The porches and other New Urbanist design elements in the plan are thought to help promote 'neighboring.' According to Michael Eisner, the planners also considered use of pneumatic tubes to remove household garbage pursuant to Disney's vision for EPCOT, but it would not have been financially feasible.[40]

True to the New Urbanism, Celebration has a town center. The 18-acre Phase One Celebration town center includes a town hall, post office, bank, cinema, retail, office space, apartments (over retail), and a hotel. Like EPCOT, Celebration's town center retail establishments currently draw heavily upon tourist expenditures. Celebration also is surrounded by a protected 4,700-acre greenbelt. Unlike EPCOT, automobiles are not banned from the town center and, perhaps fortunately for the residents, the Walt Disney World monorail does not connect with the development. While Celebration is not associated with an industrial park, it does have a 109-acre office park site. Disney was very enthusiastic about planning a school toward the end of his life and national and local educational experts continue to refine the vision of the Celebration schools.

As in any community, there is a tug-of-war between freedom and control in Celebration. Some critics have concluded that Celebration's design and community associations' controls are overly strict.[41] Others argue that the associations' rules are not unlike those found in postwar American suburbs.[42] Disney's EPCOT, with no home ownership, would have been controlled to the extreme by comparison. Celebration hardly begins to demonstrate the potential effect of control over people's lives as it was envisioned in the original EPCOT company town concept.

Not everyone enjoys life in a master-planned community. Still, the large turnout for Celebration's early sales lottery suggested that there can be strong market demand for houses in such communities. That demand continues to raise questions about the condition of many of the rest of America's communities beyond the berm of Disneyland and the New Urbanist plan of Celebration. Had Disney lived to refine his EPCOT concept and build a futuristic experimental community in the 1970s, it probably would not have looked like Celebration. Although Celebration is not designed to be an urban laboratory, it does draw upon some of the EPCOT philosophy to yield a living community with stated cornerstones, a New Urbanist plan, and community-oriented technology that may be duplicated by other communities.

The Walt Disney Company and the families of Walt and Roy O. Disney continue to profoundly impact the built environment in Southern California. For example, there is now an entire Disneyland Resort in Anaheim. The resort features the 55-acre California Adventure theme park which stands on the old Disneyland parking lot south of the original park. The resort also includes an Arts and Crafts Style-themed hotel, a 20-acre Downtown Disney, and elaborate parking and transportation facilities. In addition, there are plans to open a third 'gate' in Anaheim. The company has begun to control the land around the original park as Disney wished he could have done.

Disney's studio site in Burbank has not been quiet either. In 1990, architect Michael Grave's Team Disney Building opened. This Neo-Classical Style/fantasy headquarters features sculptures of six of Snow White's dwarfs in the entablature and the seventh dwarf, Dopey, in the pediment. Robert A. M. Stern's Feature Animation Building opened in 1995 on the site that Disney had proposed for an amusement park. The building borrows from the studios' original Streamline Moderne Style and adds playful elements such as an eight-story Sorcerer Mickey hat placed over the entrance.[43]

The company also has been involved with projects in Southern California having historic preservation components. For example, the historic renovation of the El Capitan Theatre, which reopened in 1991, was a factor in spurring Hollywood's revitalization. In addition, a 125-acre creative campus is planned in nearby Glendale to maintain the Glendale Grand Central Air Terminal. As previously noted, WED Enterprises began a long process of growth in that city in 1961.

Perhaps the grandest new project of all is the Walt Disney Concert Hall in downtown Los Angeles. A $50 million donation by Lillian Disney launched the campaign to build the Frank O. Gehry-designed hall. Diane Disney Miller has been active in this effort. As previously noted, Walt Disney and architect Welton Becket were both involved in development of the Los Angeles Music Center, a complex of live-performance theaters just a block from the Walt Disney Concert Hall site. The dramatically designed concert hall is expected to become a Los Angeles landmark. Roy E. Disney, son of Roy O. Disney, and now vice chairman of The Walt Disney Company and chairman of the feature animation division, has been active in the real estate development industry in Southern California, constructing major new studios and other types of space. In addition, his family's holding company oversees a fund to stimulate development of low–moderate income neighborhoods of Los Angeles County.

With all the entertainment industry development activity, California Dreamin' seems to be alive and well. Still, during a 1997 interview in the *Los Angeles Times*, author Jane Jacobs stated that America's cities remain in trouble: 'I'd say they're in a lot worse shape than they were in 1961, when I wrote that book. I called it *The Death and Life of the Great American City*, not the Life and Death, because I wanted to convey a sense of optimism. Today, I'm not so optimistic. I hope I'm wrong.'[44] If Disney had written a book about EPCOT in the early 1960s, it might have been called, 'Great Big Beautiful Tomorrow.' However, he did not live long enough to witness demoralizing events like Watergate and the end of the Vietnam War.

While John Hench pointed to the disadvantages of an artistic plan like Brasilia's, he also stressed that urbanites require some level of reassurance in their environment. 'The futile search for order produces anxiety, neuroses, antisocial behavior, etc.,' he said. 'Los Angeles is probably one of the best examples of a city with a lack of order. We've got to cooperate to build a life-preserving city, not a life-threatening one.'[45] Here, Imagineer Hench, in a role more akin to that of a classical urban sociologist, takes reassurance outside the berm and into a real community. The region continues to be at the forefront of addressing urban transportation issues where Disney's 'freewayphobia' now includes newer factors such as 'road rage' and gridlock. However, he would probably be tickled to see electric light-rail trains running in certain freeway medians.

Civil unrest in Los Angeles following the Rodney King police beating verdict in 1992 reminded many residents of the Watts riots of 1965. In an attempt to contribute to a solution, Frank Wells, president and chief operating officer of the company at the time, led the Disney organization to hire 230 'cast members' from the inner-city and open a new Disney Store in South Central Los Angeles. In addition, more than 3,300 West Coast employees helped raise $1 million for a revolving loan fund coordinated by First AME Church, a respected South Central institution.[46]

Former Disney advisor and Irvine Company Vice Chairman Ray Watson emphasizes that residents still are trying to create a 'sense of places' amidst the sprawl of Southern California and that the service and information revolutions are extremely geographically decentralized.[47] Planning devices such as the New Urbanism, reflected to varying degrees in Disney's 1966 transit-oriented plan and the more recent town of Celebration, Florida, attempt to address lingering problems that academia, the professions, and government identified in the 1960s. In many instances, government agencies now partner with development entities and lenders to reduce investment risk and pioneer new methods for the adaptive re-use of buildings in downtown Los Angeles and the integration of public transit in suburban and in-fill development. Architects and planners are concerned about the sustainability of their projects. Agencies like the Southern California Association of Governments coordinate the activities of the multiplicity of political jurisdictions in the region. Perhaps there is cause for some optimism after all.

A major underlying design premise of the New Urbanism is that people require non-technologically-generated, three-dimensional interaction with other community members. Marty Sklar, now vice chairman of Walt Disney Imagineering, projects what Disneyland will be like on the park's 200th anniversary in the year 2155: 'People will go beyond those electronic connections to seek out the physical experience.'[48] For the time being, Anaheim's Disneyland Resort and the omnipresent shopping mall will continue to serve as partial replacements for the lost town plaza in Southern California's decentralized Automobile/Information Age.

In the 1960s, Disney's response to the urban crisis was to conceptualize a living urban laboratory where new ways of experimenting with electronic connections for the twenty-first century and beyond might have been tested and demonstrated to visitors. As architect Peter Blake noted, perhaps that was the most intriguing aspect of the original concept – the state of becoming. Today, many high-tech products are nearly obsolete before they reach the consumer and many buildings cannot accommodate the ever-changing equipment that modern businesses require. Over more than three decades, Disney's prediction that the EPCOT concept could evolve came to pass. However, with major investments in projects like Epcot Center and Celebration, the EPCOT philosophy lives on in steel, albeit in separate components.

Disney did indeed wear many hats during his career, including the hard hat of a visionary builder. During the last filmed appearance of his life, Disney stated that there was no greater challenge than solving urban problems. Imagineer Bob Gurr, asked recently what he thought Disney would be doing now if he were still alive, replied half-seriously, 'Still struggling with EPCOT.'[49]

List of Abbreviations

Collections

AFA   Architecture and Fine Arts Library, University of Southern California, Los Angeles, California
AHR   Elizabeth J. Schultz Anaheim History Room, Anaheim Public Library, Anaheim, California
EB   Ellerbe Becket Slide Library, Ellerbe Becket, Minneapolis, Minnesota
FML   Feuchtwanger Memorial Library and Archive, Doheny Memorial Library, University of Southern California, Los Angeles, California
FSA   Florida State Archives, State Library of Florida, Tallahassee, Florida
LBJ   Lyndon B. Johnson Library, Austin, Texas
OPL   The Disney Collection, Orlando Public Library, Orlando, Florida
RN   Richard Nixon Library, Yorba Linda, California
ULI   Urban Land Institute Archives, the Urban Land Institute, Washington, D.C.
WDA   Walt Disney Archives, Walt Disney Studios, Burbank, California
WP   Special Collections Department, United States Military Academy, Library, West Point, New York

Publications

AB   *Anaheim Bulletin*
ENR   *Engineering News-Record*
LAT   *Los Angeles Times*
NYT   *New York Times*
OCR   *Orange County Register*
OES   *Orlando Evening Star*
OS   *Orlando Sentinel*
POV   *Persistence of Vision*
SEP   *The Saturday Evening Post*
TET   *The 'E' Ticket*

Notes

Introduction

1. Boyle Workman as told to Caroline Walker, *The City That Grew* (Los Angeles: The Southland Publishing Co., 1935), FML, p. 325. See David R. Smith, Inventory of Walt Disney's Offices, 3H Wing of the Animation Building, Walt Disney Studios, Burbank, California, August 23, 1971, WDA.
2. John Reddy, 'The Living Legacy of Walt Disney,' *Reader's Digest*, June 1967, p. 170.
3. Victor Gruen, *The Heart of Our Cities* (New York: Simon & Schuster, 1964). See Disney's office inventory.
4. Public Law 89-754, *Demonstration Cities and Metropolitan Development Act of 1966*, Section 101.
5. Ibid.
6. Walt Disney, *Florida Film – Final Script*, Disney's segments were filmed on October 27, 1966, WDA, p. 7.
7. Walt Disney quoted in Dave Smith, ed., *Walt Disney: Famous Quotes* (Lake Buena Vista: The Walt Disney Company, c. 1994), p. 33.
8. Ward Kimball, interview by author, December 15, 1998, transcript, p. 5.
9. Bob Thomas, 'Uncle Walt's Greatest Stand: How There Almost Was No Disneyland,' *Los Angeles*, 21, 12, December 1976, p. 164.
10. William E. Potter, 'Walt Disney World: A Venture in Community Planning & Development,' *ASHRAE Journal*, March 1972, p. 30.
11. Lillian Disney quoted by Katherine Greene and Richard Greene, interview, 1986. www.waltdisney.org, December 7, 2001, 20:00. This is the Walt Disney Family Educational Foundation museum website.
12. Harrison Price, interview by author, February 16, 1998, transcript, p.14. Anonymous, 'Disneyworld Amusement Center With Domed City Set For Florida,' *NYT*, 116, 39,822, February 3, 1967, p. 38. See also Carl Bongiorno, interview by author, February 9, 1999, transcript, p. 22 ('we always said that, based on what Walt is thinking, we have 20 to 30 years of work'). Along similar lines, Marty Sklar stated, 'He gave us enough to last 10 to 20 years.' Quoted in Jack Boettner, 'Disney's "Magical Little Park" After Two Decades,' *LAT*, July 6, 1975, p. X9.
13. E. Cardon Walker, interview by author, April 6, 1999, transcript, p. 4.

14. Marvin Davis quoted in Jack E. Janzen and Leon J. Janzen, 'Planning the First Disney Parks … A Talk With Marvin Davis,' *TET*, 28, Winter 1997, p. 17.
15. Lewis Mumford in Robert L. Carovillano and James W. Skehan, S.J., *Science and the Future of Man* (Cambridge: The MIT Press, c. 1970), p. 111.
16. John Hench, interview by author, December 18, 1997, transcript, p. 11.
17. Victor Gruen, *The Heart of Our Cities*, p. 12.
18. Sharon Disney Lund quoted in Amy Boothe Green and Howard E. Green, *Remembering Walt* (New York: Hyperion, 1999), p. 84.
19. Morgan 'Bill' Evans, interview by author, June 27, 1998, transcript, p. 16.
20. Randy Bright, *Disneyland: Inside Story* (New York: Harry N. Abrams, Inc., 1987), pp. 45, 48.
21. Peter Hall, *Cities in Civilization* (New York: Pantheon Books, 1998), p. 961.
22. Marvin Davis, interview by Richard Hubler, May 28, 1968, transcript, WDA, p. 25.
23. Lewis Mumford Introductory Essay in Ebenezer Howard, *Garden Cities of To-Morrow* (Cambridge: The MIT Press, 1965), p. 29.
24. Disney's father Elias was a Socialist. 'Dad was raised on a weekly publication called *The Appeal to Reason*.' Diane Disney Miller, as told to Pete Martin, 'Hard Times in Kansas City,' *SEP*, November 24, 1956, p. 70.
25. Ward Kimball, interview by author, December 15, 1998, transcript, p. 18.
26. Walt Disney, *Florida Film – Final Script*, Disney's segments were filmed on October 27, 1966, WDA, p. 2.

Chapter 1

1. John Hench quoted in Charlie Haas, 'Disneyland is Good For You,' *New West*, 3, 25, December 4, 1978, pp. 13–19. At that time, Hench was chief operating officer of WED Enterprises at the age of 70.
2. Elvis Lane, 'Disney Tells of $100 Million Project,' *OS*, 81, 187, November 16, 1965, p. 1. For a useful bibliography see Stephen J. Rebori, *Theme and Entertainment Parks: Planning, Design, Development and Management* (Chicago: American Planning Association, c. 1995). Also see Christopher Tunnard and Boris Pushkarev, *Man-Made America: Chaos or Control?* (New Haven and London: Yale University Press, 1963).
3. Walt Disney quoted in Van Arsdale France, *Window on Main Street … 35 Years of Creating Happiness at Disneyland Park* (Nashua: Laughter Publications, Inc., c. 1991), p. 78.

4. Marvin Davis did not care for New York City. See Marjorie Davis, interview by author, October 12, 1998, transcript, p. 4. For a classic analysis of Las Vegas, see Robert Venturi, *Learning From Las Vegas: The Forgotten Symbolism of Architectural Form* (Cambridge: MIT Press, c. 1977).

5. Walt Disney quoted in Dave Smith, ed., *Walt Disney: Famous Quotes*, p. 34.

6. See Carl Bongiorno, interview by author, February 9, 1999, transcript, p. 13.

7. Marvin Davis quoted in Jack E. Janzen and Leon J. Janzen, 'Planning the First Disney Parks ... A Talk With Marvin Davis,' p. 18. Davis was a pilot and had an interest in airports and their problems. See Marjorie Davis, interview by author, October 12, 1998, transcript, p. 13.

8. Walt Disney Productions, 'Project Florida/A Whole New Disney World,' c. 1967, paper, WDA, p. 10. Also see East Central Florida Regional Planning Council, *Airports*, Comprehensive Regional Plan Series, September 1967, OPL, pp. 7, 18, 21.

9. Walt Disney Productions, 'Project Florida/A Whole New Disney World,' p. 10.

10. Ibid., p. 3. See Marjorie Davis, interview by author, October 12, 1998, transcript, p. 4.

11. Dick Irvine, interview by Bob Thomas, April 24, 1973, transcript, WDA, p. 42. In 1965, Davis returned to WED from television to work on EPCOT and Disney World.

12. See Jack E. Janzen and Leon J. Janzen, 'Planning the First Disney Parks ... A Talk With Marvin Davis,' p. 16.

13. Marvin Davis quoted in Jack E. Janzen and Leon J. Janzen, 'Planning the First Disney Parks ... A Talk With Marvin Davis,' p. 15. See also Morgan 'Bill' Evans, interview by author, June 27, 1998, transcript, p. 15.

14. Carl Bongiorno, interview by author, February 2, 1999, transcript, p. 2.

15. Robert Price Foster, 'The Founding of a Kingdom,' manuscript, c. 1992, author's collection, p. 163.

16. Welton Becket & Associates presented an EPCOT presentation book to Disney in early 1966 and it reportedly was both rejected and lost. See Karal Ann Marling, *Designing Disney's Theme Parks: The Architecture of Reassurance* (Paris and New York: Flammarion, c. 1997), p. 149. Robert Tyler, a retired design principal of Welton Becket & Associates recalls, 'Well, I think that EPCOT and that portion of it [state of becoming] was all Disney ... .' See Robert Tyler, interview by author, March 29, 1999, transcript, p. 4.

17. Marvin Davis quoted in Anthony Haden-Guest, *The Paradise Program: Travels through Muzak, Hilton, Coca-Cola, Texaco, Walt Disney*

and Other World Enterprises (New York: William Morrow & Company, Inc., 1973), p. 309.

18. Walt Disney quoted in Dave Smith, ed., *Walt Disney: Famous Quotes*, p. 54.
19. See Elvis Lane, 'Disney Tells of $100 Million Project,' p. 1.
20. Raymond L. Watson, interview by author, November 6, 1998, transcript, p. 6.
21. John Hench, interview by author, December 18, 1997, transcript, p. 9. See also Leonard Mosley, *Disney's World* (Lanham: Scarborough House, c. 1990), p. 284.
22. Major General William E. Potter, USA, Retired, interview by Dr. Martin Reuss, Historical Division, Office of the Chief of Engineers, February 1981, WP, EP870–1–12 (July 1983), p. 192. See also Marjorie Davis, interview by author, October 12, 1998, transcript, p. 5. Also see Jack E. Janzen and Leon J. Janzen, 'Imagineering and the Disney Image ... An Interview With Marty Sklar,' *TET*, 30, Fall 1998, p. 11.
23. Walt Disney Productions, 'Project Florida/A Whole New Disney World,' p. 12.
24. General Joe Potter quoted in Anthony Haden-Guest, *The Paradise Program*, p. 299.
25. Ibid., p. 308.
26. Richard Sherman quoted in Paul F. Anderson, in Katherine Greene and Richard Greene, *Walt Disney: An Intimate History of the Man and His Magic* (Santa Monica: Pantheon Productions, Inc., 1998), CD-ROM, 'Final Vision.'
27. Walt Disney Productions, 'Project Florida/A Whole New Disney World,' pp. 12–13.
28. Economics Research Associates, 'Project Florida Planning Manual,' prepared for Walt Disney Productions, July 19, 1966, pp. VII-5, VII-9. Based on a population of 36,000 persons, not 20,000.
29. Ibid., p. VII-15.
30. See Phase One 10th Preliminary Master Plot Plan in Walt Disney Productions, 'The Story of Walt Disney World,' c. 1971, paper, OPL, p. 19.
31. Marvin Davis recorded interview in Katherine Greene and Richard Greene, *Walt Disney: An Intimate History of the Man and His Magic*, CD-ROM, 'Final Vision.'
32. Raymond L. Watson, interview by author, November 6, 1998, transcript, p. 3.
33. Karal Ann Marling, ed., *Designing Disney's Theme Parks*, p. 30. For discussions of how physical planning relates to the entire real estate development process see Richard B. Peiser with Dean Schwanke, *Professional Real Estate Development* (Washington, D.C.: Dearborn Financial Publishing, Inc. and ULI-the Urban Land Institute, c. 1992).

See also William I. Goodman, ed., *Principles and Practice of Urban Planning* (Washington, D.C.: International City Managers Association, 1968).

34. See Richard Longstreth, *City Center to Regional Mall: Architecture, the Automobile, and Retailing in Los Angeles, 1920–1950* (Cambridge and London: The MIT Press, 1997).

35. Marvin Davis quoted in Paul F. Anderson essay, in Katherine Greene and Richard Greene, *Walt Disney: An Intimate History of the Man and His Magic*, CD-ROM, 'Library.'

36. Walt Disney quoted in Dave Smith, ed., *Walt Disney: Famous Quotes*, p. 34.

37. Spiro Kostof, *The City Shaped: Urban Patterns and Meanings Through History* (Boston, Toronto, and London: Bullfinch Press, c. 1991), p. 192. There are numerous examples of the radial plan throughout history. One example in Southern California was Llano del Rio (begun 1914), located at the edge of the Mojave Desert. Designed by Alice Constance Austin, the development adhered to Howard's plan, and placed business traffic underground. See Dolores Hayden, *Seven American Utopias* (Cambridge and London: The MIT Press, c. 1976).

38. Walt Disney Productions, 'Project Florida/A Whole New Disney World,' p. 16.

39. Ibid.

40. Disney's friend, Welton Becket, designed the nearby Stanford Shopping Center.

41. Disney asked General Electric if he could put the Progress City model in the Anaheim carousel. See Carl Bongiorno, interview by author, February 9, 1999, transcript, p. 22.

42. See Paul F. Anderson, 'A Great Big Beautiful Tomorrow: Walt Disney & World's Fairs,' *POV*, No. 6/7, pp. 117–18; Jack E. Janzen and Leon J. Janzen, 'Walt Disney's Carousel of Progress,' *TET*, No. 22, Winter 1995, pp. 35–6; and University of Disneyland and General Electric Company, 'GE Carousel of Progress at Disneyland,' booklet, ca. 1967, AHR.

43. Bruce Gordon and David Mumford, *Disneyland: The Nickel Tour* (Santa Clarita: Camphor Tree Publishers, 1995), p. 238.

44. Marty Sklar quoted in Jack E. Janzen and Leon J. Janzen, 'Imagineering and the Disney Image … an Interview With Marty Sklar,' p. 8.

45. Jack E. Janzen and Leon J. Janzen, 'Walt Disney's Carousel of Progress,' p. 37.

46. Harrison Price, interview by author, December 17, 1998, transcript, p. 2.

47. Michael Broggie, *Walt Disney's Railroad Story*, pp. 45, 48.

48. John Hench, interview by author, December 18, 1997, p. 16. See WED Enterprises, Inc., 'Tomorrowland, Carousel of Progress, Progress

City Tape,' script, April 13, 1967, AHR. Also see WED Enterprises, Inc., 'Tomorrowland, Carousel of Progress,' Narration-Tape, script. See also University of Disneyland and General Electric Company, 'GE Carousel of Progress at Disneyland,' p. 16.

49. Ryman had been an art director for *Fantasia, Dumbo,* and *Pinocchio.* For an overview of Ryman's career see Bruce Gordon and David Mumford, eds., *A Brush With Disney* (Santa Clarita: Camphor Tree Publishers, 2000).

50. Ward Kimball, interview by author, December 15, 1998, transcript, p. 8.

51. Ibid., p. 9.

52. Morgan 'Bill' Evans, interview by author, June 27, 1998, p. 30.

53. Harrison Price, interview by author, February 16, 1998, transcript, p. 6.

54. See Scott Richter, 'Dr. Charles Hirt: The Miracle of Squaw Valley,' *Disney News*, Winter 1993, AHR, p. 28.

55. Marjorie Davis, interview by author, October 12, 1998, transcript, p. 6. See also Walt Disney Productions, 'Annual Report to Shareholders and Employees, Fiscal Year Ended October 2, 1965,' audited by Price Waterhouse, p. 40.

56. Dick Irvine, interview, May 1968, WDA, p. 19.

57. Harrison Price, personal communication, June 17, 2001.

58. Harrison Price, interview by author, February 16, 1998, transcript, p. 9.

59. California Institute of the Arts, 'History of California Institute of the Arts,' Steven D. Lavine, president, paper, January 1997.

60. Walt Disney Productions created a Circarama film for the 1958 Fair. See Bob Gurr, interview by author, January 25, 1999, transcript, p. 41. Walt Disney, Roger Broggie, Admiral Joe Fowler, and others went to Brussels. See also Jack E. Janzen and Leon J. Janzen, 'Disneyland on Wheels ... An Interview With Bob Gurr,' p. 34.

61. Walt Disney, *Florida Film – Final Script*, revised November 10, 1966, p. 3.

62. Victor Gruen, *The Heart of Our Cities*, p. 293.

63. Marty Sklar quoted in Amy Boothe Green and Howard E. Green, *Remembering Walt*, p. 175.

64. John M. Findlay, *Magic Lands: Western Cityscapes and American Culture After 1940* (Berkeley and Los Angeles: University of California Press, c. 1992), p. 251.

65. Harrison Price, interview by author, February 16, 1998, transcript, p. 10.

66. Richard Irvine quoted in Paul F. Anderson, 'A Great Big Beautiful Tomorrow: Walt Disney & World's Fairs,' p. 123. See also Robert A. Caro, *The Power Broker: Robert Moses and the Fall of New York* (New York: Alfred A. Knopf, 1974).

67. Ward Kimball, interview by author, December 15, 1998, transcript, p. 16.
68. See David Gelernter, *1939: The Lost World of the Fair* (New York: The Free Press, 1995), pp. 34–5. The fair also featured the radial Democracity model inside the Perisphere by Henry Dreyfuss. Its center contained a large skyscraper. Transportation was based on highways to the suburbs. Also see Helen A. Harrison, *Dawn of a New Day: The New York World's Fair, 1939/40* (New York and London: The Queens Museum and New York University Press, c. 1980), p. 14.
69. See Dan Viets, 'Mickey on the Mississippi: Walt Disney's Vision for Downtown St. Louis,' *Gateway-Heritage*, 21, 1, Summer 2000. The quarterly magazine of the Missouri Historical Society. See also Anonymous, 'Creator of Renowned Disneyland Gives His Concept of Amusement Center for St. Louis' Riverfront,' *Globe-Democrat*, Sunday Magazine, April 12, 1964, AHR, n.p.
70. Dan Viets, 'Mickey on the Mississippi,' p. 8. Also see Joe Fowler, interview by Bob Thomas, March 20, 1973, transcript, WDA, p. 41; and Robert Price Foster, 'The Founding of a Kingdom,' p. 8.
71. Robert Foster, interview by author, April 23, 1999, transcript, p. 20.
72. Marvin Davis quoted in Jack E. Janzen and Leon J. Janzen, 'Planning the First Disney Parks ... A Talk With Marvin Davis,' p. 18. See also Dick Irvine, interview, May 1968, WDA, p. 12. For detail about theme park design see Andrew David Lainsbury, 'Once Upon an American Dream: The Story of Euro Disneyland,' Volume I, Ph.D. Thesis, University of Minnesota, June 1996.
73. John Hench, interview by author, December 15, 1997, transcript, p. 23. See also Randy Bright, *Disneyland: Inside Story*, p. 61.
74. Dick Irvine, interview, May 1968, WDA, p. 11.
75. John Hench, interview by author, December 18, 1997, transcript, p. 15.
76. Ibid., p. 5.
77. James Rouse quoted in Disneyland, Inc., 'The Walt Disney Story,' Information Brochure, Spring 1973, AHR, n.p.
78. See Jack E. Janzen and Leon J. Janzen, 'Disneyland Art Director ... Bill Martin,' *TET*, No. 20, Winter 1994–1995, p. 14.
79. Liberty Street was to feature blacksmiths, crafts, wares, and a replica of Independence Hall. A near exact replica of the hall was opened by Walter Knott in 1966. Edison Square, once planned to open behind Main Street in 1959, would feature electric street lamps and period architecture from several American cities, including Boston and old St. Louis. See WED Enterprises, Inc., 'Edison Square, Disneyland, U.S.A.,' booklet, AHR, n.p.
80. Judith A. Adams, *The American Amusement Park Industry: a History of Technology and Thrills* (Boston: Twayne Publishers, 1991), p. 17.
81. John Hench quoted in Jack E. Janzen and Leon J. Janzen, '"Another

Kind of Reality": An Interview With John Hench,' *TET*, No. 17, Winter 1993–1994, p. 23.

82.   Disneyland, Inc., 'Disneyland Diary,' Publicity Department, 1966, AHR.

83.   Charles Moore, 'You Have to Pay for the Public Life,' *Perspecta*, IX, October 1964, p. 65.

84.   Richard V. Francaviglia, 'Main Street U.S.A.: A Comparison/Contrast of Streetscapes in Disneyland and Walt Disney World,' *Journal of Popular Culture*, 15, 1, Summer 1981, p. 143. See also Michael Harrington, 'To the Disney Station,' *Harper's*, 258, 1544, January 1979, pp. 35–44, 86.

85.   Michael Broggie, *Walt Disney's Railroad Story*, p. 112.

86.   Walt Disney quoted in Leonard Maltin, *The Disney Films* (New York: Crown Publishers, Inc., c. 1973), p. 89.

87.   Bob Thomas, *Building a Company:Roy O. Disney and the Creation of an Entertainment Empire* (New York: Hyperion, 1998) , p. 133. See also The Walt Disney Studios, 'The Walt Disney Studios, Preliminary Master Plan,' brochure, c. 1991, AHR.

88.   Walt Disney Productions, 'The Walt Disney Studio,' press release, c. 1967, AHR, p. 7.

89.   Joe Grant quoted in Amy Boothe Green and Howard E. Green, *Remembering Walt*, p. 118.

90.   Walt Disney Productions, 'The Walt Disney Studio,' p. 7.

91.   Diane Disney Miller quoted in Katherine Greene and Richard Greene, *The Man Behind the Magic: The Story of Walt Disney* (New York: Viking, c. 1998), p. 166.

92.   Economics Research Associates, 'Planning a New Community: Key to an Effective Approach,' prepared for Walt Disney Productions, September 30, 1966, WDA, pp. 9–11. See Disney's office inventory.

93.   For company towns see Margaret Crawford, *Building the Workingman's Paradise: The Design of American Company Towns* (London and New York: Verso, 1995). For utopias, see: Peter Hall, *Cities of Tomorrow: An Intellectual History of Urban Planning and Design in the Twentieth Century* (Cambridge and Oxford: Blackwell Publishers, 1996); and Robert Fishman, *Urban Utopias in the Twentieth Century* (New York: Basic Books, c. 1977).

94.   Peter Hall, *Cities of Tomorrow*, p. 97.

95.   Lewis Mumford, *The City in History: Its Origins, Its Transformations, and its Prospects* (New York: Harcourt Brace & Company, c. 1961).

96.   See Clarence S. Stein, *Toward New Towns for America* (New York: Reinhold Publishing Corporation, c. 1957).

97.   John Hench, interview by author, December 18, 1997, transcript, p. 9.

98.   Raymond L. Watson, interview by author, November 6, 1998, transcript, p. 4.

99.   William E. Potter, 'Walt Disney World: A Venture in Community Planning & Development,' p. 29. See also Anthony Haden-Guest, *The Paradise Program*, p. 296.

100. Bill Martin, interview by author, December 18, 1997, transcript, p. 9.

101. The Urban Land Institute, 'Reston Town Center, Reston, Virginia,' Project Reference File, 21, 11, July–September 1991, ULI, p. 1.

102. Phillip Davis, 'Columbia, Maryland: Zero to 68,000 in 20 Years,' *Urban Land*, November 1987, ULI, p. 3. Also see Robert Oliver Brooks, *New Towns and Communal Values: A Case Study of Columbia, Maryland* (New York: Praeger Publishers, 1974).

103. Harrison Price, personal communication, March 8, 2002.

104. Victor Gruen, *The Heart of Our Cities*, n.p.

105. Kevin Lynch, *Good City Form* (Cambridge and London: The MIT Press, c. 1981), p. 89.

106. Victor Gruen, *The Heart of Our Cities,* p. 286.

107. Sharon Disney Lund quoted in Amy Boothe Green and Howard E. Green, *Remembering Walt*, p. 84.

108. See Jean Paul Richter, ed., compilation, *The Notebooks of Leonardo da Vinci* (New York: Dover Publications, 1970), Plate LXXVIII, No. 2, manuscript B. First published in London in 1883.

109. Ward Kimball, interview by author, December 15, 1998, transcript, p. 5. See also Karal Ann Marling, ed., *Designing Disney's Theme Parks*, p. 219.

110. John Hench, interview by author, December 18, 1997, transcript, p. 26.

111. Ford R. Bryan, *Henry's Attic: Some Fascinating Gifts to Henry Ford and His Museum* (Dearborn: Ford Books, 1995), p. 21. See Allan Nevins, *Ford: The Times, the Man, the Company* (New York: Charles Scribner's Sons, 1954). Also see Paul Israel, *Edison: A Life of Invention* (New York: John Wiley & Sons, Inc., 1998).

112. See William H. Wilson, *The City Beautiful Movement* (Baltimore and London: The Johns Hopkins University Press, 1989).

113. Judith A. Adams, *The American Amusement Park Industry*, p. 36.

114. Walt Disney quoted in Russell Schroeder, ed., *Walt Disney: His Life in Pictures* (New York: Disney Press, c. 1996), p. 55.

115. Karal Ann Marling, ed., *Designing Disney's Theme Parks*, p. 63.

116. John Hench, interview by author, December 18, 1997, transcript, p. 2.

117. Peter Blake, 'Walt Disney World,' *The Architectural Forum*, 136, 5, June 1972, p. 40.

Chapter 2

1. Roy O. Disney quoted by Bob Thomas in Anonymous, 'Disney World Price Tag Now Reads $600 Million,' *OES*, 91, 6, January 9, 1967, p. 1.
2. Dick Irvine, interview by Bob Thomas, April 24, 1973, transcript, WDA, p. 3.
3. Diane Disney Miller, 'My Dad Walt Disney,' *SEP*, November 24, 1956, p. 75.
4. Ward Kimball quoted in Kathy Merlock Jackson, *Walt Disney: A Bio-Bibliography* (Westport: Greenwood Press, 1993), p. 149. For Disney's backyard train, see Roger Broggie, 'Walt Disney's The Carolwood-Pacific Railroad,' *The Miniature Locomotive*, May–June 1952, AHR, pp. 14–16.
5. Marjorie Davis, interview by author, October 12, 1998, transcript, p. 13. See also Walt Disney Productions, 'Project Florida/A Whole New Disney World,' p. 15.
6. Marvin Davis, 'Typical Industrial Complex,' October 19, 1966, plan, Walt Disney Imagineering Collection.
7. Walt Disney, correspondence to The Honorable Richard M. Nixon, May 8, 1959, RN.
8. Ray Bradbury, 'Los Angeles: Orange Without a Navel,' *Frontier*, 15, February 1964, p. 14. Also see Bradbury's 'Celluloid City,' *Westways*, 91, 1, January/February 1999, pp. 22–7. See also Ramon G. McLeod, 'A Marriage of Convenience,' *OCR*, June 2, 1985, p. C1.
9. Marty Sklar quoted in Jack E. Janzen and Leon J. Janzen, 'Imagineering and the Disney Image … an Interview With Marty Sklar,' *TET*, No. 30, Fall 1998, p. 15.
10. Peter Cook, ed., *Archigram* (New York: Princeton Architectural Press, c. 1999), p. 22.
11. Walt Disney Productions, 'Project Florida/A Whole New Disney World,' p. 14. The multi-level transportation hub traces to a 1964 WED Enterprises concept called SpacePort which later evolved into the Space Mountain attraction.
12. See Le Corbusier, *The City of To-Morrow* (Cambridge: MIT Press, 1971), p. 164.
13. Walt Disney Productions, 'Pirates of the Caribbean: Facts and Figures,' Confidential Memorandum, 1967, AHR, p. viii. Also see Robert R. Reynolds, *Roller Coasters, Flumes and Flying Saucers* (Jupiter: Northern Lights Publishing, c. 1999).
14. Bill Cotter, *The Wonderful World of Disney Television: A Complete History* (New York: Hyperion, 1997), p. 133.
15. Economics Research Associates, 'Experimental Prototype Community of Tomorrow, Outline of Presentation, Department of Housing and Urban Development,' prepared for Walt Disney Productions, August 15, 1966, WDA, p. 13. See Disney's office inventory.

16. Walt Disney Productions, 'Disneyland Adds Greatest Attractions for Summer '67,' *News From Disneyland*, Disneyland Publicity Release, 1967, AHR, p. 1.

17. WED Enterprises, Inc., 'Tomorrowland, Carousel of Progress, Progress City-Tape,' p. 2.

18. Marvin Davis quoted in Anonymous, 'Disney Planned a City,' *SM/Sales Meetings*, July 1969, p. 86.

19. See Disneyland, Inc., 'Disneyland-Alweg Monorail System,' Press Release, 1960, AHR, p. 1.

20. The Imagineers, *Walt Disney Imagineering: A Behind the Dreams Look at Making the Magic Real* (New York: Hyperion, 1996), p. 116.

21. Bill Martin, interview by Author, July 6, 1998, transcript, pp. 10, 30.

22. Disneyland, Inc., 'Disneyland-Alweg Monorail System,' p. 1. See also Jack E. Janzen and Leon J. Janzen, 'Disneyland on Wheels … An Interview With Bob Gurr,' p. 34.

23. WED Transportation Systems, Inc., 'Mark IV Monorail,' brochure, c. 1982, AHR, n.p.

24. Walt Disney Productions, 'The Maintenance of Magic in the "Magic Kingdom,"' University of Disneyland booklet, c. 1969, AHR, p. 18.

25. John B. Willmann, *The Department of Housing and Urban Development* (New York: Frederick A. Praeger, c. 1967), p. 97.

26. Disneyland, Inc., 'Disneyland-Alweg Monorail System,' p. 2. Standing passengers would dramatically increase the number of paying passengers in a public transit setting. The theme park called for greater comfort.

27. John Hench, interview by author, December 18, 1997, transcript, p. 8. See also Harrison Price, interview by author, February 16, 1998, transcript, p. 10.

28. Walt Disney Productions, 'Project Florida/A Whole New Disney World,' p. 14.

29. Community Transportation Services, 'Community Transportation Services, A Division of Buena Vista Distribution, Subsidiary of Walt Disney Productions,' brochure, c. 1975, OPL, n.p. Also see WED Enterprises, Inc., 'Fact Sheet: New Tomorrowland – A World on the *Move*, Disneyland, 1967,' 1967, AHR, p. 6. See also WED Enterprises, Inc., 'Profile: PeopleMover and Omnimover, WEDway Transportation Systems, New Concepts in Transportation for High Density Traffic Flow Areas,' press release, c. 1967, AHR, p. 3.

30. Jack E. Janzen and Leon J. Janzen, 'Disneyland on Wheels … An Interview With Bob Gurr,' p. 35.

31. Bob Gurr, interview by author, January 25, 1999, transcript, p. 12.

32. Walt Disney Productions, 'Disneyland Adds Greatest Attractions for Summer '67,' p. 1.

33. Walt Disney Productions, 'Project Florida/A Whole New Disney World,' p. 14.

34.   WED Enterprises, Inc., 'Profile: PeopleMover and Omnimover, WEDway Transportation Systems, New Concepts in Transportation for High Density Traffic Flow Areas,' pp. 3, 7.

35.   Ibid., p. 2.

36.   Paul F. Anderson, 'A Great Big Beautiful Tomorrow: Walt Disney & World's Fairs,' p. 33.

37.   Carl Bongiorno, interview by author, February 9, 1999, transcript, pp. 21–2.

38.   Phillip Davis, 'Columbia, Maryland: Zero to 68,000 in 20 Years,' p. 6.

39.   John Hench, interview by author, December 18, 1997, transcript, p. 6.

40.   See Disney-Turner, 'A Joint Venture in Transportation Innovation,' brochure, c. 1982, AHR, n.p.

41.   Harrison Price, interview by author, February 6, 1998, transcript, p. 10.

42.   Victor Gruen, *The Heart of Our Cities*, pp. 253–4.

43.   Peter Hall, *Cities in Civilization*, pp. 964–5.

44.   See Vance Johnston, 'State Pledges Access Roads for Disney Plan,' *Tampa Tribune*, February 3, 1967, p. 1–D.

45.   De Leuw Cather & Company of Canada Ltd, Consulting Engineers, 'Interstate 4 and SR 530,' report submitted to Hart, Krivatsy, Stubee, Planning Consultants, July 2, 1968, OPL.

46.   In Year 1 of the study, the theme park appears, but EPCOT and the industrial park are absent. By Year 10, EPCOT has 10,000 residents, 2,500 employees, and 1,000 hotel units, while the industrial park has 10,000 employees. Finally, in Year 20, EPCOT has 25,000 residents, 10,000 employees, and 4,000 hotel units. The industrial park has 20,000 employees. Ibid., Exhibits 2, 4, 5.

47.   Raymond L. Watson, interview by author, November 6, 1998, transcript, p. 4.

48.   See the following item: 'Stockholm, The City on the Water,' Forlag Aktiebolager Grafisk Konst, n.d., WDA 480. Also see Disney's office inventory.

49.   Peter Calthorpe, *The Next American Metropolis: Ecology, Community, and the American Dream* (New York: Princeton Architectural Press, 1993), p. 56. For an analysis of Calthorpe's plan see Anthony Downs, *New Visions for Metropolitan America* (Washington, D.C. and Cambridge: The Brookings Institution and Lincoln Institute of Land Policy, 1994). For New Urbanism in general, see Peter Katz, *The New Urbanism: Toward an Architecture of Community* (New York: McGraw-Hill, Inc., 1994).

50.   Bob Gurr, interview by author, September 30, 1999, transcript, p. 1.

51.   Victor Gruen, *The Heart of Our Cities*, p. 69.

52.   Judith A. Adams, *The American Amusement Park Industry*, p. 100.

Chapter 3

1. Reedy Creek Improvement District, *EPCOT Building Code*, Twelfth Edition, c. 1996, Preface.
2. Peter Cook, ed., *Archigram*, p. 36.
3. Stewart Brand, *How Buildings Learn* (New York: Penguin Group, 1994), p. 221.
4. Economics Research Associates, 'Experimental Prototype Community of Tomorrow, Outline of Presentation, Department of Housing and Urban Development,' p. 13.
5. Karal Ann Marling, ed., *Designing Disney's Theme Parks*, p. 87.
6. In general, see Leonard Pitt and Dale Pitt, *Los Angeles A to Z: An Encyclopedia of City and County* (Berkeley: University of California Press, c. 1997). Joint venture architects Luckman, Pereira, and Paul R. Williams designed the LAX Theme Building (1961).
7. Welton Becket & Associates, 'Welton Becket and Associates, Architects, Engineers,' AFA, c. 1970, n.p.
8. Tom Moses, interview by author, January 15, 1999, notes, p. 6.
9. A.L. Putnam, 'Summary of Hydrologic Conditions and Effects of Walt Disney World Development in the Reedy Creek Improvement District, 1966–73,' prepared by the United States Geological Survey, Tallahassee, Florida, 1975, OPL, p. 4.
10. Economics Research Associates, 'Experimental Prototype Community of Tomorrow, Outline of Presentation, Department of Housing and Urban Development,' p. 16.
11. Walt Disney, *Florida Film – Final Script*, revised November 7, 1966, p. 3.
12. Robert Price Foster, 'The Founding of a Kingdom,' pp. 158–61.
13. Emily Bavar, 'Girl Reporter Convinced by Walt Disney,' *OS*, 81, 161, October 21, 1965, p. 1.
14. The 1967 publication 'Project Florida/A Whole New Disney World,' stated that the office buildings and hotel 'reach skyward through EPCOT's roof.' Walt Disney Productions, pp. 12–13.
15. Christopher Alexander, Sara Ishikawa and Murray Silverstein, et al., *A Pattern Language: Towns, Buildings, Construction* (New York: Oxford University Press, 1977), p. 1160.
16. Franco Borsi, *Architecture and Utopia* (Paris: Hazan, c. 1997), p. 165.
17. Victor Gruen, *The Heart of Our Cities*, p. 190.
18. Jon Jerde, interview by author, March 4, 1999, transcript, p. 14.
19. In general, see Martyn J. Anderson, ed., *The Jerde Partnership International: Visceral Reality* (Italy: l'Arca Edizioni, c. 1998). See also Robert Kramer, *Process: Architecture* (Tokyo: Process Architecture Co., Ltd., 1994), pp. 110–11.
20. Walt Disney, quoted in Norma Lee Browning, 'Magic Cities For Young,

Old Foreseen By Disney,' *OS*, November 24, 1966, p. 1. Originally published in the *Chicago Tribune*, October 25, 1966.

21. Victor Gruen, *The Heart of Our Cities*, p. 318.
22. Bob Thomas, *Walt Disney: An American Original*, p. 344.
23. See Rick West, ed., 'Walt Disney's Pirates of the Caribbean,' *Theme Park Adventure Magazine*, 1998.
24. Walt Disney Productions, 'Project Florida/A Whole New Disney World,' p. 13.
25. After the 1964–65 New York World's Fair, with construction half-completed, Disney ordered the work on New Orleans Square torn up and re-designed. This entailed excavation under retaining walls. The pirates' boat ride would take visitors below the berm. There is a small utilidor area located under New Orleans Square. This is the first such basement WED Enterprises constructed. See Don Edgren, interview by author, January 6, 1999, p. 8.
26. Victor Gruen, *The Heart of Our Cities*, p. 255.
27. Walt Disney Productions, 'Project Florida/A Whole New Disney World,' pp. 12–13.
28. Karal Ann Marling, ed., *Designing Disney's Theme Parks*, p. 161.
29. Walt Disney Productions, 'Project Florida/A Whole New Disney World,' pp. 15–16.
30. Marvin Davis quoted in Katherine Greene and Richard Greene, *The Man Behind the Magic: The Story of Walt Disney*, p. 158.
31. Florida Statutes, Senate Concurrent Resolution No. 10–X (67), Exhibit C, p. 80.
32. Marvin Davis, 'Typical Industrial Complex,' October 1966, Walt Disney Imagineering Collection.
33. Welton Becket & Associates, 'Welton Becket & Associates, Architects, Engineers,' n.p.
34. See Disney's office inventory, No. 268. Blueprints dated 1966.
35. Harrison Price, interview by author, February 16, 1998, transcript, p. 9.
36. Donn B. Tatum, correspondence to Robert E. Kintner, December 23, 1966, LBJ (HBJ College), attachment. This document concerns a request for college housing financing.
37. United States Steel Corporation, 'United States Steel to Construct First Two 'Theme Hotels,' in Walt Disney World,' Press Release, April 30, 1969, OPL, p. 1.
38. Dick Irvine, interview by Bob Thomas, April 24, 1973, transcript, WDA, p. 42.
39. Robert Tyler, interview by author, March 29, 1999, p. 3. Welton Becket & Associates constructed a two-story lab space in its building in Century City. This space resembled the one used by WED Enterprises. The firm used the space to help plan for five hotels to be developed around Bay Lake at Disney World.

40. Walt Disney World Co., 'Contemporary Hotel Paces Theme Resort Progress,' Press Release, 1967, OPL, pp. 1–2, 4.

41. United States Steel Corporation, 'United States Steel to Construct First Two "Theme Hotels," in Walt Disney World,' pp. 1–2. Three modules were stacked atop each other and set between structural supports. WED Enterprises asked Welton Becket & Associates to investigate unitized construction and other materials, including plastic and steel. Another benefit of selecting U.S. Steel Realty Development was financial participation. See Robert Tyler, interview by author, March 29, 1999, transcript, p. 1.

42. Walt Disney World Co., 'Gigantic Mural Sets Theme of Contemporary Resort's Concourse,' Press Release, c. 1971, OPL, p. 1.

43. Don Edgren, interview by author, January 6, 1999, transcript, p. 11.

44. Paul F. Anderson, 'A Great Big Beautiful Tomorrow: Walt Disney & World's Fairs,' p. 51. See also Gereon Zimmerman, 'Walt Disney: Giant at the Fair,' p. 23.

45. Don Edgren, interview by author, January 6, 1999, transcript, p. 11.

46. Paul F. Anderson, 'A Great Big Beautiful Tomorrow: Walt Disney & World's Fairs,' p. 70.

47. The show was projected on the interior surface of the dome. In Anaheim, the second floor of that carousel would be occupied by the Progress City model.

48. Jack E. Janzen and Leon J. Janzen, '"Another Kind of Reality": An Interview With John Hench,' p. 19.

49. Walt Disney quoted by Martin A. Sklar in Richard R. Beard, *Walt Disney's EPCOT Center: Creating the New World of Tomorrow* (New York: Harry N. Abrams, Inc., 1982), p. 13.

50. Welton Becket, interview by Richard G. Hubler, July 30, 1968, quoted in Paul F. Anderson, 'A Great Big Beautiful Tomorrow: Walt Disney & World's Fairs,' p. 69.

51. John Hench quoted in Jack E. Janzen and Leon J. Janzen, '"Another Kind of Reality": An Interview With John Hench,' p. 18.

52. Jack E. Janzen, 'The Monsanto House of the Future: Putting the "Tomorrow" in Tomorrowland … ,' *TET*, 12, Winter 1991–92, p. 14.

53. Alan Hess, 'Monsanto House of the Future,' *Fine Homebuilding*, August–September 1986, p. 70.

54. Monsanto Chemical Company, 'Monsanto House of the Future: an Experimental Design Demonstrating Structural Applications of Plastics,' brochure, c. 1958, AHR, n.p.

55. Disneyland, Inc., 'Disneyland Diary,' 1957. The attraction was called the Monsanto Home in the early years and was changed to Monsanto House later.

56. Walt Disney quoted in Dave Smith, ed., *Walt Disney: Famous Quotes*, p. 62. Also see, Elvis Lane, 'Disney Tells of $100 Million Project,' p. 1.

57. Monsanto Chemical Company, 'Monsanto House of the Future: an Experimental Design Demonstrating Structural Applications of Plastics,' n.p.
58. Alan Hess, 'Monsanto House of the Future,' p. 72.
59. John Hench quoted in Jack E. Janzen and Leon J. Janzen, '"Another Kind of Reality": An Interview With John Hench,' p. 16.
60. Jack E. Janzen, 'The Monsanto House of the Future: Putting the "Tomorrow" in Tomorrowland … ,' p. 15. Also see Monsanto Chemical Company, 'Monsanto House of the Future: an Experimental Design Demonstrating Structural Applications of Plastics,' n.p.
61. Alan Hess, 'Monsanto House of the Future,' p. 75.
62. WED Enterprises, Inc., 'Edison Square, Disneyland, U.S.A.,' n.p.
63. E. Cardon Walker, interview by author, October 14, 1999, tape.
64. Diane Disney Miller, 'My Dad Walt Disney,' November 17, 1956, p. 130.
65. Walt Disney Productions, 'Crane in Disneyland,' brochure, no date, AHR, n.p.
66. See Disneyland, Inc., 'Disneyland: A Complete Guide to Adventureland, Tomorrowland, Fantasyland, Frontierland, Main Street,' paper, c. 1956, AHR N2046. Also featured was a 'bathroom in miniature.'
67. See Karal Ann Marling, ed., *Designing Disney's Theme Parks*, p. 151.
68. Charlie Haas, 'Disneyland is Good For You,' p. 17.
69. Susan Schindehette, Vicki Sheff-Cahan and Karen Grigsby Bates, 'Growing Up Disney,' *People*, 50, 23, December 21, 1998, p. 56. Disney made frequent visits, corrected site lines, changed paint colors.
70. Morgan 'Bill' Evans, interview by author, June 27, 1998, transcript, p. 16.
71. Don Edgren, interview by author, January 6, 1999, transcript, p. 1.
72. Martin A. Sklar, *Walt Disney's Disneyland* (Burbank: Walt Disney Productions, c. 1969), n.p.
73. Randy Bright, *Disneyland: Inside Story*, p. 116.
74. Karal Ann Marling, ed., *Designing Disney's Theme Parks*, p. 29.
75. Rudy Lord quoted in The Imagineers, *Walt Disney Imagineering*, p. 100.
76. John Hench quoted in Charlie Haas, 'Disneyland is Good for You,' p. 17.
77. Ibid.
78. Frank Thomas and Ollie Johnston, *Disney Animation: The Illusion of Life* (New York: Abbeville Press, c. 1981), p. 13.
79. Seymour J. Mandelbaum, 'Open Moral Communities,' in Seymour L. Mandelbaum, Luigi Mazza, and Robert W. Burchell, eds., *Explorations in Planning Theory* (New Brunswick: Center For Urban Policy Research, 1996), p. 83.
80. Ward Kimball, interview by author, December 15, 1998, transcript, p. 12.

81. Bob Thomas, *Building a Company*, p. 132.
82. Ward Kimball, interview by author, December 15, 1998, transcript, p. 12.
83. Walt Disney Productions, 'The Walt Disney Studio,' p. 8. See also The Walt Disney Company, 'The Walt Disney Studios: Facilities, Production & Post Production Services,' booklet, c. 1992, AHR. Also see The Walt Disney Studios, 'The Walt Disney Studios: 50 Magical Years in Burbank, 1940–1990,' brochure, 1990, AHR. For a glimpse into the new studios, see the film *The Reluctant Dragon* (1941).
84. Walt Disney Productions, 'The Walt Disney Studio,' p. 10. The Animation Building was one of the first major buildings to be air conditioned in Southern California.
85. David R. Smith, 'Disney Before Burbank: The Kingswell and Hyperion Studios,' *Funnyworld*, 20, Summer 1979, p. 37.
86. Walt Disney Productions, 'First Amendment to Registration Statement, Form A-2, Securities and Exchange Commission,' March 1940, AHR, p. 1. This figure may not include buildings moved to the Burbank location.
87. Bob Thomas, *Building a Company*, p. 54.
88. Ibid., pp. 125–6.
89. Steve Proffitt, 'Jane Jacobs: Still Challenging the Way We Think About Cities,' *LAT*, October 12, 1997, p. M3.
90. Stewart Brand, *How Buildings Learn*, p. 194.
91. Ibid., p. 213.

Chapter 4

1. Howard P. Segal, *Technological Utopianism in American Culture* (Chicago: University of Chicago Press, 1985), p. 10.
2. Robert Price Foster, 'The Founding of a Kingdom,' p. 7. See also Harrison Price, interview by author, February 16, 1998, transcript, p. 4.
3. Anonymous, 'Disney Land Purchase Story Reads Like Bond Thriller,' *OS*, 81, 187, November 16, 1965, p. 2–A. For a useful summary of the land acquisition process, see Leonard E. Zehnder, *Florida's Disney World* (Tallahassee: The Peninsular Publishing Company, c. 1975), OPL.
4. Hammer and Company Associates, 'Current and Projected Economy of East Central Florida,' prepared for East Central Florida Regional Planning Council, May 1965, OPL, pp. iv, v.
5. Edward L. Prizer, 'The Disney Decade,' *Orlando Magazine*, 35, 12, October 1981, p. 31. See also Franklin A. Baumann, 'Disney World: A Modern Feudal Kingdom?,' M.A. Thesis, Department of Geography, University of Florida, 1973, OPL, p. 97.

6. Phil Smith, interview by author, April 2, 1999, transcript, p. 6. See also E. Cardon Walker, interview by author, September 10, 1999, tape.
7. Phil Smith, interview by author, April 2, 1999, transcript, p. 6. In 1975, 1,100 acres of the City of Bay Lake (where the EPCOT site is located) were in use for cattle production. See Arthur C. Bravo, 'Environmental Systems at Walt Disney World,' *Journal of the Environmental Engineering Division*, ASCE, 101, EEG, p. 887. See also Tom Moses, interview by author, January 15, 1999, transcript, p. 6. Also see Reedy Creek Improvement District, 'Comprehensive Plan, Data and Analysis and Adoption Documents, As Amended Through Amendment 97–1,' printed September 1998, Figures 2–7.
8. Anonymous, 'Building a Disney Dream,' *Industry Week*, 205, 4, May 26, 1980, p. 59. See also Tishman Realty and Construction Co., Inc., 'Walt Disney World EPCOT Center,' *ENR*, special advertising section, November 25, 1982, n.p.
9. Jack E. Janzen and Leon J. Janzen, 'Planning the First Disney Parks … A Talk With Marvin Davis,' p. 16.
10. Elvis Lane, 'Disney Tells of $100 Million Project,' p. 16–A.
11. Spessard Holland to Lyndon B. Johnson, telephone conversation, March 25, 1964, tape, LBJ, No. 2650. See also Robert C. Weaver, Memorandum to Bill Moyers, February 7, 1964, LBJ, Box 18.
12. Walt Disney quoted in Norma Lee Browning, 'Magic Cities For Young, Old Foreseen by Disney,' p. 1.
13. Harrison Price, interview by author, December 17, 1998, transcript, p. 2. On the West Coast, Disney and ERA considered involvement in a large planned project to be developed on the Del Monte Ranch near Monterey, California.
14. Robert Price Foster, 'The Founding of a Kingdom,' p. 29.
15. Bob Thomas, *Building a Company*, p. 277.
16. Robert Price Foster, 'The Founding of a Kingdom,' pp. 247–52.
17. Anonymous, 'Huge Tract Completed: $1.5 Million Paid in Big Land Deal,' *OS*, 80, 356, May 4, 1965, p. 1. See also Anonymous, 'Mystery Industry Land Buying Tops $5 Million: 47 Deals Detailed by Broker,' *OES*, 89, 124, May 28, 1965, p. 1.
18. Anonymous, 'Huge Tract Completed: $1.5 Million Paid in Big Land Deal,' p. 1. The larger transaction, 8,380 acres was recorded by Paul Helliwell on May 3, 1965, with a tax stamp value of $900,000. The seller was Bronsons, Inc. The article mentions 'rumors' that the buyer would build a large industrial complex.
19. Anonymous, 'Mystery Industry Land Buying Tops $5 Million: 47 Deals Detailed by Broker,' p. 1.
20. Ken Klug, interview by author, January 20, 1999, transcript, p. 3.
21. Anonymous, 'We KNOW We'll Get It, But We Don't Know WHAT,' *OS*, 81, 10, May 23, 1965, p. 1. Also see H. Bailey Thomson, 'Martin

Andersen and the Rise of Modern Orlando,' Ph.D. dissertation, University of Alabama, 1994.

22. Anonymous, '"Mystery" Site Deal Completed,' *OS*, 81, 43, June 25, 1965, p. 1.

23. Anonymous, 'How Our Mystery Grew,' *OS*, 81, 164, October 24, 1965, p. 20–A.

24. See Roy O. Disney letter in Walt Disney Productions, 'Annual Report to Shareholders and Employees, Fiscal Year October 2, 1965,' audited by Price Waterhouse, n.p. Also see Sources and Uses. This figure is based on the fiscal year.

25. Thomas Murray, 'The Men Who Followed Mickey Mouse: Walt Disney Productions is Blazing New Trails of Growth,' *Dun's Review*, December 1969, p. 38.

26. Emily Bavar, 'Girl Reporter Convinced by Walt Disney,' p. 1.

27. Ibid. See also Emily Bavar, 'Mystery Site Left Up in Air: Disney Hedges Big Question,' *OS*, 81, 157, October 17, 1965, p. 1.

28. Anonymous, 'We Say: "Mystery" Industry Is Disney,' *OS*, 81, 164, October 24, 1965, p. 1.

29. Donn B. Tatum, correspondence to Robert E. Kintner, December 23, 1966, LBJ, HS 1 College, p. 1.

30. Harrison A. Price, William M. Stewart, and Redford C. Rollins, 'An Analysis of Location Factors for Disneyland,' prepared for Walt Disney Productions, August 28, 1953, by Stanford Research Institute, AHR, Appendix C. The first site was located at Harbor Boulevard and Interstate 5.

31. Ramon G. McLeod, 'A Marriage of Convenience,' p. C11.

32. David R. Smith, 'Disney Before Burbank: The Kingswell and Hyperion Studios,' pp. 34–5.

33. Walt Disney Productions, 'The Walt Disney Studio,' p. 2. Also see David R. Smith, 'Disney Before Burbank: The Kingswell and Hyperion Studios,' p. 38.

34. Joe Fowler, interview by Richard Hubler, July 23, 1968, transcript, WDA, pp. 10–11.

35. Don Edgren, interview by author, January 6, 1999, transcript, p. 26.

36. Franklin A. Baumann, 'Disney World: A Modern Feudal Kingdom?,' p. 92.

37. Anonymous, 'Delicate Hydraulics Keep Mickey Mouse's Feet Dry,' *ENR*, 188, 4, January 27, 1972, p. 25.

38. Franklin A. Baumann, 'Disney World: A Modern Feudal Kingdom?,' p. 60.

39. A.L. Putnam, 'Summary of Hydrologic Conditions and Effects of Walt Disney World Development in the Reedy Creek Improvement District, 1966–73,' p. 3.

40. Tom Jones, interview by author, January 7, 1999, transcript, pp. 5, 9.

41. Anonymous, 'Disney Clearing Starts,' *OS*, 81, 169, October 29, 1965, p. 1.
42. Gee and Jenson, 'Plan of Reclamation for Reedy Creek Drainage District,' report, June 1966, WDA. See Disney's office inventory. See also Bob Bobroff, '$8.4 Million Disney Area Proposal Studied,' *OS*, 82, 91, August 12, 1966, p. 1–C.
43. Ken Klug, interview by author, January 20, 1999, transcript, p. 6.
44. Anonymous, 'Delicate Hydraulics Keep Mickey Mouse's Feet Dry,' p. 25.
45. Economics Research Associates, 'Experimental Prototype Community of Tomorrow, Outline of Presentation, Department of Housing and Urban Development,' p. 13.
46. Anonymous, 'Delicate Hydraulics Keep Mickey Mouse's Feet Dry,' p. 58.
47. Franklin A. Baumann, 'Disney World: A Modern Feudal Kingdom?,' p. 59.
48. Tishman Realty & Construction Co., Inc., 'Walt Disney World EPCOT Center,' n.p.
49. John Hench, interview by author, December 18, 1997, transcript, p. 9.
50. Ken Klug, interview by author, January 20, 1999, transcript, p. 8.
51. Don Edgren, interview by author, January 6, 1999, transcript, p. 10
52. Marty Sklar quoted in Jack E. Janzen and Leon J. Janzen, 'Imagineering and the Disney Image … an Interview With Marty Sklar,' p. 15.
53. John Hench, interview by author, December 18, 1997, transcript, p. 10.
54. Walt Disney Productions, 'Project Florida/A Whole New Disney World,' p. 16.
55. Bill Martin quoted in Jack E. Janzen and Leon J. Janzen, 'Disneyland Art Director … Bill Martin,' p. 17.
56. Robert Tyler, interview by author, March 29, 1999, transcript, p. 5. See also Walt Disney Productions, 'Preview Edition of Walt Disney World,' paper, c. 1970, OPL, p. 21.
57. Anonymous, 'Disney Planned a City,' p. 89.
58. Donn Tatum quoted in Walt Disney World Co., 'The Story of Walt Disney World,' Commemorative Edition, c. 1971, OPL, p. 15.
59. Tom Moses, interview by author, January 15, 1999, notes, p. 6.
60. Marvin Davis quoted in Jack E. Janzen and Leon J. Janzen, 'Planning the First Disney Parks … A Talk With Marvin Davis,' p. 16.
61. John Hench quoted in Jack E. Janzen and Leon J. Janzen, '"Another Kind of Reality": An Interview With John Hench,' p. 18.
62. E. Cardon Walker, interview by author, September 10, 1999, tape.
63. Walt Disney quoted in Dave Smith, ed., *Walt Disney: Famous Quotes*, p. 11.
64. Wathel Rogers quoted in Robert De Roos, 'The Magic Worlds of Walt Disney,' *National Geographic*, August 1963, p. 207.

65. John Hench, interview by author, December 18, 1997, transcript, p. 7.

66. Robert B. Sherman and Richard M. Sherman, *Walt's Time: From Be-fore to Beyond* (Santa Clarita: Camphor Tree Publishers, 1998), p. 34.

67. WED Enterprises, Inc., 'Tomorrowland, Carousel of Progress,' Narra-tion-Tape, script.

68. Walt Disney quoted in Dave Smith, ed., *Walt Disney: Famous Quotes*, p. 47.

69. Richard Shale, *Donald Duck Joins Up: The Walt Disney Studio During World War II* (Ann Arbor: UMI Research Press, c. 1982), Appendices B and C.

70. Ernst Stuhlinger and Frederick I. Ordway, III, *Wernher von Braun, Crusader for Space: A Biographical Memoir* (Malabar: Krieger Pub-lishing Company, 1994), p. 115.

71. Ward Kimball, interview by author, December 15, 1998, transcript, p. 3.

72. Ernst Stuhlinger and Frederick I. Ordway, III, *Wernher von Braun, Crusader for Space*, p. 116.

73. Marty Sklar quoted in Jack E. Janzen and Leon J. Janzen, 'Imagineering and the Disney Image … an Interview With Marty Sklar,' p. 13.

74. Eugene M. 'Gene' Poirot, *Our Margin of Life* (New York: Vantage Press, 1964). See Disney's office inventory.

75. Carl Bongiorno, interview by author, February 9, 1999, transcript, p. 10.

Chapter 5

1. Charles W. Moore, William J. Mitchell, and William Turnbull, Jr., *The Poetics of Gardens* (Cambridge: MIT Press, c. 1988).

2. WED Enterprises, Inc., 'Tomorrowland, Carousel of Progress, Progress City-Tape,' script, n.p.

3. Jack E. Janzen, 'The Monsanto Home of the Future … Putting the Tomorrow in Tomorrowland,' *TET*, 12, Winter 1991–92, p. 15.

4. Martin A. Sklar, *Walt Disney's Disneyland*, n.p.

5. McKeever, J. Ross, ed., *The Community Builders Handbook* (Wash-ington, D.C.: Urban Land Institute, 1968), p. 172.

6. Bookout, Lloyd W. et al., *Residential Development Handbook* (Wash-ington, D.C.: Urban Land Institute, 1990), pp. 231–49.

7. Christopher Alexander, et al., *A Pattern Language*, p. 136.

8. Morgan 'Bill' Evans quoted in Jack E. Janzen and Leon J. Janzen, 'Creating the Disney Landscape: An Interview With Bill Evans,' *TET*, Spring 1996, p. 4.

9. Morgan 'Bill' Evans, interview by author, June 27, 1998, transcript, pp. 11–12. See also Anonymous, 'A Gardener's Visit to Disneyland,' *Sunset*, 126, 3, March 1961, pp. 100–101.

10. Morgan 'Bill' Evans, interview by author, June 27, 1998, transcript, p. 11.
11. Karal Ann Marling, ed., *Designing Disney's Theme Parks*, p. 105. Many Jungle Cruise and Disneyland trees were saved from the 'jaws' of bulldozers in 1954–1955. Evans had contacts inside the California Department of Transportation and purchased trees in the path of the expanding freeway system for $25 apiece. See Morgan 'Bill' Evans, interview by author, June 27, 1998, transcript, p. 67.
12. Disneyland, Inc., 'Disneyland Dimensions and 1995 Fact Sheet,' Press Release, 1995, AHR, p. 2.
13. Morgan 'Bill' Evans quoted in Jack E. Janzen and Leon J. Janzen, 'Creating the Disney Landscape ... ,' p. 8.
14. Morgan 'Bill' Evans, interview by author, June 27, 1998, transcript, p. 21.
15. Ibid., p. 3.
16. Ibid., p. 72.
17. See Dee Hansford, *Gardens of The Walt Disney World Resort* (Burbank: The Walt Disney Company, c. 1988), OPL. Also see Robert H. Stamps and Loretta N. Satterthwaite, eds., *Common Native Plants of Central Florida* (Jacksonville: Florida Native Plant Society, c. 1994), OPL.
18. Morgan 'Bill' Evans, interview by author, June 27, 1998, transcript, p. 15.
19. Anne Whiston Spirn, *The Language of Landscape* (New Haven: Yale University Press, 1998), p. 225.

Chapter 6

1. William Pereira quoted in Lawrence S. Martz, 'The Wide World of Walt Disney,' *Newsweek*, 60, 27, December 31, 1962, p. 49.
2. Harrison Price, interview by author, December 17, 1998, transcript, p. 4.
3. Ibid., p. 5.
4. Economics Research Associates, 'The Economic Impact of the Disneyland Recreation Complex on the City of Anaheim,' p. 8.
5. Economics Research Associates, 'Economic Impact of Disneyworld, Florida,' prepared for Walt Disney Productions, January 20, 1967, FSA, Series 697, Carton 3, p. I-2.
6. Harrison Price, interview by author, February 16, 1998, transcript, p. 6.
7. Card Walker, 'Walt Disney World: Master Planning for the Future,' speech to the Urban Land Institute, October 5, 1976, WDA, p. 2. See also Tom Jones, interview by author, January 7, 1999, transcript, p. 2.
8. Harrison Price, interview by author, February 16, 1998, transcript, p. 11.

9.   Richard Peiser and Soumyajit Mukherjee, 'Interview: Raymond Watson,' *Lusk Review*, IV, 1, Spring/Summer 1998, p. 38.
10. Raymond L. Watson, interview by author, November 6, 1998, transcript, p. 2.
11. Harrison Price, interview by author, December 17, 1998, transcript, p. 6.
12. Raymond L. Watson, interview by author, November 6, 1998, transcript, p. 2.
13. Ibid.
14. Economics Research Associates, 'Economic Impact of Disneyworld, Florida,' p. I-3.
15. Ibid.
16. Economics Research Associates, 'Project Florida Planning Manual,' p. VII-13.
17. Phillip Davis, 'Columbia, Maryland: Zero to 68,000 in 20 Years,' p. 2.
18. Economics Research Associates, 'Project Florida Planning Manual,' p. VII-13.
19. Real Estate Research Corporation, *Economic and Financial Feasibility Models for New Community Development*, prepared for the Office of New Communities, Department of Housing and Urban Development, August 1971, p. 16.
20. Economics Research Associates, 'Project Florida Planning Manual,' pp. VIII-5, VIII-7.
21. Ibid., p. IV-21.
22. Richard J. Roddewig, Steven P. Schiltz and Gary Papke, 'Appraising Theme Parks,' p. 99.
23. This estimate is based on total retail sales less 65 percent for operating expenses and a conservative range of capitalization rates.
24. Economics Research Associates, 'Project Florida Planning Manual,' p. VII-5. Compare with Urban Land Institute, *The Dollars and Cents of Shopping Centers: A Study of Receipts and Expenses* (Washington, D.C.: Urban Land Institute, 1966), ULI Archives, p. 68.
25. Marvin Davis quoted in Jack E. Janzen and Leon J. Janzen, 'Planning the First Disney Parks ... A Talk With Marvin Davis,' p. 16.
26. Raymond L. Watson, interview by author, November 6, 1998, transcript, p. 3.
27. John McDonald, 'Now the Bankers Come to Disney,' *Fortune*, 73, 5, May 1966.
28. John Hench, interview by author, December 18, 1997, transcript, p. 20.
29. Steven Watts, *The Magic Kingdom*, p. 157.
30. Walt Disney Productions, First Amendment to Registration Statement, Form A-2, Securities and Exchange Commission, March 1940, Exhibit A-2.
31. Randy Bright, *Disneyland: Inside Story*, p. 89.

32. Disneyland, Inc., 'Disneyland Data,' report prepared by Lessee Relations Division, June 1961, AHR, pp. 7–8.

33. Joanne Potter-Heine, interview by author, March 31, 1999, transcript, p. 8. Representative companies at the fair include: American Express Co., National Cash Register Co., RCA, Equitable Life Assurance Society, IBM, Coca-Cola, Dupont, AT&T, S.C. Johnson & Son, Inc., Eastman Kodak Co., General Motors Corp., and U.S. Steel. See Gereon Zimmermann, 'Walt Disney: Giant at the Fair,' p. 85.

34. Marty Sklar quoted in Christopher Finch, *The Art of Walt Disney* (New York: Harry N. Abrams, Inc., 1995), p. 423.

35. See Jack E. Janzen and Leon J. Janzen, 'Tomorrowland 1967,' *TET*, No. 17, Winter 1993–1994, p. 6.

36. Bob Gurr, interview by author, January 25, 1999, transcript, p. 16.

37. Ibid., p. 17.

38. E. Cardon Walker, interview by author, April 6, 1999, transcript, p. 2.

39. Bob Gurr, interview by author, January 25, 1999, transcript, p. 2.

40. Ibid., p. 17.

41. Bob Gurr quoted in Jack E. Janzen and Leon J. Janzen, 'Disneyland on Wheels … An Interview With Bob Gurr,' p. 38.

42. Major General William E. Potter, USA, Retired, interview by Dr. Martin Reuss, Historical Division, Office of the Chief of Engineers, p. 188.

43. Walt Disney Productions, 'Annual Report to Shareholders and Employees, Fiscal Year Ended October 1, 1966,' audited by Price Waterhouse, p. 24.

44. General Joe Potter quoted in Anthony Haden-Guest, *The Paradise Program*, p. 297.

45. Major General William E. Potter, USA, Retired, interview by Dr. Martin Reuss, Historical Division, Office of the Chief of Engineers, p. 188.

46. William E. Potter, 'Walt Disney World: A Venture in Community Planning & Development,' March 1972, p. 31.

47. General Joe Potter quoted in Anthony Haden-Guest, *The Paradise Program*, p. 297.

48. John P. Evans, correspondence to Max E. Wettstein, May 17, 1966, FSA, Series 131, Carton 18.

49. John Hench, interview by author, December 18, 1997, transcript, p. 20.

50. Jim Hampton, 'All Smiles at the Gaylord Palms; What Walt Wanted,' *Orlando Business Journal*, December 14, 2001, p. 1.

51. Anonymous, 'Disneyworld Amusement Center With Domed City Set For Florida,' p. 38. In this *NYT* article, the cost of the city is estimated at $75 million by Roy O. Disney. Also see Anonymous, 'Disney World Price Tag Now Reads $600 Million,' p. 1. See also Walt Disney Productions, 'Walt Disney Productions Announces Plans for a Whole

New 'Disney World' Development Near Orlando, Florida,' Press Release, February 2, 1967, OPL, p. 2.

52. Carl Bongiorno, interview by author, February 9, 1999, transcript, p. 10. See also Harrison Price, interview by author, February 16, 1998, transcript, p. 15. Economics Research Associates did estimate construction costs for selected structures in the 'Project Florida Planning Manual.'

53. Card Walker, 'Walt Disney World: Master Planning for the Future,' p. 2.

54. Roy O. Disney quoted in Don Rider, 'Florida's Disney World Unveiled," p. 1.

55. Marvin Davis quoted in Jack E. Janzen and Leon J. Janzen, 'Planning the First Disney Parks ... A Talk With Marvin Davis,' p. 17.

56. Economics Research Associates, 'Project Florida Planning Manual,' Table I.

57. Harrison Price, interview by author, February 16, 1998, transcript, p. 11.

58. Harrison Price, interview by author, December 17, 1998, transcript, p. 3.

59. John A. Andrew, III, *Lyndon Johnson and the Great Society* (Chicago: Ivan R. Dee, Inc., 1998), p. 135. See also Irving Bernstein, *Guns or Butter: The Presidency of Lyndon Johnson* (New York and Oxford: Oxford University Press, 1996).

60. *United States Code*, Public Law 89–754, Section 101(a)(2).

61. Ibid., Sections 204(a)(1) (regional), 208(8) (special district), 204(a)(2) (unit of general local government).

62. Claude Kirk, correspondence to Roy Disney, May 3, 1968, FSA, Series 923, Carton 31.

63. Ibid. By the end of 1966, Donn Tatum was working to obtain a college housing loan on behalf of the Disney Foundation through HUD for CalArts. See Donn B. Tatum, correspondence to Robert E. Kintner, December 23, 1966, LBJ, HS1 College, p. 1.

64. John Hench, interview by author, December 18, 1997, transcript, p. 19.

65. Carl Bongiorno, interview by author, February 9, 1999, transcript, pp. 18–19.

66. Walt Disney Productions, 'Annual Report to Shareholders and Employees, Fiscal Year Ended September 30, 1961,' audited by Price Waterhouse, n.p. See also Walt Disney Productions, 'Annual Report to Shareholders and Employees, Fiscal Year Ended October 1, 1966,' audited by Price Waterhouse, n.p.

67. John McDonald, 'Now the Bankers Come to Disney,' p. 139.

68. Walt Disney Productions, 'Disneyland Adds Greatest Attractions for Summer '67,' p. 4.

Chapter 7

1. Disneyland, Inc., 'First Annual Report to Disneyland Lessees,' Public Relations Division, April 1956, AHR.
2. Harrison Price, interview by author, October 14, 1999, tape.
3. Marty Sklar quoted in Jack E. Janzen and Leon J. Janzen, 'Imagineering and the Disney Image ... an Interview With Marty Sklar,' p. 6.
4. Marty Sklar quoted in Jean Lee, 'Marty Sklar: Promoting Walt's Dreams With Imagination,' *Disney Magazine*, 30, 3, June, July, August, 1995, AHR, pp. 51–2.
5. Anonymous, 'It's Official: This is Disney's Land,' *OS*, 81, 166, October 26, 1965, p. 1.
6. Anonymous, 'Walt Disney to Wave His Magic Wand Over Us,' *OS*, 81, 164, October 24, 1966.
7. Elvis Lane, 'Disney Tells of $100 Million Project,' p. 16–A. See also Anonymous, 'Recreation: Disneyland East,' *Newsweek*, November 29, 1965, p. 82. Also see Walt Disney, Haydon Burns, and Roy O. Disney, Press Conference, November 15, 1965, videotape, FSA. Also of interest is WFTV (ABC), 'Disney Plans to be Revealed by TV Pool Coverage,' Press Release, November 10, 1965, FSA, Series 131, Carton 18. Also refer to Walt Disney Productions, 'Walt Disney Outlines Preliminary Concepts for His "Disney World" Community Near Orlando Fla.,' Press Release, November 15, 1965, FSA, Series 131, Carton 18.
8. Elvis Lane, 'Disney Tells of $100 Million Project,' p. 16–A. See also Jack E. Janzen and Leon J. Janzen, 'Imagineering and the Disney Image ... an Interview With Marty Sklar,' p. 8.
9. Don Rider, 'Florida's Disney World Unveiled,' p. 1.
10. Stan Roberts, 'Top Financial Men Here,' *OS*, 82, 26, February 3, 1967, p. 4. Walt Disney Productions, 'Walt Disney Productions Announces Plans for a Whole New "Disney World," Development Near Orlando, Florida,' p. 5.
11. Walt Disney Productions, 'Walt Disney Productions Announces Plans for a Whole New "Disney World," Development Near Orlando, Florida,' p. 5.
12. Marty Sklar quoted in Jack E. Janzen and Leon J. Janzen, 'Imagineering and the Disney Image ... an Interview With Marty Sklar,' p. 12.

Chapter 8

1. *Florida Statutes*, Chapter 67–764, House Bill No. 486, Reedy Creek Improvement District, p. 5. The Disney organization legislation was divided into three acts. The other two acts created the municipalities.
2. *Florida Statutes*, Chapter 67–764, p. 5.

3. Prior to passage of the district legislation, the state Circuit Court approved formation of the Reedy Creek Drainage District for the Disney organization property in May 1966. See *Florida Statutes*, Chapter 67–764, Section 1. The RCID legislation ratifies the Reedy Creek Drainage District but alters its name and boundaries.
4. Helliwell, Melrose and DeWolf, 'Memo on the Establishment of Special Taxing Districts and Municipalities on the Walt Disney Productions Property,' with map, May 23, 1966, WDA. See Disney's office inventory.
5. Robert Foster, interview by author, April 23, 1999, transcript, p. 11.
6. Ibid., p. 12.
7. *Florida Statutes*, Chapter 67–764, Section 9.16.
8. Ibid., Section 9.17.
9. Ibid., Section 9.20.
10. Advisory Commission on Intergovernmental Relations, *The Problem of Special Districts in American Government*, Commission Report, Washington, D.C., May 1964.
11. *Florida Statutes*, Chapter 67–764, Section 1.
12. Tom Moses, interview by author, January 15, 1999, notes, p. 2.
13. Robert Foster, interview by author, April 23, 1999, transcript, p. 4.
14. William E. Potter, 'Walt Disney World: A Venture in Community Planning & Development,' p. 31.
15. Advisory Commission on Intergovernmental Relations, *The Problem of Special Districts in American Government*, p. 8.
16. Judith A. Adams, *The American Amusement Park Industry*, p. 139. Walt Disney Company security works in conjunction with the sheriff. Only the sheriff can make arrests.
17. *Florida Statutes*, Chapter 67–764, Section 10.2.
18. Ibid., Section 9.3.
19. Ibid., Section 1.
20. Ibid., Section 9.5.
21. Ibid., Section 9.11.
22. Ibid., Section 1.
23. Ibid., Section 23.
24. Ibid., Section 1.
25. Ibid., Section 30 (liens), Section 31 (foreclosure of liens).
26. Ibid., Preamble, p. 2.
27. Ibid., Section 9.7.
28. Ibid., Section 9.10.
29. Ibid., Section 18.3.
30. Ibid., Section 33.1. Not to exceed 50 percent of the assessed valuation of the taxable property within the district. Requires a vote of the landowners.
31. Ibid., Section 34.1. No limit to amount. Not secured by taxes or full faith and credit. No election of landowners required.

32. Ibid., Section 35. No limit to amount. Not secured by taxes or full faith and credit. No election of landowners required.
33. Ibid., Section 40. Notice and hearing process.
34. Ibid., Section 41.
35. Ibid., Section 43.
36. Critics point out that the few full-time residents on the district property are sympathetic to the landowner and often employees. For example, see Stephen M. Fjellman, *Vinyl Leaves: Walt Disney World and America* (Boulder and Oxford: Westview Press, Inc., c. 1992), pp. 12, 121.
37. See Reedy Creek Improvement District, 'Comprehensive Plan, Data and Analysis and Adoption Documents, As Amended Through Amendment 97–1,' p. 8–2.
38. Robert Foster, interview by author, April 23, 1999, transcript, p. 17.
39. *Florida Statutes*, Chapter 67–1104, Section 3.
40. Ibid., Section 5(12).
41. Ibid., Section 5(15).
42. Ibid., Section 5(29).
43. Ibid., Section 5(30).
44. Ibid., Section 7.
45. Ibid., Section 12(2).
46. Harrison Price, interview by author, December 17, 1998, transcript, p. 4.
47. Robert G. Smith, *Public Authorities, Special Districts and Local Government* (Washington, D.C.: National Association of Counties Research Foundation, c. 1964), pp. ix, 196.
48. Advisory Commission on Intergovernmental Relations, *The Problem of Special Districts in American Government*, p. 2.
49. Tom Moses, interview by author, January 15, 1999, notes, pp. 4–5.
50. Economics Research Associates, 'Experimental Prototype Community of Tomorrow, Outline of Presentation, Department of Housing and Urban Development,' p. 22. For context, see Mary McLean, ed., *Local Planning Administration* (Chicago: The International City Managers' Association, 1959).
51. *Florida Statutes*, Chapter 67–764, Section 23.7(b).
52. Ibid., Section 23.2. Some of the current regulations are found in Reedy Creek Improvement District, 'Reedy Creek Improvement District, Land Development Regulations,' amended December 1997.
53. Reedy Creek Improvement District, *EPCOT Building Code*, Preface.
54. Marty Sklar quoted in Christopher Finch, *The Art of Walt Disney*, p. 406.
55. Tom Moses, interview by author, January 15, 1999, notes, p. 3.
56. Stephen M. Fjellman, *Vinyl Leaves*, p. 118.
57. Kenneth T. Jackson, *Crabgrass Frontier: The Suburbanization of the United States* (New York and Oxford: Oxford University Press, c. 1985), p. 300.

58. Randy Bright, *Disneyland: Inside Story*, p. 68.
59. Disneyland, Inc., 'Walt Disney Presents Views on High-Rise Proposal,' Press Release, 1964, AHR, p. 3.
60. Ramon G. McLeod, 'A Marriage of Convenience,' pp. C1, C11. The ordinance provided for pre-construction balloon tests with Disneyland personnel in attendance to determine if the proposed building would be visible from inside the park.
61. Bob Gurr quoted in Jack E. Janzen and Leon J. Janzen, 'Disneyland on Wheels … An Interview With Bob Gurr,' pp. 36–7.
62. *Florida Statutes*, Chapter 67–764, Section 23.8(b).
63. *United States Code*, Public Law 89–754, Section 201(a).
64. Economics Research Associates, 'Experimental Prototype Community of Tomorrow, Outline of Presentation, Department of Housing and Urban Development,' p. 3.
65. Richard Lacayo, 'The Brawl Over Sprawl,' *Time*, 153, 11, March 22, 1999, p. 48.
66. Robert Foster, interview by author, April 23, 1999, transcript, p. 20.
67. Raymond L. Watson, interview by author, November 6, 1998, transcript, p. 3.
68. Walt Disney quoted in Dave Smith, ed., *Walt Disney Famous Quotes*, p. 27.
69. Paul Goldberger, 'Mickey Mouse Teaches the Architects,' *NYT*, magazine, 122, 41,910, October 22, 1972, p. 93.
70. Norma Lee Browning, 'Magic Cities for Young, Old Foreseen by Disney,' p. 1.
71. Ibid.
72. Ibid.
73. Marvin Davis in Katherine Greene and Richard Greene, *Walt Disney: An Intimate History of the Man and His Magic*, CD-ROM, 'Final Vision'.
74. William E. Potter, 'Walt Disney World: A Venture in Community Planning & Development,' p. 32.
75. Thomas R. Larmore, personal correspondence, September 16, 1999.
76. Robert Foster, interview by author, October 19, 1999, tape.
77. Marvin Davis quoted in Anthony Haden-Guest, *The Paradise Program*, pp. 309–10.
78. Marvin Davis, interview by Richard Hubler, May 28, 1968, transcript, WDA, p. 26. See also Walt Disney Productions, 'Project Florida/ A Whole New Disney World,' p. 11.
79. John Hench, interview by author, December 18, 1997, transcript, p. 21. See also Raymond L. Watson, interview by author, November 6, 1998, transcript, p. 3.
80. Carl Bongiorno, interview by author, February 9, 1999, transcript, p. 5.
81. Bob Gurr, interview by author, January 25, 1999, transcript, p. 27.

82. Economics Research Associates, 'Experimental Prototype Community of Tomorrow, Outline of Presentation, Department of Housing and Urban Development,' pp. 20–2.

83. See Disney's notes in Helliwell, Melrose and DeWolf, 'Memo on the Establishment of Special Taxing Districts and Municipalities on the Walt Disney Productions Property.' Refer to Richard E. Foglesong, *Married to the Mouse: Walt Disney World and Orlando* (New Haven and London: Yale University Press, 2001).

84. Robert Foster, interview by author, April 23, 1999, p. 15.

85. Robert Foster, personal communication, February 23, 2001.

86. WED Enterprises, Inc., 'Tomorrowland, Carousel of Progress,' Narration-Tape, script, p. 13.

87. E. Cardon Walker, interview by author, September 10, 1999, tape.

88. Marvin Davis quoted in Anthony Haden-Guest, *The Paradise Program*, pp. 308–9. See also Economics Research Associates, 'Experimental Prototype Community of Tomorrow, Outline of Presentation, Department of Housing and Urban Development,' p. 4.

89. DeMolay International is a branch of Freemasonry. Disney became a member in Kansas City in 1923. www.demolay.org, March 3, 1999, 13:59.

90. William E. Potter, 'Walt Disney World: A Venture in Community Planning & Development,' p. 30.

91. The studio made a film entitled, *Family Planning* (1967) for the Agency for International Development. Disney's office contained the book, Anonymous, *Family Planning and Population Programs* (Chicago: University of Chicago Press, 1966). See Disney's office inventory.

92. Robert D. Putnam, *Bowling Alone: The Collapse and Revival of American Community* (New York: Simon & Schuster, c. 2000), p. 283.

93. Christopher Jencks and Paul E. Peterson, eds., *The Urban Underclass* (Washington, D.C.: The Brookings Institution, c. 1991), p. 19.

94. Walt Disney quoted in Bob Thomas, *Walt Disney: An American Original*, p. 338.

95. Walt Disney quoted in Dave Smith, ed., *Walt Disney: Famous Quotes*, p. 44.

96. Joe Fowler, interview by Richard Hubler, July 23, 1968, transcript, WDA, p. 11.

97. Ken Klug, interview by author, January 20, 1999, transcript, p. 5.

98. *United States Code*, Public Law 89–754, Section 103(a)(2).

99. Arthur D. Little, Inc., *Strategies for Shaping Model Cities* (Washington, D.C.: Communication Service Corporation, c. 1967), p. 22.

100. William E. Potter, 'Walt Disney World: A Venture in Community Planning & Development,' p. 31.

101. Ibid.

102. Diane Disney Miller, Introduction to Russell Schroeder, ed., *Walt Disney: His Life in Pictures*, p. 7.
103. Steven Watts, *The Magic Kingdom*, p. 295.
104. Bob Gurr, interview by author, January 25, 1999, transcript, p. 30.
105. WED Enterprises, Inc., 'Tomorrowland, Carousel of Progress,' Narration-Tape, script, p.14.
106. James March and Johan Olsen, *Democratic Governance* (New York: The Free Press, 1995), p. 252.
107. Economics Research Associates, 'Experimental Prototype Community of Tomorrow, Outline of Presentation, Department of Housing and Urban Development,' p. 5. Biographer Steven Watts concludes that 'Walt Disney was neither a crusader for civil rights nor a virulent race-baiter, but a typical white American of his time who harbored a benign, genteel bias against blacks.' See Steven Watts, *The Magic Kingdom*, p. 279.
108. Robert Foster, interview by author, April 23, 1999, transcript, pp. 20–1.

Chapter 9

1. Van Arsdale France, *Window on Main Street*, p. 110.
2. Norma Lee Browning, 'Magic Cities for Young, Old Foreseen by Disney,' p. 1.
3. Walt Disney Productions, 'The Maintenance of Magic in the "Magic Kingdom,"' p. 6.
4. Michael Sorkin, ed., *Variations on a Theme Park: The New American City and the End of Public Space* (New York: Hill and Wang, c. 1992), p. xiv.
5. Walt Disney quoted by John Hench in Jack E. Janzen and Leon J. Janzen, '"Another Kind of Reality": An Interview With John Hench,' p. 20.
6. Walt Disney Productions, 'The Maintenance of Magic in the "Magic Kingdom,"' p. 5.
7. Ibid., p. 24. The park had 4,500 tons of chiller capacity and was repainted every two years.
8. Walt Disney quoted in Dave Smith, ed., *Walt Disney: Famous Quotes*, p. 37.
9. WED Enterprises, Inc., 'Disneyland Dictionary,' c. 1968, AHR, p. 32.
10. Walt Disney Productions, 'University of Disneyland Newsletter,' August 1966, AHR, pp. 1–2.
11. Van Arsdale France, *Window on Main Street*, p. 71.
12. Walt Disney Productions, 'The Walt Disney Traditions at Disneyland,' University of Disneyland Handbook, c. 1967, AHR, n.p.
13. Walt Disney quoted in Kathy Merlock Jackson, *Walt Disney: A Bio-Bibliography*, pp. 130–4.

14. Disneyland, Inc. 'Your Disneyland: a Guide for Hosts and Hostesses,' booklet, c. 1955, AHR, p. 8. Also see Kathryn Bold, 'Corporate Cleanup,' *LAT*, May 9, 1996, pp. E1, E5.
15. Bill Martin quoted in Jack E. Janzen and Leon J. Janzen, 'Disneyland Art Director ... Bill Martin,' p. 12.
16. Harrison Price, interview by author, July 6, 1998, transcript, p. 33.
17. Charles Moore, 'You Have to Pay for the Public Life,' p. 65.
18. David R. Smith, 'Disney Before Burbank: The Kingswell and Hyperion Studios,' p. 33.
19. Carl Bongiorno, interview by author, February 9, 1999, transcript, p. 1.
20. Bob Thomas, *Walt Disney: an American Original*, p. 171.
21. Diane Disney Miller quoted in Amy Boothe Green and Howard E. Green, *Remembering Walt*, p. 68.
22. Walt Disney Productions, 'The Maintenance of Magic in the 'Magic Kingdom," p. 2.
23. Harrison Price, interview by author, December 17, 1998, transcript, p. 6.

Chapter 10

1. See C.E. Wright, 'Florida's Disney World Aims at '70 Opening,' *NYT*, 116, 39,838, February 19, 1967, p. XX-4.
2. Walt Disney Productions, 'Annual Report to Shareholders and Employees, Fiscal Year Ended September 30, 1967,' audited by Price Waterhouse, p. 7. See also Walt Disney World Company, 'Walt Disney World-Florida,' brochure, 1968, OPL, n.p.
3. Marty Sklar quoted in Christopher Finch, *The Art of Walt Disney*, p. 406.
4. Bob Thomas, *Building a Company*, p. 316.
5. Roy O. Disney quoted in Walt Disney Productions, 'Preview Edition, Walt Disney World,' p. 21.
6. William E. Potter, 'Walt Disney World: A Venture in Community Planning & Development,' p. 32.
7. Paul Goldberger, 'Mickey Mouse Teaches the Architects,' p. 93.
8. Peter Blake, 'Walt Disney World,' p. 39. The estimates show 25,000 EPCOT residents in 1991, with 20,000 industrial employees. See also Anonymous, 'Disney Ready to Construct "Community of Tomorrow,"' *AB*, May 25, 1974, p. C1.
9. Bob Gurr, interview by author, January 25, 1999, transcript, p. 23. See also Jack E. Janzen and Leon J. Janzen, 'Imagineering and the Disney Image ... an Interview With Marty Sklar,' p. 12.
10. Marvin Davis quoted in Jack E. Janzen and Leon J. Janzen, 'Planning the First Disney Parks ... A Talk With Marvin Davis,' p. 17.

11. Michael Eisner quoted in Christopher Finch, *The Art of Walt Disney*, p. 423.
12. John Hench, interview by author, December 18, 1997, transcript, p. 19.
13. Raymond L. Watson, interview by author, November 6, 1998, transcript, p. 12.
14. Ibid., p. 11.
15. John Hench, interview by author, December 18, 1997, transcript, p. 22.
16. John Hench quoted in Sally Davis, 'Should We Let Disney Redesign Los Angeles,' *Los Angeles*, 19, 7, July 1974, p. 46.
17. Spiro Kostof, *The City Shaped*, p. 159. See also Paolo Soleri, *The Bridge Between Matter and Spirit is Matter Becoming Spirit: The Arcology of Paolo Soleri* (Garden City, New York: Anchor Books, c. 1973).
18. Spiro Kostof, *The City Shaped*, p. 162.
19. Bob Gurr, interview by author, January 25, 1999, transcript, p. 19.
20. Walt Disney Productions, 'Annual Report 1974, Fiscal Year Ended September 30,' audited by Price Waterhouse, p. 23.
21. Walt Disney Productions, 'Annual Report 1975, Fiscal Year Ended September 30,' audited by Price Waterhouse, p. 1.
22. Ibid., pp. 2–3.
23. Card Walker, 'Walt Disney World: Master Planning For the Future,' pp. 7–10.
24. WED Enterprises, 'EPCOT: What it Is, How it Works, Values of Participation,' paper, c. 1976, OPL.
25. Richard Beard, *Walt Disney's EPCOT Center*, pp. 40, 113.
26. Kofi Annan, Press Release SG/SM/6758, 19 October 1998. www.un.org/news/press/docs.
27. E. Cardon Walker, 'Security Analysts Meeting, Walt Disney World, Excerpts From Remarks,' January 15, 1975, OPL, p. 12.
28. Walt Disney Productions, 'Houston Chooses Disney PeopleMover,' Press Release, July 19, 1979, AHR, p. 1.
29. Disney-Turner, 'A Joint Venture in Transportation Innovation,' n.p. Also see Community Transportation Services, 'Community Transportation Services, A Division of Buena Vista Distribution, Subsidiary of Walt Disney Productions,' p. 10. See also Walt Disney Productions, *Disney Newsreel*, 11, 16, April 16, 1982, AHR, p. 3. See WED Transportation Systems, Inc., 'WEDway PeopleMover,' brochure, c. 1982, AHR, n.p. The technology for the PeopleMover and monorails was later sold to a Canadian company, Bombardier, Inc.
30. In general, see WED Transportation Systems, Inc., 'Mark IV Monorail,' n.p.
31. Martin Wachs in Allen J. Scott and Edward W. Soja, eds., *The City: Los Angeles and Urban Theory at the End of the Twentieth Century*

(Berkeley and Los Angeles: University of California Press, 1996), p. 156.

32. Joe Fowler, interview by Richard Hubler, July 23, 1968, transcript, WDA, p. 12.

33. Marty Sklar quoted in Christopher Finch, *The Art of Walt Disney*, p. 434.

34. Other 'EPCOT-like' projects include the Water Hyacinth Project, developed in conjunction with NASA and the EPA, begun in 1978, which treats sewage. This technology has been borrowed by San Diego, Austin, and Orlando. See Jeff Kurtti, *Since the World Began: Walt Disney World, The First 25 Years* (New York: Hyperion, 1996), p. 101. In addition, Walt Disney World featured the first all-electronic telephone system using underground cable and the first to use fiber optics in a commercial venture.

35. Reedy Creek Improvement District, 'Reedy Creek Improvement District: Thirtieth Anniversary Report,' brochure, 1999, p. 10. See also The Walt Disney Company, 'Walt Disney World: Innovation in Action,' brochure, 1989, AHR.

36. John Hench, interview by author, December 18, 1997, transcript, p. 10.

37. Bob Gurr, interview by author, January 25, 1999, transcript, p. 31. The company's plans for a residential complex in the eastern portion of the property were announced in 1973. Ultimately, 133 rental townhouses were constructed as well as houses, apartments, and a retirement community. The voting rights issue became a concern. Most of the units became part of the Disney Institute in 1995. See Walt Disney Productions, 'The National Champion: A Report to Participants in Disneyland and Walt Disney World,' October 1972, OPL, pp. 12–13.

38. Peter Rummell quoted in Adrienne Schmitz and Lloyd W. Bookout, *Trends and Innovations in Master-Planned Communities* (Washington, D.C.: Urban Land Institute, c. 1998), p. 144. Communities that influenced Celebration designers are: Winter Park, Kissimmee, Charleston, Savannah, East Hampton, Nantucket, and Mount Dora. According to Lillian Disney, Disney was knowledgeable enough about Charleston that he could conduct tours there. Quoted in Amy Boothe Green and Howard E. Green, *Remembering Walt*, p. 37.

39. Economics Research Associates, 'Experimental Prototype Community of Tomorrow, Outline of Presentation, Department of Housing and Urban Development,' p. 17.

40. Michael Eisner with Tony Schwartz, *Work in Progress* (New York: Random House, 1998), p. 409.

41. For example, see John Beardsley, 'A Mickey Mouse Utopia,' *Landscape Architecture*, February 1997, p. 76. For two accounts written by early residents of Celebration, see Douglas Frantz and Catherine Collins, *Celebration, U.S.A.: Living in Disney's Brave New Town* (New York:

Henry Holt and Company, 1999), and Andrew Ross, *The Celebration Chronicles* (New York: The Ballantine Publishing Group, 1999).

42. Andres Duany, 'In Celebration,' *Urban Land*, 61, 1, January 2002, p. 60.

43. See Beth Dunlop, *Building a Dream: The Art of Disney Architecture* (New York: H.N. Abrams, 1996).

44. Jane Jacobs quoted in Steve Proffitt, 'Jane Jacobs: Still Challenging the Way We Think About Cities,' p. M3.

45. John Hench quoted in Sally Davis, 'Should We Let Disney Redesign Los Angeles,' p. 65.

46. The Walt Disney Company, 'Annual Report to Shareholders and Employees, 1992,' audited by Price Waterhouse, p. 6.

47. Raymond L. Watson, interview by author, November 6, 1998, transcript, p. 8.

48. Marty Sklar quoted in Bruce Gordon and David Mumford, *Disneyland: The Nickel Tour*, p. 359. Also see Manuel Castells, *The Rise of the Network Society* (Malden and Oxford: Blackwell Publishers, 1996); and William J. Mitchell, *City of Bits: Space, Place, and the Infobahn* (Cambridge and London: The MIT Press, 1995).

49. Bob Gurr, interview by author, January 25, 1999, transcript, p. 35.

Biographical References

Adams, Lee. In charge of the Walt Disney Studios' central plant and was familiar with high-voltage power generation and storage. Visited Westinghouse with Disney in January 1966 for EPCOT.

Becket, Welton. Principal in Welton Becket & Associates, a major commercial architecture firm. Neighbor of Walt Disney's. Worked on designs for the Carousel of Progress, Contemporary Resort, and undoubtedly had some influence on the EPCOT concept.

Blair, Mary. Started with the company in 1939. Was instrumental in the design of 'It's a Small World.' Designed exterior graffiti-resistant tile murals for Tomorrowland in 1967 and the large mural in the Contemporary Resort.

Bongiorno, Carl. Started with the company in 1963 and worked at the Celebrity Sports Center in Denver as controller. Became treasurer of WED Enterprises in 1964. Named president of WED Enterprises in 1979 and retired from Walt Disney Imagineering in 1988.

Bradbury, Ray. Science fiction author and friend of Disney's. He later worked on the conceptualization of Epcot Center.

Broggie, Roger. Joined the company in 1939 and established the machine shop. Helped Disney with his backyard train hobby. Oversaw all WED Enterprises transportation systems and played a large role in most mechanical aspects of Imagineering. He visited companies with Disney in 1966. Retired in 1975.

Davis, Marjorie. Wife of Marvin Davis and niece of Walt Disney.

Davis, Marvin. Joined WED Enterprises in 1953 and developed the master plan of Disneyland and worked on designs for Main Street, U.S.A. In 1965, he began work on Florida master planning, including EPCOT, and contributed to the design of the Contemporary Resort. Davis also developed plans for the proposed St. Louis redevelopment project.

DeWolf, Tom. Director, Board of Supervisors, Reedy Creek Improvement District. Partner in the Florida law firm of Helliwell, Melrose & DeWolf, which provided Disney with the memorandum, 'Establishment of Special Taxing Districts and Municipalities … ' in May 1966.

Disney, Lillian. Wife of Walt Disney, married in 1925. In 1987, she announced that she would give $50 million to help build the Walt Disney Concert Hall in downtown Los Angeles.

Edgren, Don. Did structural engineering work at Disneyland for an outside firm beginning in 1954. Joined WED Enterprises in 1960. Project engineer for New Orleans Square. Worked on Magic Kingdom utilidors and Contemporary Resort. Became vice president of engineering at WED Enterprises. Chief engineer for Tokyo Disneyland.

Eisner, Michael. Chairman and chief executive officer of The Walt Disney Company since 1984. Eisner's interest in architecture has influenced the built environment on company property around the world. He was actively involved in the planning and development of the town of Celebration, Florida.

Ellenshaw, Peter. An artist initially hired by Disney in England. He painted one of the original bird's-eye views of Disneyland for the Disneyland television show. He received an Oscar for his special visual effects in *Mary Poppins*.

Evans, Morgan 'Bill.' Designed the landscaping for Disney's Holmby Hills home with his brother, Jack. Landscape architect for Disneyland. His family introduced many plant species into the United States and Evans established landscaping standards in the theme park industry.

Foster, Robert. Attorney who coordinated acquisition of the Florida land parcels and the drafting and establishment of the state legislative package. Became general counsel of Walt Disney World Company and developed some of the Walt Disney World properties.

Fowler, Admiral Joseph. Joined the Disney organization in 1954 to oversee construction of Disneyland. Fowler also oversaw construction at the 1964–65 New York World's Fair. He was in charge of construction at Walt Disney World until 1972. His nickname was 'Can Do.'

France, Van. Began work at Disneyland in 1955 and created Disney University where he taught innovative concepts in customer service.

Gurr, Robert. Director of special vehicle development. Industrial designer. Designed most of the vehicles in Disneyland, including the WEDway and monorail. Traveled with Disney in 1966 to promote the EPCOT concept to industry. Also worked on Audio-Animatronics and the sale of company monorails for use in Las Vegas. Graduate of Art Center College of Design. Retired in 1981.

Hench, John. Joined the company in 1939. Moved to WED Enterprises in 1955 to work on Tomorrowland. Became a WED Enterprises director in 1966. Instrumental in the Monsanto House of the Future attraction and Ford pavilion at the 1964–65 New York World's Fair. Led the development of Epcot Center with Marty Sklar. Has worked on most aspects of Imagineering.

Irvine, Richard. Art director who came to WED Enterprises from Twentieth Century Fox, and later became its president. Helped Roy O. Disney sell Disneyland to financiers and headed the Disneyland development team for Disney. With John Hench, convinced new company management of WED Enterprises' capabilities after Disney's death. Retired in 1973.

Jones, Colonel Tom. Aide to General Joe Potter in the Panama Canal Zone and worked with him in Florida for Disney. Rose to become a vice president of Walt Disney Imagineering.

Kimball, Ward. One of Disney's 'Nine Old Men.' Confidant of Disney's. Fellow train enthusiast and visited Greenfield Village with Disney in 1948. Worked on World War II military films. Produced a television space series in the mid-1950s. Joined the company in 1934 as an animator. His wife Betty worked in the Ink and Paint department.

Klug, Ken. Civil designer who began work at Disneyland in 1962 and transferred to WED Enterprises in 1966. Worked on construction of the Magic Kingdom in Florida.

Lund, Sharon Disney. Disney's younger daughter.

Luske, Ham. Joined the company in 1931. Animated the character of Snow White. Became director for military training films in 1943. Produced the Florida Film in 1966.

Martin, Bill. Joined the company in 1953. Fantasyland art director. He took Herbert Ryman's castle concept and refined it into architectural drawings. He is associated with many attractions including the monorail. In 1971, as a vice president of WED Enterprises, he supervised the master layout of the Magic Kingdom in Florida.

Martin, Lucille. Joined the company in 1964 and has served as an executive assistant for Walt Disney, Ron Miller, and Michael Eisner. She is currently a vice president.

Miller, Diane Disney. Disney's older daughter. She married Ronald Miller, who later served as president of Walt Disney Productions, and they had seven children. She has been active in the planning and development of the Walt Disney Concert Hall in Los Angeles.

Miller, Ronald. Disney's son-in-law. Joined the company in 1957 and produced films and television programs. Served as president from 1980 to 1984 and was elected to the board of directors in 1966.

McGinnis, George. Joined WED Enterprises in 1966. He created artwork for EPCOT's international themed shopping area and the Tomorrowland Rocket Jets wienie.

McKim, Sam. Began at WED Enterprises in 1954. Is one of the key designers of Main Street, U.S.A. and New Orleans Square. In addition, he helped shape the Carousel of Progress.

Morrow, Richard. One of the first company insiders to be informed of Disney's plans for Project X. General Counsel of Walt Disney Productions.

Moses, Thomas. Administrator, Reedy Creek Improvement District. Hired by Roy O. Disney in 1969. Former official of the Southern Building Code Congress.

Nunis, Richard. Began as an assistant to Van France in orientation training at Disneyland in 1955. Became vice president of Disneyland Operations in 1968 and rose to become chairman of Walt Disney Attractions.

Potter, Major General William 'Joe.' Former governor of the Panama Canal Zone, U.S. Army Corps of Engineers. Was executive vice president under Robert Moses at the 1964–65 New York World's Fair. Joined the company in 1965 and became vice president of EPCOT Planning. First manager of the Reedy Creek Improvement District.

Potter-Heine, Joanne. A daughter of General Joe Potter.

Price, Harrison 'Buzz.' An economist originally with Stanford Research Institute, where he performed locational analyses for Disneyland in 1953. Later, Disney urged him to form his own firm, Economics Research Associates. He helped Disney evaluate scores of projects, including Mineral King, CalArts, and EPCOT/Disney World. Price has been involved with CalArts for nearly 40 years.

Rester, George. WED Enterprises designer who assisted Marvin Davis with plans for EPCOT and developed the design of the ever-sleeker EPCOT hotel.

Ryman, Herbert. Art director and designer, joined the company in 1954. He helped Disney design the original concept rendering for Disneyland. Most of the original EPCOT concept art was done by Ryman and he also helped conceptualize Epcot Center. Graduate of the Art Institute of Chicago.

Sayers, Jack. Joined the company in 1955 and rose to become Disneyland's vice president of lessee relations. In 1966, he visited industries with General Joe Potter as part of EPCOT research.

Sherman, Richard and Robert. Songwriters, known primarily for their Disney work including *Mary Poppins* and *There's a Great Big Beautiful Tomorrow* (Carousel of Progress). Their work earned nine Academy Award nominations.

Sklar, Martin. Began working for the company in 1955 in Disneyland Public Relations. Worked directly with Disney almost immediately. Wrote the Florida Film script with Disney. Led the Epcot Center development team with John Hench. Currently vice chairman and principal creative executive of Walt Disney Imagineering.

Smith, Phil. Former associate in the Helliwell, Melrose & DeWolf law firm. Joined Walt Disney Productions in 1965. Assisted with property acquisition and legislation. Became first company resident on the Florida property. Rose to become a Walt Disney World Company executive.

Stewart, Max. Produced the Florida Film with Ham Luske and developed its storyboards.

Tatum, Donn. Joined the company in 1956 and rose to vice president of administration. In 1968, he became president of Walt Disney Productions. With Card Walker, he led the company after Roy O. Disney's death.

Tyler, Robert. Design principal at Welton Becket & Associates. Started at the firm in 1956. Worked with WED Enterprises on the design of the Contemporary Resort and worked closely with Marvin Davis.

Walker, E. Cardon 'Card.' Joined the company in 1938 and is currently a director. In 1965, he became vice president of marketing and assisted in the production of the Florida Film. He became president of the company in 1971 and was chairman when Epcot Center opened in 1982. Disney's protégé.

Watson, Raymond. In 1966, he was the chief planner and executive vice president of the Irvine Company. He advised Disney on two occasions regarding the EPCOT plan. Currently he is a director of The Walt Disney Company and vice chairman of the Irvine Company.

EPCOT Chronology

December 5, 1901	Disney is born in Chicago, Illinois.
1918–19	Disney in France as Red Cross ambulance driver.
1923	The Disney brothers establish West Coast animation studio in their Uncle Robert's garage in the Los Angeles community of Silverlake.
1926	Hyperion studio completed.
1937	Premier of *Snow White and the Seven Dwarfs*.
1938	Disney's mother, Flora, dies of carbon monoxide poisoning due to improper furnace installation.
1939	New York World's Fair, 'World of Tomorrow.'
1940	Disney visits Greenfield Village in Dearborn, Michigan. Walt Disney Studios in Burbank completed. Release of *Fantasia*.
1941	Strike at studios.
1941–45	Walt Disney Studios produces highly technical military training films.
1944	Disney produces *The Amazon Awakens*, which includes footage of Henry Ford's 17,000-acre cleared jungle plantation in Brazil.
1948	Disney and Ward Kimball visit Chicago Railroad Fair and Greenfield Village.
1949	Disney purchases Holmby Hills property. Would feature a miniature railroad and nostalgic setting in the backyard.

1952	Disney presents proto-Disneyland plans to the Burbank City Council. WED Enterprises, Inc., is established.
October 27, 1954	Disney promotes Disneyland on television show of same name.
July 17, 1955	Disneyland opens.
1955–57	Ward Kimball produces space series for television in conjunction with scientist Wernher von Braun.
1956–58	Plans drawn for an International Street at Disneyland.
1957	Monsanto House of the Future opens at Disneyland.
1958	Brussels World's Fair.
1959	Vice President Richard Nixon dedicates the monorail at Disneyland. General Electric asks Disney to produce a show for the 1964–65 New York World's Fair. Walt Disney Productions considers a land deal with RCA including a city of tomorrow component.
1960	Disney approaches Las Vegas city officials with the idea of running a monorail down the Strip and is rejected.
1961	CalArts is established with strong support from Disney.
November 1961	First-generation PeopleMover test track is tested at the Burbank studios using Lincoln Continentals.
April 21, 1962	Seattle Century 21 Exposition opens. Many WED Enterprises staff visit the exposition in preparation for the 1964–65 New York World's Fair.
November 1963	Disney views property in the Reedy Creek Basin in central Florida.
1964	Architect Victor Gruen publishes *The Heart of Our Cities*. Marvin Davis submits plans for the St. Louis Riverfront Square redevelopment proposal.

April 22, 1964	1964–65 New York World's Fair opens. Robert Moses is president and General Joe Potter is executive vice president. An early proposal for the fair influences Disney's EPCOT plans.
September 1964	Disney receives the Medal of Freedom from President Lyndon Johnson.
1965	Land in the Mineral King Valley is purchased. HUD is established. President Lyndon Johnson's Task Force on Urban Problems advocates a demonstration cities program. Ebenezer Howard's *Garden Cities of To-Morrow* is republished. Architect Le Corbusier dies.
Summer 1965	Watts riots break out in Los Angeles.
June 1965	Florida land acquisition program completed. Disney holds a Project Future seminar. *Orlando Sentinel* article mentions Disney and a city of the future.
September 1965	General Joe Potter is formally hired by Disney and becomes vice president of EPCOT Planning.
November 15, 1965	Walt Disney, Roy O. Disney, and Florida Governor Haydon Burns conduct a press conference to discuss the company's early plans for the Florida property, including creation of a city of 'Yesterday' and a city of 'Tomorrow.'
January 1966	Disney and select team members visit Westinghouse and General Electric on an early industry junket for EPCOT. They bring brown-line drawings with them.
July 1966	Economics Research Associates presents Disney with the 'Project Florida Planning Manual,' which includes preliminary EPCOT economic estimates.
July 24, 1966	New Orleans Square dedicated at Disneyland. Includes basement component.
August 1966	ERA presents Disney with the EPCOT presentation outline for HUD.
October 27, 1966	Disney's portions of the Florida Film are shot.

November 3, 1966   President Lyndon Johnson signs Model Cities legislation.

November 7, 1966   Disney undergoes surgery.

December 15, 1966   Disney dies.

April 17, 1967   Disney's Florida Film is screened before both houses of the state Legislature.

May 12, 1967   Florida Governor Claude Kirk signs legislative package.

Summer 1967   Tomorrowland 'A World on the Move' opens at Disneyland. It features the EPCOT prototype WEDway PeopleMover and station as well as the massive Progress City model on the second floor of the Carousel of Progress building.

1970   EPCOT Building Code set is adopted.

1971   CalArts campus in Valencia, California, opens.

October 1, 1971   Walt Disney World opens in Florida.

December 20, 1971   Roy O. Disney dies.

1972   General Joe Potter discusses 'mini-EPCOT planning' to help cities until EPCOT can be developed.

1973–1974   WED Enterprises executive Marty Sklar convenes EPCOT planning meetings with many of the original team members. The Progress City model is removed from Disneyland. The EPCOT concept begins its evolution into Epcot Center.

1975   Company President Card Walker announces that EPCOT would be a system based on the communication of new ideas and not a living community.

1981   WEDway system installed at the Houston Intercontinental Airport.

October 1, 1982   Epcot Center theme park opens on the site originally planned for Disney's EPCOT concept.

June 1996   First residents move into the town of Celebration, Florida.

Bibliographical Essay

This book's endnotes present a complete list of the research materials used to prepare this publication. The reader is now directed to essential source material, including some of the collections as well as academic and professional literature.

The Walt Disney Archives were established in 1970 by their director, David R. Smith. The archives serve primarily as a resource for company employees. The primary collection deals with Disney and the Disney family, but other files cover such fields as motion pictures, theme parks, character merchandise, publicity, promotion, publications, and recordings. Smith's inventory of Disney's private offices indicates that they contained personal papers relating to EPCOT. These documents are proprietary in nature and remain for future research.

Retired company attorney Robert Foster notes that the original Project Florida team members exercised strict confidentiality and used as few memoranda as possible. These practices limited the historical record of the EPCOT concept's early incarnations. The archival research for this book was supplemented with original interviews with company veterans familiar with the EPCOT concept and the theme parks. In addition, Imagineers have written books over the years and these sources are useful. Authors include Bruce Gordon, David Mumford, Randy Bright, Martin A. Sklar, and The Imagineers (Kevin Rafferty with Bruce Gordon). The following 'Disneyana' publications are immensely helpful resources. Jack Janzen and Leon Janzen publish *The 'E' Ticket* (P.O. Box 800880, Santa Clarita, California 91380). Their periodicals often feature interview transcripts from conversations with company veterans. Paul F. Anderson publishes *Persistence of Vision* which frequently contains articles researched in the Walt Disney Archives. The Walt Disney Family Educational Foundation maintains a history website at www.waltdisney.org.

The Disney Collection, a company depository, is located in the Orlando Public Library's Social Science Department. The collection includes a fairly complete book section, press clippings, news releases, pamphlets, brochures, and catalogs. The press clippings date to January 1971. Logging reports from radio and television are also available. Librarians Tracey Covey and Angela Jacoby were especially helpful. Another company depository is located in the Elizabeth J. Schultz Anaheim History Room in the Anaheim Public Library. Much material relating to Disneyland and its relationship with Anaheim is available in the Anaheim History Room. Of particular assistance were Jane Newell, Sal Addotta, and Opal Kissinger.

The Florida State Archives in Tallahassee, Florida, contain useful information about the company's early dealings with Florida. For example, these archives yielded correspondence from the administration of Governor Haydon Burns. Documents also are available concerning Governor Claude Kirk's administration. Jody Norman and Patricia Robertson were generous with their research time. The Lyndon B. Johnson Library in Austin, Texas, holds material relating to the company's contacts with the administration.

Ellerbe Becket, a commercial architecture firm, is a descendant of Welton Becket & Associates. The firm maintains a slide library in Minneapolis and holds images from Walt Disney Production's early Florida years. Members of the firm who were especially helpful include Jim Takamune, Janet Rhee, and Robert Albachten.

An academic historical analysis of Disneyland is contained in John M. Findlay's *Magic Lands: Western Cityscapes and American Culture After 1940* (Berkeley, 1992). It is also a useful research tool for EPCOT because it examines cityscapes directly related to Disney's concept: industrial parks, retirement communities, and world's fairs. Stephen J. Rebori's bibliography, *Theme and Entertainment Parks: Planning, Design Development, and Management* (Chicago, 1995) is an invaluable resource in the area. Amusement park historian Judith A. Adams' *The American Amusement Park Industry* (Boston, 1991) is a standard reference and includes details about Walt Disney World.

Many books about things Disney were published during the course of this research. This includes the first academic biography of Disney, *The Magic Kingdom: Walt Disney and the American Way of Life,* by Steven Watts (New York, 1997). This book was exhaustively researched in the Walt Disney Archives and has a strong cultural orientation, as most Disney academic works do. This book is now a prerequisite to the scholarly study of Disney. Also made available was the Canadian Centre for Architecture's exhibit catalog, *Designing Disney's Theme Parks: The Architecture of Reassurance*, edited by art historian Karal Ann Marling (Paris and New York, 1997). The exhibit toured Canada and the United States. Marling, the exhibit's curator and project's director of research, took on a daunting task: the history of Disney theme park design. The book is heavily illustrated with many treasures of Disney design. Still, its focus was design and other multidisciplinary aspects of the 'Imagineering process' could not be addressed. An outgrowth of this research was a dissertation and, ultimately, a book by one of Marling's doctoral candidates, Andrew David Lainsbury, titled *Once Upon an American Dream: The Story of Euro Disneyland* (Lawrence, 2000). As the title suggests, the book has a cultural focus. Nevertheless, by virtue of Lainsbury being a participant in the Canadian Centre project, the book is rich with information about the history of Disney design, based on archival research as well as interviews.

Anthropologist Stephen M. Fjellman wrote the widely-known, *Vinyl Leaves: Walt Disney World and America* (Boulder, 1992). The book criticizes Walt Disney World as a symbol of American corporate control and also addresses urban planning issues in some detail. Duke University's Project on Disney produced *Inside the Mouse: Work and Play at Disney World* (Durham and London, 1995). This work's emphasis is on issues such as the consumption of leisure opportunities in America and the controlled façade of theme parks. Similarly, sociologist Sharon Zukin's *Landscapes of Power: From Detroit to Disney World* (Berkeley, 1991) emphasizes corporate control in Walt Disney World and the need for more authentic urban space. Architect Michael Sorkin, editor of *Variations on a Theme Park: The New American City and the End of Public Space* (New York, 1992), offers similar viewpoints and argues that cities essentially are becoming privately-controlled theme parks.

Urban environments are also a function of the set of constraints builders must confront in realizing their visions. Because 1966 is not long ago in historical terms, many professional books and periodicals are available to consult. For example, it is useful to compare the Urban Land Institute's (ULI) *Community Builder's Handbook* (Washington, D.C., 1968) with the more recent *Residential Development Handbook* (Washington, D.C., 1990). Similarly, the International City Managers' Association planning 'green books' also are available to compare.

Professional texts enabled the analysis of data. For example, ULI's *Dollars and Cents of Shopping Centers: A Study of Receipts and Expenses* (Washington, D.C., 1966), available in the ULI Archives, is a simpler version of the same resource published today. Rick Davis was generous with his research time. These figures permitted analysis using some of the same tools used by Economics Research Associates in EPCOT estimating. In addition, 'Appraising Theme Parks,' an important article in the *Appraisal Journal* (Chicago, January 1986), provided tools to assess the financial magnitude of some of what Disney envisioned. Where possible, period professional literature was consulted, particularly in such areas as special districts and architecture.

Two books, written by architects 30 years apart, were especially interesting. Disney chose to read Victor Gruen's *The Heart of Our Cities: The Urban Crisis: Diagnosis and Cure* (New York, 1964). In this book, the father of the enclosed shopping mall called for revitalization of downtowns and greater urban mass transit orientation. Peter Calthorpe's *The Next American Metropolis: Ecology, Community, and the American Dream* (New York, 1993) offers transit-oriented development at dense urban nodes. While different in some respects, these two visions of the future show one thing very clearly: progress can take time.

Index

Miller, Ronald 54, 182
Milton Keynes 23
Mineral King project 14, 48, 72–3,
    110–12, 116, 187
Mitchell, William J. 83
Mitsu 38
Model Cities program 95–6, 109, 112
Monsanto (company) 93
Monsanto House of the Future 52–4,
    62–3, 83, 89, 186
Moore, Charles 19, 83, 124, 135–6
Morrow, Richard 6, 102, 106, 182
Moses, Robert 15, 36, 40, 68, 117, 187
Moses, Tom 45, 77, 108–9, 182
Mumford, Lewis xvi–xvii, 21, 25, 127
Murdy, John 111

National Aeronautics and Space
    Administration (NASA) 79, 133
National Endowment for the Arts 134
National Lead Company 93
neighborhood participation in govern-
    ment 117
neighborhood planning 9, 20–21
Nestlé 133
New Deal 21
new towns in Britain xviii, 23, 39,
    108–9, 114
New Urbanism 139–40
New York City: planning 20; rent
    control 114
New York World's Fair (1964–65) xv,
    6, 15, 31, 36, 38, 51, 67–8, 76, 78,
    90, 93, 100, 186–7
Newhall Land and Farming Company
    73
Nixon, Richard 32, 123, 182, 186

Olmsted, Frederick Law 25, 28
Olsen, Johan 118
Orlando Sentinel 67–8, 72, 101–2, 187
Orwell, George 67

Packard, David 78
The Parent Trap 54
Parker, Bryan 20
Pelli, Cesar 135
Pereira, William 6, 12, 15, 44, 55, 89
Perry, Clarence 20–21

Peterson, Paul E. 116
philosophy behind EPCOT xiv–xv, 6–7,
    89, 130, 133–4, 138
Plater-Zyberk, Elizabeth 135
Portman, John 47
Potter, Joe xvi, 6, 8, 15, 23, 74, 77,
    93–4, 100–101, 106, 109, 116–17,
    128, 182, 187–8
Potter-Heine, Joanne 182
Price, Harrison xvi, 6, 15, 20, 36, 38,
    44, 48, 67, 73, 89–91, 95, 100,
    108, 112–15, 124–5, 182
privacy for residents 9
Progress City 12–14, 34, 45, 47, 83,
    128, 188
Progressland 51–2
Putnam, Robert 116, 118

Radburn, New Jersey 21, 23, 32
radial plans for physical environment
    11–12
Rawn, William 135
RCA 51, 67, 77–8, 128
Reagan, Ronald 99
Reedy Creek Improvement District
    105–9, 112, 115, 130, 134
Rester, George 6, 47, 102, 182
Reston, Virginia 24
Retlaw Enterprises 72, 97
Richfield (company) 93
Robertson, Jacquelin 135
Rogers, Wathel 78
Roosevelt Island 134
Rosenberg, Joe 96–7
Rouse, James 17, 24, 38, 91, 117
Rummell, Peter 135
Ryman, Herbert 14–19 *passim*, 34, 47,
    57, 83, 97, 102, 183

Savio, Mario 105
Sayers, Jack 94, 102, 183
Seattle World's Fair (1962) 36
Segal, Howard P. 67
Sheraton Hotels 110
Sherman, Richard 8, 78, 183
Sherman, Robert 78, 183
shopping malls 46–7
Siegel, Robert 135
Sierra Club 110